The Sense of Dissonance

The Sense of Dissonance

Accounts of Worth in Economic Life

David Stark

with

Daniel Beunza,

Monique Girard,

and

János Lukács

PRINCETON UNIVERSITY PRESS
Princeton and Oxford

Copyright © 2009 by Princeton University Press
Requests for permission to reproduce material from this work should be sent to Permissions,
Princeton University Press

Published by Princeton University Press, 41 William Street, Princeton, New Jersey 08540
In the United Kingdom: Princeton University Press, 6 Oxford Street, Woodstock, Oxfordshire
OX20 1TW

Library of Congress Cataloging-in-Publication Data

Stark, David, 1950-
  The sense of dissonance : accounts of worth in economic life / David Stark.
    p. cm.
  Includes bibliographical references and index.
  ISBN 978-0-691-13280-8 (hbk. : alk. paper) 1. Industrial sociology. 2. Organizational
sociology. 3. Value. I. Title.
  HD6955.S785 2009
  306.3—dc22

                                                              2008052647

British Library Cataloging-in-Publication Data is available

This book has been composed in Minion and Myriad
Printed on acid-free paper. ∞
press.princeton.edu
Printed in the United States of America

10 9 8 7 6 5 4 3 2 1

for my parents

Non tener pure ad un loco la mente

Fix not thy mind
On one place only.

—Dante Alighieri, *The Divine Comedy: Purgatory*, canto 10,
ca. 1308–1321, trans. Henry Cary

A good investigator doesn't know what he's looking for till he sees it.

—Elmore Leonard, *Mr. Paradise*, 2004

Dissonance
(if you are interested)
leads to discovery

—William Carlos Williams, *Paterson IV*, 1951

Contents

Preface

In retrospect, this book began with a dissertation that went unwritten. As a graduate student at Harvard in the late 1970s working in the field of comparative sociology, I was especially interested in understanding how industrial organization differed in capitalist and socialist economies. While exploring how I might develop this interest into a dissertation topic, I learned about the phenomenon of "peasant-workers" in socialist Eastern Europe. I recognized that peasant-workers could be an analytically strategic social group because their workdays spanned the world of socialist industry and the world of privately held agricultural plots organized along entirely different principles. Of course, the natural experiment would have been even better had the peasant-workers moved on a daily basis from socialist to capitalist *industrial* forms. Still, the topic was a good opportunity to explore what happens when people live in two social worlds organized around very different modes of production.

With dissertation traveling fellowships, my wife Monique Girard, who was a graduate student in anthropology at Harvard, and I left for research in Yugoslavia in 1979–80. We had studied Serbo-Croatian together and, just married, we looked forward to sharing the adventure of dissertation field research. A week after we arrived in Zagreb, Marshal Tito, Communist leader of Yugoslavia, was hospitalized, and he lay dying throughout our research visit. Although we were part of an exchange program that granted us permission to conduct research, legal formalities were the least of our problems. With the political situation completely uncertain, no academics, even those who advised us informally, could offer official assistance. Moreover, with our phones tapped, our apartments bugged, our landladies (three in nine months) harassed, and our friends reluctant to tell us that they were being questioned, we could not jeopardize field research informants. Yugoslavia, "socialism with a human face," was a police state; and our dissertations were the most minor victims of its eventual demise.

I returned to Harvard to consider my options. The independent trade union Solidarność (Solidarity) had recently been recognized in Poland, and it made sense to convert my knowledge of an Eastern European country and my background in a Slavic language to study this new development. So I enrolled in an introductory Polish course taught by Stanislav

Barancsak, one of the founders of KOR (Committee to Defend the Workers) and a personal friend of Lech Walesa. On the morning I was supposed to take the final exam for the course, I was awakened by a Polish friend: "Martial law has just been declared in Poland," she said. "There's no way you'll be able to do dissertation research there." I did not take the exam.

With a supportive committee and a sympathetic department, I did complete a dissertation on the organization of work under capitalism and socialism[1]—but without carrying out the ethnographic research that I had wanted to do on the collision of competing and coexisting organizational principles. Several months before leaving Cambridge, I met the eminent Hungarian economist János Kornai. Over many cups of coffee in a Mass Ave café, we talked about several of his books, and I recounted the story of my dissertation misadventures. "You're a persistent young man," János said upon hearing that I still wanted to do fieldwork after my Yugoslav and Polish disappointments. "Come to Hungary and we'll do what we can to help you get access to firms."

A year later, in the summer of 1983, I arrived in Budapest on the Orient Express from Paris. Csaba Makó, a sociologist with whom I was well acquainted, met me at the Kelleti train station. I can recall the moment as if it were yesterday. We were not even out of the station when Csaba began talking excitedly about a new development in Hungarian labor relations: through a measure initiated by the Politburo of the Hungarian Communist Party a year earlier in 1982, workers had received the right to form "intra-enterprise partnerships." In the partnerships, workers were running factory equipment on the "off-hours" and on weekends, subcontracting to the parent enterprise and getting orders from outside firms. Not entirely unlike the peasant-workers that I had wanted to study in Yugoslavia, the partners were working in two forms of social organization. But the partnership form was an even more extraordinary social laboratory for an organizational sociologist: in the same factory, using the same technology, workers were moving on a daily basis from bureaucratic to nonbureaucratic organizational forms as the selection of supervisors, the organization of work, and methods of internal payment were left to the discretion

[1] Based on library and archival research, my dissertation focused on a comparison of Taylorism and Leninism—not in the conventional way that Lenin was fascinated by the prospects of introducing Taylorism into state-owned firms, but on each as new class projects tied to "scientific" knowledge claims in different domains. Whereas the scientific management of the firm claimed legitimacy on the basis of the "laws" derived from "time and motion studies," the attempt to manage an economy scientifically rested on claims to knowledge of the "laws of motion of history." The irony was that the attempt to scientifically manage an economy through the budgetary instruments of central planning made it impossible to introduce rationalized principles of scientific management within the firm.

of the work partners. "From six to two we work for them," Csaba told me was the expression he had heard, and "from two to six we work for ourselves." This was an opportunity I could not fail to recognize. "I have to study this," I told him as we got onto the subway.

Csaba introduced me to his assistant, János Lukács, and we immediately set to work. During that summer, we conducted dozens of interviews with workers and managers in a number of factories to learn more about the work partnership "experiment," always with an eye to spot one or more settings where we could do in-depth ethnographic work. We found such an opportunity at "Minotaur,"[2] a producer of tires and other rubber products and one of the very largest state-owned enterprises in Hungary, where we were welcomed by a work partnership in its machine-tool factory. The toolmakers had formed their partnership to gain recognition of their worth as highly skilled craftsmen, bringing them into conflict with Minotaur management but also leading to new challenges of finding an internal payment system to allocate their "entrepreneurial fee."

Over the following years I returned frequently to Minotaur, supported by fellowships that allowed me to take research leaves. In the fall of 1986 I traveled back and forth between Budapest and Paris, where I was a visiting fellow at the Centre de Sociologie Politique et Morale at the invitation of its founder, Luc Boltanski. I wrote the first draft of "Work, Worth, and Justice" (chapter 2 of this book) in Paris while Luc and his collaborator, Laurent Thévenot, were preparing the manuscript for their book *De la Justification: Les Économies de la Grandeur* (discussed in chapter 1). Our conversations about their work helped to clarify my ideas. Whereas the language of my graduate student days had been one of "modes of production," I now saw that economic sociology and organizational theory could benefit from the vocabulary of "orders of worth" (my translation of the French, *les ordres de la grandeur*). In place of the grand historic clash of modes of production, I now heard another noisy encounter in the workplace: the clash of contending principles of evaluation.

But while I was on a steep learning curve with my French colleagues, I was also grappling with my field notes, for there I kept returning to something that I felt missing in the drafts of *De la Justification*. Whereas Boltanski and Thévenot saw orders of worth as conventions that made calculable action possible, the experiment in the machine-tool factory presented considerably more ambiguity. In fact, at Minotaur, action was made possible precisely because there was uncertainty about which order of worth was in operation. Some actors, moreover, were attempting to benefit, not

---

[2] All names of firms and individuals are pseudonymous.

from asserting or fixing their worth in one order, but by maintaining an ongoing ambiguity among the coexisting principles. This ongoing rivalry produced an organizational reflexivity, grossly distorted by the confines of the command economy and a closed political system but incipient nonetheless, pointing to possibilities for the real entrepreneurial activity of recombination.

After leaving Paris, I sent my "Work, Worth, and Justice" paper to Pierre Bourdieu, who accepted it for publication in French in his journal *Actes de la Recherche en Sciences Sociales*. At the encouragement of Bourdieu and Boltanski, I decided to write a book based on my research at Minotaur and other Hungarian factories. A wonderful opportunity to do so presented itself when I was invited to be a Visiting Fellow at Cornell University's Society for the Humanities starting in the fall of 1989. But some other wonderful things also happened in the fall of 1989. There I was, in my office in Ithaca in upstate New York, poring over my field notes for as long as I could before being pulled away to follow fast-breaking political developments in Poland, Hungary, and East Germany. The world I was writing about was undergoing a momentous change.

In early October my friend László Bruszt came through Ithaca brimming with news from Eastern Europe. Throughout the summer of 1989, László had been a participant in the "Roundtable" negotiations in which representatives of Hungary's Communist government and those of the political opposition hammered out an agreement on the transition to free elections. As a delegate of the Hungarian League of Independent Trade Unions (founded in his apartment in Budapest), he had been sent to consult with his counterparts in Poland where similar Roundtable talks had taken place earlier in the year. To say his story was exciting would be an understatement.

László proposed that I come to Hungary, that we interview all the key Communist and opposition figures who had participated in the political negotiations, and that we do so immediately, while their memories were fresh and before election outcomes selectively modified their recollections. I seriously considered his proposal. On one hand, I was an untenured assistant professor with a book to write and with the data to do so. But, on the other, I was on leave from my teaching duties. Several days later the Berlin Wall was toppled. I recognized that the opportunity to do real-time research on an epochal transformation on a topic that my previous ten years had prepared me to understand would not come more than once in a lifetime. The fascinating story of the Minotaur toolmakers was now being played out on a much larger historical stage that I could study firsthand. By December I was in Budapest.

In place of a book on workplace politics in the socialist period, my research with Bruszt led to a quite different book, *Postsocialist Pathways: Transforming Politics and Property in East Central Europe*, addressing the distinctive challenge of postsocialist politics: Could the transformation of property rights and the expansion of citizenship rights be achieved simultaneously?[3] During this period I continued my research in economic sociology, returning to several of the firms where I had studied the work partnerships during the 1980s and augmenting the case studies by systematically collecting data on the ownership structure of the two hundred largest Hungarian enterprises to chart network ties among these firms. That research led me to question the notion of market transition as a toggle switch from public to private property. I did find property transformation, but I found that it took forms of "recombinant property" in which the boundaries of public and private as well as the boundaries of firms were blurred in networks of intercorporate ownership.[4]

Whether it occurs in politics or in the economy, I concluded that change, even fundamental change, of the social world cannot be understood as the passage from one order to another but should be seen as rearrangements in the patterns of how these orders are interwoven. That is, instead of thinking about institutional change or organizational innovation as replacement, I examined them as reconfigurations of institutional elements. In short, I thought of organizational innovation as recombination, a theme that reappears throughout the present book.

I completed my paper "Recombinant Property" as well as my book *Postsocialist Pathways* while a Visiting Fellow at the Center for Advanced Study in the Behavioral Sciences in Palo Alto in 1996–97. Near the end of my stay, I was watching my daughter's soccer practice on a late afternoon and struck up a conversation with another parent. He was curious about my research in Hungarian firms and asked me to describe what I had been finding. "Well, I sometimes have difficulty knowing where one firm ends and another one begins," I began. He nodded an encouragement to continue. I went on to mention the blurring of public and private and then how firms sometimes collaborate on projects without getting all the property arrangements settled at the outset. At each step he kept me going with an encouraging "Yeah, and . . . ?" After four or five such promptings, he interrupted, "You're not talking about Hungary. You're talking about Silicon Valley."

[3] David Stark and László Bruszt, *Postsocialist Pathways: Transforming Politics and Property in East Central Europe*, 1998.

[4] David Stark, "Recombinant Property in East European Capitalism," 1996.

The comic-strip version of this narrative would now show a big light-bulb glowing in a bubble over my head. Indeed, I am aware that it seems almost comical that I could be standing on the side of a playing field and suddenly realize that while I had been studying a major social transformation elsewhere, another one was taking place in the society in which I lived. I knew that the two processes could not be the same, but the possibility of understanding that difference sparked my curiosity. If I had learned anything from my research on the democratic revolutions in Eastern Europe, it was that if I wanted to study the so-called digital revolution it would have to be by getting right into the middle of it. How do you study a hurricane or a tornado? You fly into it and gather data while it is happening.

In the fall of 1997 I joined the faculty of Columbia University, attracted by the prospect of participating in the rebuilding of a renowned department and also by the opportunities that New York City posed as a research site. It was not Silicon Valley, but it did have its own version of that phenomenon called Silicon Alley, home to thousands of new start-up companies in the field that came to be known as "new media." With Monique Girard, I conducted several years of ethnographic research among programmers and interactive designers in one these new-media start-ups, a firm we call NetKnowHow. That ethnography forms the basis of chapter 3 of this book. Toolmakers of a different sort from my Minotaur machinists, the new-media workers at NetKnowHow were building the tools of the digital economy. And, like the Minotaur toolmakers, the new-media toolmakers were using the ambiguity of multiple evaluative principles to navigate through uncharted territory—in this case the Internet land rush in what was then known as the new economy.

While we were studying NetKnowHow, we were also learning that our predecessors at Columbia University had put together a model research program on which we could attempt to build. At midcentury, organizational analysts at Columbia, led by Robert Merton and Paul Lazarsfeld, launched two ambitious research programs. On one track, Merton and his graduate students examined the origins and functioning of bureaucracy using various research methods (Peter Blau, small groups; Alvin Gouldner, ethnography; James Coleman, survey research). On a second, parallel track, Merton and Lazarsfeld established the Bureau of Radio Research to examine the dynamics of mass communication, pioneering in the use of focus groups and methods to study the demography of audience reception.

The idea of studying an organizational form *and* a form of communication, in a period when each was being reconfigured, stimulated a series of conversations with my graduate students. Whereas our Columbia predecessors had charted the structure of bureaucratic organizations in the era of mass communication, we realized that our research challenge would be to chart the emergence of collaborative organizational forms in an era of new interactive technologies. But the difference between the earlier and the current Columbia projects goes beyond the fact that our predecessors studied hierarchy and we study heterarchy, or that they studied the social technologies of mass production and mass communication and we study the social technologies of collaborative production and collaborative communication. The important difference, as Bob Merton emphasized in our conversations, is that the two tracks of research (organizational forms on one side, communication technologies on the other) can no longer be conducted along parallel lines. As we shall see in chapter 3 and especially in chapter 4, in our era the design of heterarchical organization cannot be separated from design of the digital interface.

The newly founded Columbia Center on Organizational Innovation provided an institutional platform for this research program. One of our first activities was a yearlong speakers' series and graduate seminar titled "Heterarchy." With all the talk about "multiple evaluative principles" in the seminar, we wondered whether it might be interesting to establish a baseline by studying an organization in which there was no ambiguity or disagreement about value. Such a study would provide a kind of standard against which we could better understand the workings of heterarchical organizations where value was in contention. With Daniel Beunza, one of the grad students in the seminar, we took up this project and secured access to what we assumed would be the gold standard of a single metric of value—the arbitrage trading room of a major international investment bank on Wall Street, the scene of chapter 4.

In ethnographic field research, as in any research method, nothing is more productive than surprise. And the biggest and best surprise is the one that goes against the research design. But precisely because it is research—that is, not a search for the already known—you can never anticipate what it will be, and, on that account, you can never deliberately design your project for that surprise. The best you can do is be prepared so you will be able to recognize the opportunity for novel insight. Chapter 4 reports such an occasion of surprise. Traders know that they are looking for value, for profits, but the specific instances of such rewarding opportunities cannot be known in advance. Arbitrage operates by making novel associations across highly abstracted qualities of securities and their derivatives. But within arbitrage there are multiple principles for searching for value, and the trading room is organized as a kind of cognitive ecology exploiting the diversity of these principles to recognize (in fact, as we shall see, re-cognize) novel associations.

• • •

As an epigraph, I quote a passage where Dante advises, "Fix not thy mind / On one place only." Certainly not advice that I consciously followed from the outset, it does account, after the fact, for a process repeatedly at work in the zigs and zags, the false starts, the seized opportunities, and the sudden turns in this intellectual journey. But if there were abrupt turns, surely they could just as well be cast as *returns*: going to Hungary, yet returning to the problem I had not been able to study in Yugoslavia; shifting from an outdated, decaying industrial setting to high tech, yet returning to the notion of entrepreneurial recombination that I had found only in incipient and distorted form in Hungary; going downtown to the trading room, yet returning to the notion of diversity of principles as key for recognition and re-cognition. So, yes, returns, many happy returns. Because in these *ritornellos* (here the musical term), the theme is not simply repeated but returns—recognizable, yet in a different form. And the more disconcerting the difference, the more delightful the recognition. A curious, and I hope you will find a generative, fixed idea this: to fix not thy mind on one place only.

The key insight, however, is not that sociologists should search in diverse settings. I bring these three cases together to make a broader argument about search. The idea, in its most simple form, is that organizations can see more, search better, with a sociological double vision. Stated succinctly: The Minotaur toolmakers recognize their worth and their identities in the discrepancies between competing orders of the worth; the new-media firm recognizes opportunities in the contention over what is a resource; the traders recognize value in the diversity of principles of valuation. A society recognizes its potential when it truly gives recognition to a multiplicity of ways of defining what is valuable. Our wealth—no, even better, our worth is increased when there is open disagreement about what is worthy.

Durham, England, December 2007

Heterarchy: The Organization of Dissonance

Searching Questions

Search is the watchword of the information age. Among the many new information technologies that are reshaping work and daily life, perhaps none are more empowering than the new technologies of search. With a few keywords at the toolbar, we can access enormous databases to find an obscure article by a long-distant colleague, identify the supplier of a critical component, read about the benefits and side effects of new pharmaceutical products or medical procedures, or find the fact that immediately settles a dispute about the performance of an opera, an athlete, or a mutual fund. Whereas the steam engine, the electrical turbine, the internal combustion engine, and the jet engine propelled the industrial economy, search engines power the information economy.

Search is among the key concepts of this book because search is the process that best exemplifies the challenges of contemporary organization. Ironically, those challenges cannot be solved by the search technologies that are transforming how we work, how we shop, and even how we locate ourselves in social and physical space. Certainly, new search technologies have become invaluable for how organizations manage knowledge. But the results they yield are of precisely the wrong kind to answer the more fundamental problems confronting organizations today. The more challenging type of search does not yield coordinates for a preidentified entity or category, as, for example, when I search for an e-mail address or for a recent paper that I heard presented at a conference. Nor is it even a search for solutions to clearly defined problems. The fundamental challenge is the kind of search during which you do not know what you are looking for but will recognize it when you find it.

Academics are familiar with the process. In fact, to distinguish it from the search for the already known, we have a ready term: *research*.[1] In other

---

[1] If you are a reader searching for a dissertation topic, you are familiar with this kind of search. If you already knew precisely what you were looking for, chances are it has already been done. Innovative research expands the problem field. The challenge therefore is to work enough outside the already known while casting the research such that the new problem, concept, method, insight will be recognized by others.

fields, the process goes by a different name: *innovation*. John Dewey, one of the founders of the pragmatist school of American philosophy, used another term: *inquiry*.[2]

Dewey was emphatic that inquiry, as a distinctive mode of search, should be distinguished from problem solving. His clarification merits quoting at length because it so nicely turns our attention from a well-defined problem to the more interesting case of a perplexing situation:

> [I]t is artificial, so far as thinking is concerned, to start with a ready-made problem, a problem made out of whole cloth or arising from a vacuum. In reality such a "problem" is simply an assigned *task*. There is not at first a situation *and* a problem, much less just a problem and no situation. There is a troubled, perplexed, trying situation, where the difficulty is, as it were, spread throughout the entire situation, infecting it as a whole. If we knew just what the difficulty was and where it lay, the job of reflection would be much easier than it is. . . . In fact, we know what the problem *exactly* is simultaneously with finding a way out and getting it resolved.[3]

Dewey's evocation of perplexed and troubling situations will ring true to any reader who has faced the challenge of knowing that sometimes you must search even when you do not know what you are looking for. We grasp the difference between an assigned task, as Dewey labels a simple search, and a challenging situation. We sense that there is a difference between occasions when we look for solutions within a set of established parameters and other occasions (Dewey would say situations) rife with uncertainty and yet, precisely because of that, also ripe with possibilities.[4] Life would be blessedly simple if we could solve our searching questions with a few clicks at the toolbar. But it would be neither interesting nor satisfying.

In their study of new-product development in cellular telephones, blue jeans, and medical devices, Richard Lester and Michael Piore succinctly capture the difference between the two types of search.[5] In the *analytic* mode, the task of the good manager is to clearly identify the problem, break it down into independent components, and organize a series of decisions about how best to solve them. But Lester and Piore conclude that the

---

[2] Dewey was working in the pragmatist tradition that began with Charles Sanders Peirce's idea of communities of inquiry to account for the ways that people construct knowledge in collaboration with others.

[3] John Dewey, "Analysis of Reflective Thinking," [1933] 1998, p. 140 (emphasis in the original).

[4] Ann Mische and Harrison White, "Between Conversation and Situation: Public Switching Dynamics across Networks," 1998.

[5] Richard K. Lester and Michael J. Piore, *Innovation: The Missing Dimension*, 2004.

most important component of innovation is a process that is not directed toward the solution of well-defined problems. This second mode is characterized by *interpretation*. Whereas problem solving involves the precise exchange of information, the interpretive model fosters open-ended, unpredictable conversation. Where the former seeks clarity, the latter seeks spaces of ambiguity since the challenge is to integrate knowledge across heterogeneous domains. Lester and Piore demonstrate that each of their cases of radical innovation involves combinations across disparate fields: Fashion jeans are the marriage of traditional workmen's clothing and laundry technology borrowed from hospitals and hotels. Medical devices draw on the basic life sciences as well as clinical practice. And cellular phones recombine in novel form radio and telephone technologies. They conclude that "without integration across the borders separating these different fields, there would have been no new products at all."[6]

Because innovation, in this view, involves bringing together incompatible traditions, we should not expect that the process will be harmonious. With hindsight, it is easy to see that high-fashion faded blue jeans are a recombination of workmen's clothing and laundry technology. If we can say that "of course!" cellular phones are the marriage of the radio and the telephone, it is only because, as Lester and Piore show, the respective communities worked from the starting point of their differences. In hindsight, we infer that they must have known all along what they were looking for whereas, in fact, as Dewey and the pragmatists argued, it was only in the conflictual process of attempting to make a transformation in the world that the problem could even be formulated.[7] Working broadly from within this same tradition, Lester and Piore observe:

> In many industries, innovations can be identified that did not, at least initially, address a particular need or problem, or for which the problem became apparent only after the product was in use. In such cases, *the product developer frequently starts out without really knowing what she is trying to create.* (p. 41, emphasis added)

The search problems that this book addresses are thus different from the everyday notion of exploration, if that term calls to mind a process like exploring for petroleum or similar searches for a good that is known in advance. Following James March, I shall use the term *exploration* narrowly to refer to processes that break from successful, familiar routines to

---

[6] Lester and Piore, *Innovation*, pp. 14–15.
[7] For a similar account of discovering the world through the conflictual process of attempting to transform it, see Tracy Kidder, *The Soul of a New Machine*, 1981.

search into the unknown.[8] That is, if exploring for territory is your metaphor of choice, the challenging searches would be efforts to recognize the terrae incognitae.

Stated as recognition of the incognita, the process of innovation is paradoxical, for it involves a curious cognitive function of recognizing what is not yet formulated as a category. It is one thing to recognize an already-identified pattern, but quite another to make a new association. To take some mundane yet now ubiquitous examples: gas for industrial lighting in the nineteenth century (recognizing a waste product of the process of converting coal to coke as a valuable resource);[9] the shopping cart (a basket on wheels);[10] the parking meter (a hitching post with a clock-type mainspring); the car radio (pioneered by a family firm, now famously Motorola, that had made accessories for carriages and sought a market in accessories for the new automobile); the airport shopping mall (combining consumption and travel); and, more troubling, the megachurch of American exurbia (combining Wal-Mart architecture, televangelism, and highly niched small groups or cells from the repertoire of underground movements to create a new form of spirituality as mass-customized consumption). Each example of recombination or repurposing involved a category switch, obvious now in retrospect precisely because each could be recognized with little cognitive difficulty by the user.

Whether we refer to the process as research, innovation, exploration, or inquiry, the kind of search that works through interpretation rather than simply managing information requires *reflective cognition*. Whether in science, politics, civic associations, or business, it is not enough just to embark on a search for an unknown breakthrough; you must also be able to recognize it when you find it. And you must present the category-breaking solutions in forms that are recognizable to other scientists, citizens, activists, investors, or users. This is a tall challenge, for the more ambitious the project, the more deliberately ill defined the initial process of search; and the more demanding the processes of eventual recognition, the greater is the discomforting ambiguity facing the innovating organization. Innovation, as Joseph Schumpeter observed, is recombination; but, as Schumpeter argued as well, it is also deeply disruptive of cultural taken-for-granteds and routines of organizational cognition.

We can now appreciate again Dewey's characterization of inquiry as provoked by "troubled, perplexed, trying situations." Organizations fac-

---

[8] James G. March, "Exploration and Exploitation in Organizational Learning," 1991.

[9] Wolfgang Schivelbusch, *Disenchanted Night: The Industrialization of Light in the Nineteenth Century*, 1995, p. 18.

[10] Catherine Grandclément, "Wheeling One's Groceries around the Store," 2008.

ing such perplexing situations have several options. The first temptation for the leaders of science projects, corporate projects, or civic projects is to immediately address ambiguous situations pregnant with interpretive search by using the clearly defined problem-solving strategy of analytic search. But such a managerialist strategy of early top-down control entails the risk of forgoing the big opportunities represented in innovations such as cellular phones, fashion jeans, and breakthrough medical equipment. Although problem solving eventually came into the picture, interpretation was the dominant mode of product development that led to innovative success in each of these cases.[11]

The alternative strategy is more in line with John Dewey's notion of inquiry as a guide for innovation. Dewey's attention to the productive possibilities of situations is the lesson that I try to keep in mind throughout this book. Instead of avoiding perplexing situations, organizations can embrace them. Even more radically, organizations can take the next step: If perplexing situations provoke innovative inquiry, then why not build organizations that generate such situations? Instead of merely responding to external situations as they happen to present themselves, why not foster organizational forms that regularly and recursively produce perplexing situations within the organization itself? Organizations that adopt such forms will then be poised to undertake the challenging task of ongoing innovation.

At the most elementary level, a perplexing situation is produced when there is principled disagreement about what counts. Organizations that seek to generate productive, perplexing situations can work from this basic starting point. Instead of enforcing a single principle of evaluation as the only legitimate framework, they recognize that it is legitimate to articulate alternative conceptions of what is valuable, what is worthy, what counts. Such organizations have heterogeneous criteria of organizational "goods." To signal that this organizational form is a mode of governance that differs from a hierarchy of command and a conceptual hierarchy of cognitive categories, I refer to it as a *heterarchy*. As the case ethnographies in the following chapters demonstrate, heterarchies are cognitive ecologies that facilitate the work of reflexive cognition.

Such organizations, we shall see, are not frictionless. But friction is not something to be avoided at all costs. We all prefer a smooth ride, but as you and your tire dealer know, when taking a sharp curve, we count on friction to keep us on course. Friction can be destructive. But, as the

---

[11] Lester and Piore, *Innovation.*

designers of the U.S. Constitution well understood when they built the friction of checks and balances into our system of government, it can also be a principled component of a functioning system with productive outcomes. That is, having multiple performance criteria can produce a resourceful dissonance. If you are confident that you know precisely what resources your organization will need in the indefinite future to meet stable and predictable markets (or continue to get grants to meet your unchanging mission as a nonprofit or a research operation), then dissonance is an avoidable headache that you need not abide. But for many organizations the "foreseeable future" is not long distant. Where the organizational environment is turbulent and there is uncertainty about what might constitute a resource under changed conditions, contending frameworks of value can themselves be a valuable organizational resource. Entrepreneurship then, in this view, exploits uncertainty. Not the property of an individual personality but, instead, the function of an organizational form, entrepreneurship is the ability to keep multiple principles of evaluation in play and to benefit from that productive friction.

For a Sociology of Worth

What counts? Each of us confronts this question on a daily basis. Faced with decisions involving incommensurable frameworks—work versus family life, career opportunities versus loyalty to friends or attachment to a locality, vacations versus investments for retirement, and so on—we ask ourselves what really counts. What is valuable, and by what measures? As our lives are a search to find out what is really valuable, we try, we fail, and we try again to learn from our mistakes.

In our roles as actors in organizations we face similar questions. In these organizational settings we need to sift through a barrage of information—seemingly growing at an exponential rate—to select what counts, what matters, what is of true relevance. More fundamentally, organizations are engaged in a search for what is valuable. What new products can be brought to market? What new technologies or production processes should be pursued? Which will prove to be valuable and which will be a costly dead end? And how should the performance of units, of teams, and of the individual employees within them be evaluated? Nonprofits might be tax-exempt, but they are not exempt from similar questions. Which campaigns and projects are worthy of pursuit? Will our members, constituents, activists, targeted communities, and donors recognize their value, perhaps quickly, or perhaps too late?

Within the sociological discipline, economic sociology is the specialization that deals with societal and organizational questions of the valuable. The field's founding moment took place more than a half century ago
at Harvard, where Talcott Parsons was developing his grand designs for
sociology. Parsons's ambitions were imperial, with the aim of reshaping
much of the social sciences. But his instincts in academic politics led him
to be wary of economics as the discipline that could thwart his agenda if
his program was perceived as encroaching on its territory. Whereas sociology, psychology, and anthropology could be claimed outright, economics
would have to be maneuvered around. To dispel any doubt about his intentions, Parsons walked down the hall in Harvard's Littauer Center to his
colleagues in the Economics Department, alerting them to his ambitious
plans and assuring them that he had no designs on their terrain.[12] Thus, Parsons made a pact. In my gloss: You, economists, study value; we, the sociologists, will study values. You will have claim on the economy; we will stake
our claim on the social relations in which economies are embedded.[13]

Although Parsons's Pact suggests that we must choose a single vantage
point—value *or* values, economy *or* social relations—I adopt an analytic
strategy of fusing the two notions across this divide.[14] The key concept in
this fusion is the notion of worth. The polysemic character of the term—
worth—signals concern with fundamental problems of value while recognizing that all economies have a moral component. Rather than the
static fixtures of value and values, it focuses instead on ongoing processes
of *valuation*—whether in assessing the value of firms under competing

---

[12] Charles Camic, "The Making of a Method: A Historical Reinterpretation of the Early Parsons," 1987. Although he characterizes it slightly differently, Velthuis similarly argues that in the
mid-1930s Parsons and the economist Lionel Robbins agreed on the terms of a disciplinary division of labor. Olav Velthuis, "The Changing Relationship between Economic Sociology and
Institutional Economics: From Talcott Parsons to Mark Granovetter," 1999.

[13] Parsons's Pact thus imposed a jurisdictional division of the social sciences that placed constraints on sociology by limiting its range. Yet, by delimiting a legitimate object of study—society,
though not the economy—it ensured that the discipline would flourish in the great postwar expansion of the social sciences.

[14] Economic sociologists have adopted various strategies to break with Parsons's Pact. In *Markets from Networks* (2002) Harrison White basically turns the tables on the terms of the pact.
Markets, he argues, are not *embedded in* social relations; they *are* social relations. Instead of accepting the economists' conception of markets, White has developed a sociological theory of
markets. As the counterpart to Harrison White, Viviana Zelizer pointed out a way to escape
from Parsons's Pact along the value/values dimension. In *Pricing the Priceless Child* (1985) Zelizer examines the interrelation between market or price and personal or moral values in a rich
historical study of child labor, adoption, and insurance. Zelizer's later work on the social meaning
of money, on payment systems, and circuits of commerce boldly transgresses and transcends the
disciplinary divide.

metrics of performance, or in studying the incommensurable assessments made in everyday life. "What are you worth?" is a question that can be unambiguous when constrained by context (as, for example, when applying at a bank for a mortgage). But the same question in an art gallery—"Yes, but what is it worth?"—already suggests that value might be different from price. And when the question comes up among friends—"Honey, do you really think he's worth it?"—we know that several opposed evaluative criteria have been brought into play.

Worth is a wonderful word with deep roots (*wort*) in the old Anglo-Saxon tongue before the Norman invasion brought the Latinate separation of value and values into the English language. With its double connotations of an economic good and a moral good, *worth* is a difficult noun to translate into Italian, for example. None of the candidate terms has that twinned salience, as each is heavily loaded toward either the value or the values side. On the other hand, there is no such verb as "to worth" in English. We can "value something as worth a great deal" or "judge someone as worthy," but we cannot "worth" something or someone. Meanwhile Italian has a perfectly apt verb, *stimare*. In this case, it was English that separated the verbs "to estimate" (on the value side) and "to esteem" (on the values side)—connotations that are equally salient in the Italian verb.[15]

Perhaps more than anyone on this topic, John Dewey was aware not only of how everyday language constrains our thinking but also of how it can reveal insights about the concepts we deploy. In his *Theory of Valuation*, Dewey explores the double meanings in ordinary speech and points to words such as *praise* and *appraise* that parse in different directions from a common root. After noting the twins *estimate* and *esteem*, Dewey observes that it is suggestive "that praise, prize and price are all derived from the same Latin word; that appreciate and appraise were once used interchangeably; and that 'dear' is still used as equivalent both to 'precious' and to 'costly' in monetary price."[16]

With Dewey, I agree that we cannot appeal to everyday language to solve analytic problems. But I also take his point that when we see some commonsense terms pulling apart and others joining together, we should pay attention, for we will usually find a problem worth studying. In particular, we can often see how ideas from ordinary language become incor-

---

[15] I recently encountered this problem when giving a simultaneously translated public lecture at the University of Modena and later when my essay "For a Sociology of Worth" was translated for an Italian journal. On a more general note, writers who make words work very hard should give them due recognition—or, at least, follow the lead of Humpty-Dumpty in *Alice in Wonderland*: "When I make a word do extra work, I'm always sure to pay it very well."

[16] John Dewey, Theory of Valuation, 1939, pp. 5–6.

porated in the false dichotomies that we use in analysis—for example, in viewing ends as values that are prized while regarding means as objects that are appraised. For Dewey, it makes as much sense to see means as prized and ends appraised. His pragmatic theory of inquiry as action shatters these dichotomies.

In the closing section of his *Theory of Valuation* Dewey provides a diagnosis of the crisis of his time. Writing in 1939, he observes that emotional loyalties and attachments are not linked to scientific debate, while ideas with their origin in scientific inquiry have not succeeded in gaining emotional force.[17] For Dewey this is a practical problem, and an analytic one. In the penultimate paragraph he highlights this problem by returning to the discussion of common speech with which he began his study.

> In fact, and in net outcome, the previous discussion does not
> point in the least to supersession of the emotive by the intellectual.
> Its only and complete import is the need for their integration in
> behavior—behavior in which, according to common speech, the
> head and the heart work together, in which, to use more technical
> language, prizing and appraising unite in direction of action. (p. 65)

It is, then, with Dewey that we embark on an analysis of worth to develop tools for understanding a richer calculus that integrates value and values, the intellectual and the emotive, valuation and the evaluative. When we see that acts of estimation entail practices of esteem, we see that payment systems are about recognition as well as about monetary rewards. When we see inquiry as action, we see search less as a process of finding what we already know to be valuable than as distributed practices for recognizing opportunities by re-cognizing resources. When we regard calculation as not separated from judgment, we see that what counts in the processing of information is the capacity for interpretation.

Following Dewey will require that economic sociology's preoccupation with the analysis of *institutions* should be augmented by close study of indeterminate *situations*. In making this shift, economic sociology can draw lessons from developments in the field of science and technology studies (STS). During its inaugural stage, the sociology of science, led by

---

[17] "We are living in a period in which emotional loyalties and attachments are centered on objects that no longer command that intellectual loyalty which has the sanction of the methods which attain valid conclusions in scientific inquiry, while ideas that have their origin in the rationale of inquiry have not as yet succeeded in acquiring the force that only emotional ardor provides. The practical problem that has to be faced is the establishment of cultural conditions that will support the kinds of behavior in which emotions and ideas, desires and appraisals, are integrated." Dewey, *Theory of Valuation*, p. 65.

Robert Merton, carved out a distinctive place for sociology by focusing on the institutions of science—the structure of rewards and careers, patterns of citations, and the norms of scientific life. Departing from this tradition, the next generation of STS researchers moved into the laboratories to study scientists at work, observing the difficult labor of stabilizing facts, the challenges of replicating experiments, and the ongoing controversies of science in the making.[18]

Just as post-Mertonian studies of science moved from studying the institutions in which scientists were embedded to analyzing the actual practices of scientists in the laboratory, so can economic sociology move from studying the institutions in which economic activity is embedded to analyzing the actual evaluative and calculative practices of actors at work.

In making this move, I draw on insights by Luc Boltanski and Laurent Thévenot, whose book *On Justification: The Economies of Worth*, only recently translated, was originally published in France in 1991.[19] Boltanski, a sociologist, and Thévenot, an economist, are part of a group of French economic sociologists[20] whose work is collectively known as "the economics of convention."[21] Just as Harrison White has developed a sociological theory of markets, Boltanski and Thévenot are developing a sociological theory of value. Their first move is to demonstrate that there is not just

[18] Bruno Latour and Steve Woolgar, *Laboratory Life: The Social Construction of Scientific Facts*, 1979; Trevor Pinch, *Confronting Nature: The Sociology of Solar-Neutrino Detection*, 1986; and Bruno Latour, *Science in Action: How to Follow Scientists and Engineers through Society*, 1987.

[19] Luc Boltanski and Laurent Thévenot, *On Justification: The Economies of Worth*, 2006. For an accessible introduction to the major concepts in article form, see Boltanski and Thévenot, "The Sociology of Critical Capacity," 1999. Michèle Lamont together with Thévenot led an exciting project involving a set of empirical studies, pairing French and American researchers, that demonstrates the fruitful application of these ideas. See their edited collection, *Rethinking Comparative Cultural Sociology: Repertoires of Evaluation in France and the United States*, 2000.

[20] For a recent collection in English, see *Conventions and Structures in Economic Organization: Markets, Networks and Hierarchies*, edited by Olivier Favereau and Emmanuel Lazega, 2002. Introductions to the economics of conventions are provided in John Wilkinson, "A New Paradigm for Economic Analysis?" 1997; and Thierry Levy, "The Theory of Conventions and a New Theory of the Firm," 2001.

[21] The French conventionalist school began with the idea that the qualities of labor were unknown prior to hiring, but soon extended this idea to other commodities that suffered from deficiencies of "incomplete contracts." (The market for used cars is now a well-known example; see George A. Akerlof, "The Market for 'Lemons': Quality Uncertainty and the Market Mechanism," 1970.) Guidance systems and other instrumentation in space vehicles provide a different kind of example in which the buyer cannot know in advance how the qualities of the product will perform in extreme conditions. Of even greater interest are cases in which the parties embark on complex collaborations in which the fundamental characteristics of the joint product are not known in advance but are themselves the key aim of the collaboration. In this case, the critical quality is the ability to collaborate. On discursive quality standards, see especially Charles Sabel and Jane Prokop, "Stabilization through Reorganization?" 1996.

one way of making value but that modern economies comprise multiple principles of evaluation. A modern economy (and note that the word is not society but economy) is not a single social order but contains multiple "orders of worth."

One might object that this is not an escape from Parsons's Pact. After all, as soon as you make a plural out of value, you get *values*. But the orders of worth of the French school, in fact, differ from the cultural systems of Parsonsian values and from the classificatory codes of the new institutionalists. For my colleagues in American economic sociology, values are counterposed to calculation; they are outside and distant from calculation. More precisely, if cultural taken-for-granteds are the embeddings for value, they make calculation possible precisely because they are a kind of antimatter to calculation.[22] For my French conventionalist colleagues, on the other hand, orders of worth are not values counterposed to value but are constitutive of value. Orders of worth are the very fabric of calculation, of rationality, of value.

Boltanski and Thévenot's work refuses a dichotomy of value and values; instead, it fuses them in the concept of worth. Although we are accustomed to thinking about "moral economies" as opposed to market economies—for example, in the norms of close-knit communities that embodied precapitalist traditions of the just and fair[23]—Boltanski and Thévenot see all economies as moral economies. Each of the orders of worth operating in the domain that we conventionally denominate as "the economy" is an economy. And, as an economy, each is a moral order.

Boltanski and Thévenot delineate six discrete orders of worth, each epitomized by a particular moral philosopher. From their perspective, I would be mistaken to say that I live in a market economy. Markets are, indeed, one of the organizing principles of the U.S. economy. But, as they show in their study of the domain of the corporation, in addition to a *market* rationality (exemplified by the moral philosophy of Adam Smith), a modern economy also has an *industrial* or technological rationality (Saint Simon), another organized around a *civic* logic (Rousseau), and still

---

[22] Paul J. DiMaggio and Walter W. Powell, "Introduction," in *The New Institutionalism in Organizational Analysis*, 1991. In this agenda-setting statement for the "new institutionalism" in economic sociology, DiMaggio and Powell present a sharp critique of Parsons (pp. 15–22), making clear that whereas the old institutionalism was about "values, norms, attitudes," the new institutionalism analyzes "classifications, routines, scripts, schema." Emphasizing the importance of "unreflective activity," DiMaggio and Powell explicitly counterpose such cultural taken-for-granteds to calculative behavior (p. 22).

[23] Social historian E. P. Thompson emphasized the force of such traditions in his pioneering article "The Moral Economy of the English Crowd in the Eighteenth Century," 1971.

others arrayed according to principles of *loyalty* (Bossuet), *inspiration* (Augustine), and *renown* or fame (Hobbes).

Boltanski and Thévenot are emphatic that their orders of worth do not map to separate domains.[24] Inspiration, for example, is not the special province of the world of art; nor does a civic rationality correspond to the public sphere; and the market order can operate as well in the domains of academia and religion. In the second part of *On Justification*, Boltanski and Thévenot illustrate the operation of each of the orders of worth within a single domain, that of the large corporation, through a content analysis of six best-selling guidebooks to being a good manager—each written from the perspective of a different order respectively.

As an example that each of the orders of worth is salient in the world of academia, take letters of recommendation for faculty appointments. You do not need to read a great many such letters to recognize that recommenders frequently refer to multiple principles of evaluation. In fact, a given letter might include performance criteria from each of the six orders of worth. We would not be surprised, for example, to read that a given candidate is "very creative" (the order of inspiration); that she is incredibly "productive" (the industrial); and that she is a "good citizen" (the civic). Moreover, the same letter could note that her work is "frequently cited" (the order of fame or renown) and that she is fiercely "loyal to her graduate students" (check off another). Has the letter writer neglected the market order? We are not likely to hear about an academic as the author of a "best-selling" book. Look through the letter again and you might find that the candidate "has a strong record of getting grants."

As coherent principles of evaluation, each of the orders of worth has distinctive and incommensurable principles of equivalence. Each defines the good, the just, and the fair—but according to different criteria of judgment. Each qualifies persons and objects with a distinctive grammar or logic. As principles of evaluation, the orders involve systematic associations of concepts; but the entities that populate an order of worth are not

---

[24] Despite the similarity of a notion of multiple rationalities, Boltanski and Thévenot's framework differs markedly from that of Roger Friedland and Robert Alford, who identify several institutional domains, each with its distinctive "logic of action" ("Bringing Society Back In: Symbols, Practices, and Institutional Contradictions," 1991). Whereas Friedland and Alford parse logics to domains (e.g., affective in the family, cognitive in the market, etc.), Boltanski and Thévenot's respective orders of worth are not isolated to specific societal domains. Although it shares a similar intuition, their view also differs from that of Wendy Espeland and Mitchell Stevens, who argue that "because societies are complexes of multiple institutions, they are characterized by multiple modes of valuing" ("Commensuration as a Social Process," 1998, p. 332). Because Boltanski and Thévenot's orders of worth do not parse to separate institutions, all can be operating in the economy.

limited to persons and ideas. *On Justification* shows in rich detail how the principles of evaluation established in each order of worth entail discrete metrics, measuring "instruments," and proofs of worth objectified in artifacts and objects in the material world.

In this view, rational calculation is not opposed to moral judgment; instead, rationality works within orders of worth. As such, I interpret Boltanski and Thévenot's work as casting new meaning on the term "bounded rationality." Whereas we conventionally think about bounded rationality as the cognitive limits on rationality (as, for example, in the usage of the term by economist Oliver Williamson), in Boltanski and Thévenot's work rationality is possible only insofar as it takes place within the boundaries and through the social technologies of particular orders of worth. In this latter sense we should speak—and with a very different meaning—of bounded *rationalities*.

Drawing from Boltanski and Thévenot, as well as from Michel Callon and his colleagues,[25] in the framework that I adopt in this book, the familiar culturalist *versus* materialist opposition becomes meaningless. All economic objects are thoroughly cultural, and no moral order could operate without specific material objects. Moreover, rationality is not something "above" the preconscious, nor is calculation somehow "below" moral orderings. From my field research in Hungary, where I found a plurality of economic forms operating in a single factory (see chapter 2), I was predisposed to the idea that organizations are settings where multiple principles of evaluation are at play. But because I do not confine these to the six moral orders of *On Justification*, I specify the evaluative principles differently from one case to another, as is appropriate for each case. Most importantly, my field research leads me to different conclusions from those of Boltanski and Thévenot. As I shall argue in the next section and develop in the subsequent substantive chapters, whereas they see orders of worth as making action possible by resolving problems of uncertainty, my case ethnographies led me to see the mix of evaluative principles as creating uncertainty and therefore as opening opportunities for action.

Entrepreneurship at the Overlap

Economic sociology, like many fields in the discipline, is populated with dualisms. In addition to the dichotomy of value and values and the perennial

---

[25] See especially Michel Callon and Fabian Muniesa, "Economic Markets as Calculative Collective Devices," 2005.

"structure versus agency," we also find notions of calculation versus trust, and efficiency versus legitimacy. One particularly productive distinction that continues to generate insights was formulated by economist Frank Knight as the problem of *risk versus uncertainty*.[26] For Knight, uncertainty and risk are both shaped by the fact that the future is unknown. But the two are not the same. In circumstances of risk, chances are calculable; that is, the distribution of outcomes can be expressed in some probabilistic terms. Uncertainty, however, lacks calculation: "All bets are off."

The problem of uncertainty, it must be emphasized, is not a function of the limited calculative power of the human actors confronting it. Instead it is a property of the situation. The situation is indeterminate. John Dewey, writing about the same time as Knight but in a different context, nicely expresses the problem of indeterminate situations:

> A variety of names serves to characterize indeterminate situations. They are disturbed, troubled, ambiguous, confused, full of conflicting tendencies, obscure, etc. It is the *situation* that has these traits. *We* are doubtful because the situation is inherently doubtful.[27]

Santa Fe Institute economist David Lane succinctly summarizes the situation of uncertainty: "the question is not what we do not know, but what cannot be known."[28]

Although economists are now giving renewed attention to the problem of uncertainty,[29] the typical view in the discipline, institutionalized in the neoclassical framework, was to frame all economic action as cases of risk.[30] Knight could see the direction that his discipline was moving, and in his view the tendency to see all situations as those in which the distribution of outcomes could be expressed in probabilistic terms would deprive economists of the ability to grasp a problem that should be at the core of the discipline. Knight argued that a world of generalized probabilistic knowledge of the future leaves no place for profit and, as a consequence, no place for the entrepreneur. For Knight, what defines profit is that it cannot be measured ex ante—as distinct from rents, which constitute contractualizable residual revenue. In Knight's framework, the entrepreneur,

---

[26] Frank H. Knight, *Risk, Uncertainty and Profit*, 1921.

[27] John Dewey, "The Pattern of Inquiry," [1938] 1998, p. 171, emphasis in the original.

[28] David Lane, "Models and Aphorisms," 1995.

[29] Adam Brandenburger, "The Power of Paradox: Some Recent Developments in Interactive Epistemology," 2007; Sheila Dow and John Hillard, eds., *Keynes, Knowledge and Uncertainty*, 1995; and Edward Fullbrook, ed., *Intersubjectivity in Economics: Agents and Structures*, 2001.

[30] Jens Beckert, "What Is Sociological about Economic Sociology? Uncertainty and the Embeddedness of Economic Action," 1996.

properly speaking, is not rewarded for risk taking but, instead, is rewarded for an ability to exploit uncertainty.

In Boltanski and Thévenot's framework, there is little space for entrepreneurial activity. For this French school of economic sociology, conventions (of which orders of worth are a particularly well-elaborated variant) are a way of dealing with uncertainty. They are engines for turning situations into calculative problems. Orders of worth can be considered as social technologies to transform uncertainty into risk.[31] The limitation of this view—and here is my departure from Boltanski and Thévenot—is that it does not give adequate attention to the problem that orders of worth cannot eliminate uncertainty. In particular, they cannot eliminate the possibility of uncertainty about which order or convention is operative in a given situation.

Taking this into account, we are in a position to restate the insight of Knight, but now in new terms: it is precisely *this* uncertainty that entrepreneurship exploits. *Entrepreneurship is the ability to keep multiple evaluative principles in play and to exploit the resulting friction of their interplay.*

In exploiting the uncertainty about which order of worth is operative, entrepreneurship involves *asset ambiguity.*[32] From ambiguity it makes an asset; and in creating assets that can operate in more than one game, it makes assets that are ambiguous. In the subsequent chapter, for example, we shall see how a group of highly skilled machinists, working in Communist Hungary, exploited the ambiguity of the "economies" of redistribution, market, and reciprocity that were operative in their factory. Their strategy was not without limits and was not always successful, but it

---

[31] The coordination problems in Boltanski and Thévenot differ from Schelling's case of a couple who get separated in a large department store but who do not have a predefined meeting place (Thomas C. Schelling, *The Strategy of Conflict*, 1960). The couple succeed in coordinating not despite the circular specularity but because each knows that the other is trying to coordinate with him/her. Schelling's case is more like the common knowledge framework in Lewis's notion of convention. (David K. Lewis, *Conventions: A Philosophical Study*, 1969. For discussion see especially Jean-Pierre Dupuy, "Common Knowledge, Common Sense," 1989.) Boltanski and Thévenot's orders of worth are not about the application of *rules* and hence differ from "institutions" either in game theory or in the new institutionalism.

[32] Asset ambiguity, thus, contrasts sharply with the concept of asset specificity developed by the economist Oliver Williamson. By *asset specificity* Williamson referred to the extent to which investment in a given asset was specific to a particular transaction. The degree of asset specificity was critical, Williamson argued, in the decision to make or buy. (Oliver Williamson, "The Economics of Organization: The Transaction Cost Approach," 1981.) Charles Sabel and Bruce Kogut, by contrast, explored the problem of asset interdependence, demonstrating that, under conditions of extraordinarily rapid technological change, actors engage in hedging strategies vis-à-vis other organizations (partners or competitors) in their organizational field. (Charles F. Sabel, "Moebius-Strip Organizations and Open Labor Markets," 1990; and Bruce Kogut, Weijan Shan, and Gordon Walker, "The Make-or-Cooperate Decision in the Context of an Industry Network," 1992.)

well-illustrates the possibilities and the difficulties of playing in multiple games simultaneously. In chapter 3, we encounter a new-media firm in Manhattan's Silicon Alley that attempts to stay ahead of the curve of a very rapidly changing market by benefiting from the friction between multiple, incompatible principles for assessing the company's products—sophisticated e-commerce websites. In chapter 4, we shall see how a Wall Street trading room is organized as a cognitive ecology in which the friction among competing principles of arbitrage generates new ways of recognizing opportunities. That is, although very different in their settings, the ethnographies will demonstrate how an entrepreneurial rivalry of performance principles makes assets of ambiguity by keeping open multiple ways of redefining, and hence recombining and redeploying, resources.

Entrepreneurship exploits the indeterminate situation by keeping open diverse performance criteria rather than by creating consensus about one set of rules. As such, my conception of entrepreneurship differs considerably from the strategic action of Neil Fligstein's "institutional entrepreneur." For Fligstein, "Strategic action is the attempt by social actors to create and maintain stable social worlds (i.e., organizational fields). This involves the creation of rules to which disparate groups can adhere."[33] Rather than involving the creation of rules for stability, my concept of entrepreneurship draws from Harrison White, for whom the problem is not "how is there social order?" but that of "getting action" in worlds that are already too ordered and rule governed.[34]

In more general terms, whereas the "new institutionalism" in economic sociology during the 1980s developed concepts of classificatory rules, scripts, and cultural taken-for-granteds to explain how organizations gain legitimacy to operate in stabilized institutional environments, today organizations in rapidly changing environments face the problem that their taken-for-granteds can soon be out-of-date. In this situation, entrepreneurship is less about creating stability (building on success) than about creating disruptions that prevent the path-dependent effects of locking in to early successes.[35] That is, in fast-breaking fields, among the many challenges facing firms is the problem of coping with success. Organizations that keep multiple evaluative principles in play, I argue and demonstrate in my case studies, foster a generative friction[36] that disrupts

[33] Neil Fligstein, "Social Skill and Institutional Theory," 1997, p. 398.

[34] See especially Harrison C. White, *Identity and Control*, 1992.

[35] I elaborate these ideas further in chapter 5.

[36] On the notion of "creative abrasion," see Dorothy Leonard-Barton, *Wellsprings of Knowledge: Building and Sustaining the Sources of Innovation*, 1995; and John Seely Brown and Paul Duguid, "Knowledge and Organization: A Social-Practice Perspective," 2001.

received categories of business as usual and makes possible an ongoing recombination of resources.

My perspective thus combines Knight's notion that entrereneurship exploits uncertainty with Schumpeter's emphasis that entrepreneurship is disruptive and recombinatory. My conception of entrepreneurship as keeping multiple evaluative principles in play and exploiting the resulting dissonance thus differs from brokerage.

Brokerage, as Ron Burt powerfully demonstrates, exploits "structural holes" in the social field, strategically locating gaps and profiting from the ability to broker among units that are otherwise disconnected.[37] Brokerage is frequently mistaken for entrepreneurship, but the two roles and their corresponding social processes are distinct. Whereas the broker is an insider to none and taxes flows, the entrepreneur is an insider to multiple games and recombines assets.

For Burt, the key problem is access to *information*. Bridging ties provide access to new ideas that are free-floating in the network environment—access that, in Burt's view, is not possible through redundant, cohesive ties. In my view, by contrast, the most innovative ideas are not "out there" in the environment of the group. Instead of waiting to be found, they must be generated.[38] When the problem is the production of new *knowledge* rather than simply access to information, the bridging ties of brokerage are insufficient. Generating new knowledge of the Schumpeterian recombinant type requires more intimate familiarity than can be produced by weak ties.

Recall Lester and Piore's observations, mentioned at the outset of this chapter, about cellular phones as a novel recombination of radio and telephone technologies: "without integration across the borders separating these different fields, there would have been no new products at all."[39] For me, the telling phrase in this passage is "integration across the borders." Lester and Piore do not refer to "contacts" across borders, for it is not enough for different communities to be *in contact*. Recombinant innovation requires that they *interact*. In network analytic terms, this suggests that entrepreneurship occurs at the overlap of cohesive structures where different communities (defined by their cohesive ties) intersect

---

[37] Ronald Burt, *Structural Holes: The Social Structure of Competition*, 1995.

[38] "When entry-deterring benefits are absent, competition switches from traditional elements of market structure to the comparative capabilities of the firm to replicate and generate new knowledge." Bruce Kogut and Udo Zander, "Knowledge of the Firm, Combinative Capabilities, and the Replication of Technology," 1992.

[39] Lester and Piore, *Innovation*, pp. 14–15.

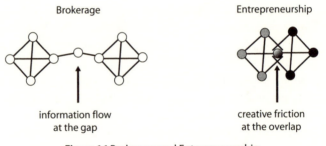

Figure 1.1 Brokerage and Entrepreneurship

without dissolving their distinctive network identities.[40] The network diagrams in figure 1.1 represent these differences between brokerage and entrepreneurship.

In addition to deep familiarity about resources, the work of recombinant innovation also requires diversity. What is overlapping are not simply cohesive network structures but also diverse, even disparate, evaluative principles. Thus, the diagram in figure 1.1 maps diverse discursive frames as well as network ties.[41] Within the same domain space, even within the same organization, diverse performance criteria are colliding and competing. Because there are multiple codes to evaluate performance, codified knowledge can be broken up and recoded. With analogy to genetics, think of the friction of rivaling principles as increasing the rate of mutation. But the dissonance of diverse evaluative frameworks does more than simply speed up the production of novelty. The coexistence of multiple, principled standpoints means that no standpoint can be taken for granted as the natural order of things. Creative friction yields an organizational reflexivity.

From this perspective, entrepreneurship, as an enabling capacity, proves productive not so much by encouraging the smooth flow of information or the confirmation of fixed identities as by fostering a productive friction

---

[40] To date, network analysts have typically defined cohesion as exclusive; that is, a given node can be a member of only one cohesive structure. This view was driven more by methodological limitations than by sociological insight. Georg Simmel, one of the founding figures of network analysis in the early decades of the twentieth century, had recognized that an individual could simultaneously participate in more than one cohesive group. Balazs Vedres and I adopt new methods consistent with this insight to identify a distinctive network position, "intercohesion," at the intersection of cohesive group structures. Using historical network analysis of the ties among the largest 1,800 enterprises in Hungary from 1987 to 2001, we demonstrate that the entrepreneurial opportunities created by such overlap significantly contribute to high group performance. Balazs Vedres and David Stark, "Opening Closure: Intercohesion and Entrepreneurial Dynamics in Business Groups," forthcoming.

[41] As such, my notion of entrepreneurship resonates with Mische and White's notions of situations and publics (Mische and White, "Between Conversation and Situation").

that disrupts organizational taken-for-granteds, generates new knowledge, and makes possible the redefinition, redeployment, and recombination of resources. In short, entrepreneurship occurs not at the gap but through the generative friction at the overlap of evaluative frameworks.[42]

As an ability to promote productive friction, entrepreneurship is not the property of an individual—it is not, for example, the personality trait of tolerating ambiguity. Instead of seeing entrepreneurs as individuals, I consider entrepreneurship as a property of organizations. That is, organizational forms will differ in their capacity to sustain an ongoing and productive rivalry among performance criteria making it possible to break out of the lock-in of habituated, unreflective activity. I use the term "heterarchy" to refer to the organizational forms with a capacity for reflexive cognition.

Heterarchy

Heterarchy[43] represents an organizational form of distributed intelligence in which units are laterally accountable according to diverse principles of evaluation. Two key features are at work here. In contrast to the vertical authority of hierarchies, heterarchies are characterized by more crosscutting network structures, reflecting the greater interdependencies of complex collaboration. They are heterarchical, moreover, because there is no hierarchical ordering of the competing evaluative principles. Here I discuss the first feature of heterarchies—distributed intelligence coordinated through lateral accountability. I then turn to the second, related feature of heterarchies—the organization of diversity enacted through the friction of competing performance principles.

[42] Espeland and Stevens offer a related perspective: "We suspect that claims about incommensurables are likely to arise at the borderlands between institutions, where what counts as an ideal or normal mode of valuing is uncertain, and where proponents of a particular mode are entrepreneurial" (Espeland and Stevens, "Commensuration," p. 332). My position has two points of similarity with this view, emphasizing, first, uncertainty about principles of valuation and, second, that this occurs at the borderlands (especially if we understand this not as boundary but overlap). But there are two very important points of difference: First, because entrepreneurship is not between institutions but between principles of evaluation, it can take place within an institution. As my cases demonstrate, it can take place within a single organization. Second, entrepreneurs are not proponents of a particular mode of valuing but are exploiting the uncertainty of multiple modes of valuing.

[43] As I discuss in more detail in the next section, the term *heterarchy* was first used by neurologist Warren McCulloch in 1945. Gunnar Hedlund introduced the term to the social sciences with application to the multinational corporation. See Gunnar Hedlund, "The Hypermodern MNC: A Heterarchy," 1986; and Gunnar Hedlund and Dag Rolander, "Action in Heterarchies: New Approaches to Managing the MNC," 1990.

Distributing Intelligence

Heterarchy's twinned features are a response to the increasing complexity of the firm's environment, in which it becomes difficult to project future states of the world from current trends. Analysts at the Santa Fe Institute have several terms to refer to these complexities. David Lane and Robert Maxfield denote them as "limited foresight horizons," in which the strategy horizon of the firm is so unpredictable that the firm cannot even be certain about what product it will be producing in the near future.[44] Stuart Kauffman adopts the language of the irregular shape of "rugged fitness landscapes" with multiple optimal solutions.[45] A smooth fitness landscape is highly regular and single peaked, reflecting a single optimal solution possessing a higher fitness value than any other potential solution. A more complex or "rugged" fitness landscape, by contrast, is not amenable to linear programming models (e.g., lower unit costs through economies of scale), because the topography is jagged and irregular, with multiple peaks corresponding to multiple optimal solutions.[46]

As an example of such complexities, think of the scrambling that is taking place among firms that are producing in fields that were once previously separated into the relatively discrete categories of computers, telecommunications, software, media, or banking. When a major computer electronics company markets songs and videos (Apple) or when major software companies (Microsoft and Google) collide with newspapers and broadcast giants over the delivery of news and entertainment, we know that competition is not taking place within the boundaries of Standard Industrial Classification (SIC) categories. In retrospect, we might say that the problem was simple: the industries listed above are all converging. That retrospective view would suffer from the typical problem of 20/20 hindsight, assuming that what we see now could have been anticipated by the actors involved. But it would also be incorrect; whatever else is happening, the rearrangements have not been a case of simple convergence, as the key multimedia artifacts continue to morph. Most critically, we cannot assume that our retrospective view, with its promise of stabilization, offers guidance for the future. It does not. Because just when we have figured out the intersecting paths among the list of industries above,

---

[44] David Lane and Robert Maxfield, "Strategy under Complexity: Fostering Generative Relationships," 1996.

[45] Stuart Kauffman, "Adaptation on Rugged Fitness Landscapes," 1989.

[46] On the use of genetic algorithms designed to explore initially unpromising paths and thereby avoid the danger of "climbing to the nearest peak," which might simply be the highest point in a valley surrounded by yet higher peaks, see John Holland, "Complex Adaptive Systems," 1992; and Kauffman, "Adaptation."

along will come new developments in such fields as genetics, linguistics, biophysics, mapping, and even social network analysis to add to the mix of new recombinations.

The situation in "old" manufacturing sectors is scarcely different. Not so long ago, firms like General Motors (GM) were easily categorizable. Then, the major materials were steel, rubber, and plastic; the major costs were equipment and labor; and these firms made automobiles and other vehicles. Today, an automobile can be viewed as an entertainment system that we travel in;[47] various computer components, taken together, account for the greatest share of the value of a car; financing contributes the greatest share of profits; and pension plans and medical insurance for retired employees are among the highest costs. GM, doubtless, makes automobiles. But it could well be seen as being in the computer business, the finance business, the insurance business, or even the entertainment business.

Thus, in an increasing number of areas, many firms literally do not know what products they will be producing in the not so distant future. To cope with these uncertainties, instead of concentrating their resources for strategic planning among a narrow set of senior executives or delegating that function to a specialized department, heterarchical firms embark on a radical decentralization in which virtually every unit becomes engaged in innovation. That is, in place of specialized search routines in which some departments are dedicated to exploration while others are confined to exploiting existing knowledge, the functions of exploration are generalized throughout the organization.[48]

These developments increase interdependencies between divisions, departments, and work teams within the firm. But because of the greater complexity of these feedback loops, coordination cannot be engineered, controlled, or managed hierarchically. The results of interdependence are to increase the autonomy of work units from central management.[49] Yet, at the same time, more complex interdependence heightens the need for fine-grained coordination across the increasingly autonomous units.

These pressures are magnified by dramatic changes in the sequencing of activities within production relations. As product cycles shorten from years to months, the race to new markets calls into question the strict sequencing of design and execution.[50] Because of strong first-mover advantages,

[47] John Urry, "The 'System' of Automobility," 2004.

[48] The search for new markets, for example, is no longer the sole province of the marketing department, if units responsible for purchase and supply are also scouting the possibilities for qualitatively new inputs that can open up new product lines.

[49] Luc Boltanski and Ève Chiapello, *The New Spirit of Capitalism*, 2005.

[50] The still-definitive statement on the transformation from the long production runs of mass production to the customized production of flexible specialization is Michael Piore and

in which the first actor to introduce a new product (especially one that establishes a new industry standard) captures inordinate market share by reaping increasing returns, firms that wait to begin production until design is completed will be jeopardized in competition. Like the production of "B movies" in which filming begins before the script is completed, successful strategies integrate conception and execution, with significant aspects of the production process beginning even before design is finalized.

Production relations are even more radically altered in the processes analyzed by Sabel and Dorf as simultaneous engineering.[51] Conventional design is sequential, with subsystems that are presumed to be central designed in detail first, setting the boundary conditions for the design of lower-ranking components. In simultaneous engineering, by contrast, project teams develop all the subsystems concurrently. In such concurrent design, the various project teams engage in an ongoing mutual monitoring, as innovations produce multiple, sometimes competing proposals for improving the overall design.

Thus, increasingly rugged fitness landscapes yield increasingly complex interdependencies that in turn yield increasingly complex coordination challenges. Where search is no longer departmentalized but is instead generalized and distributed throughout the organization, and where design is no longer compartmentalized but deliberated and distributed throughout the production process, the solution to the nonhierarchically distributed intelligence of heterarchical firms is distributed authority.[52]

Under circumstances of simultaneous engineering where the very parameters of a project are subject to deliberation and change across units, authority is no longer delegated vertically but instead emerges laterally. As one symptom of these changes, managers socialized in an earlier regime frequently express their puzzlement to researchers: "There's one thing I can't figure out. Who's my boss?" Under conditions of distributed authority, managers might still "report to" their superiors, but increasingly they are accountable to other work teams. A young interactive designer whom we shall meet in chapter 3 expressed this succinctly: When asked to whom he was accountable, he replied, "I report to [the project manager] but I'm

---

Charles F. Sabel, *The Second Industrial Divide*, 1984. Whereas mass production uses specialized tools to make standardized products (think of the dedicated tools of the Fordist car assembly line, replaced each year to make a new line of nearly identical automobiles), flexible specialization uses standardized tools to make specialized products.

[51] Michael C. Dorf and Charles F. Sabel, "A Constitution of Democratic Experimentalism," 1998.

[52] Walter W. Powell, "Inter-organizational Collaboration in the Biotechnology Industry," 1996.

accountable to everybody who counts on me." Thus, corresponding to the patterns of knowledge and communication that are recombined laterally rather than flowing vertically, authority in the heterarchical firm takes the form of lateral accountability.

Organizing Dissonance

Mid–twentieth century, there existed a general consensus about the ideal attributes of the modern organization: it had a clear chain of command, with strategy and decisions made by the organizational leadership; instructions were disseminated and information gathered up and down the hierarchical ladder of authority; design preceded execution, with the latter carried out with the time-management precision of a Taylorist organizational machine. This consensus was still strong thirty years later when economist Oliver Williamson published an article in the *American Journal of Sociology* confidently assuming that he could embrace all economic activity within only two logics of coordination—"markets and hierarchies."[53] By the end of the century, the main precepts of that ideal organizational model would be challenged. The primacy of relations of hierarchical dependence within the firm and relations of market independence between firms was giving way to relations of interdependence among networks of firms and among units within the firm.[54]

Heterarchical forms do not take the boundaries of the firm and the boundaries of its internal units as fixed parameters. As Walter Powell and others show, the boundaries of the firm, especially those in fast-breaking sectors, are crisscrossed by dense ties of interlocking ownership and complex patterns of strategic alliances.[55] Where the environment is most volatile and uncertain, the real unit of economic action is increasingly not the isolated firm but networks of firms. Turning to network ties inside the firm, Peter Dodds, Duncan Watts, and Charles Sabel show that top-down patterns of organizational communication perform much more poorly than decentralized networks on tasks of distributed problem solving. In a simulation of network perturbation (comparable to an attack or other serious disruption), they further demonstrate that "multi-scale networks"—with

---

[53] Williamson, "The Economics of Organization."

[54] Kogut and Zander, "Knowledge of the Firm"; Gernot Grabher and David Stark, "Organizing Diversity: Evolutionary Theory, Network Analysis, and the Postsocialist Transformations," 1997; and Paul DiMaggio, ed., *The Twenty-First Century Firm: Changing Economic Organization in International Perspective*, 2001.

[55] Kogut, Shan, and Walker, "The Make-or-Cooperate Decision"; Powell, "Inter-organizational Collaboration"; and Walter W. Powell, Douglas R. White, Kenneth W. Koput, and Jason Owen-Smith, "Network Dynamics and Field Evolution," 2005.

enough pockets of cohesion and enough random ties among them—have the robust connectivity required to recover rapidly and respond effectively in episodes of crisis.[56] Networks dissolve boundaries external and internal to the firm.

At this point, the reader is likely wondering why I am proposing another term—*heterarchy*—to label the emerging organizational form. If these forms exhibit distinctive network properties, then why not label them as "network organizations"? Similarly, if the emerging organizational forms are characterized primarily by their nonbureaucratic features, then terms such as "nonhierarchical" or "postbureaucratic" would come more readily to hand.

Within the triplicate of markets, hierarchies, and networks, the term *network* stands for an alternative coordinating mechanism.[57] This alone would be enough to account for the path dependency exhibited by the field in continuing to deploy "network" as a term to denote changes in organizational form. But, however fruitful in stimulating more than a decade of research, the problem of labeling these forms as "networks" conflates the name for an organizational form with an analytic approach. That is, as the literature also abundantly demonstrates, not only the emergent network form but also markets and hierarchies can be analyzed in network terms.

But there is an even more important reason for not adopting the "network" label. In economic sociology and organizational studies, social network analysis typically refers to patterns of ties among persons (or anthropomorphized entities such as firms). But actors in and across organizations do more than communicate with, or link to, others. They also evaluate performance, justify their actions, and offer reasons to explain why things should be done this way instead of that.[58] When they do so, they refer either explicitly or (more often) implicitly to principles of evaluation. Organizations can be seen as patterns of ties, but they should also be seen as sites in which actors engage in practices of justifying worth. Network ties are mechanisms of coordination but always alongside performance criteria and the evaluative principles on which they are based.

A similar logic holds for rejecting the "postbureaucratic" label. Organizations can be analyzed as patterns of authority; but all relations of authority, whether vertical or lateral, must rest on principles of account-

---

[56] Peter Sheridan Dodds, Duncan J. Watts, and Charles F. Sabel, "Information Exchange and the Robustness of Organizational Networks," 2003.

[57] Walter W. Powell, "Neither Market Nor Hierarchy: Network Forms of Organization," 1990.

[58] Charles Tilly, *Why?* 2006.

ability. And the more lateral the patterns of authority, the more diverse the principles of accountability.

When authority is distributed along lines of lateral accountability, we need to study those who make and keep accounts (and who, most emphatically, are not simply the accountants). To analyze the processes of evaluation that are central to the problems of worth in organizations, we must thus first explore the concept of *accounts*. Etymologically rich, the term simultaneously connotes bookkeeping and narration. Both dimensions entail evaluative judgments, and each implies the other: Accountants prepare story lines according to established formulas, and in the accounts given by a good storyteller we know what counts.

In organizations, as in everyday life, we are all bookkeepers and storytellers. We keep accounts and we give accounts, and, most importantly, we can be called to account for our actions. It is always within accounts that we "size up the situation," for not every form of worth can be made to apply and not every asset is in a form mobilizable for a given situation. We evaluate the situation by maneuvering to use scales that measure some types of worth and not others, thereby acting to validate some accounts and discredit others. How am I accountable? What counts? Who counts? Can you be counted on? Will you credit my account? By which accounting?

Heterarchies flatten hierarchy. But they are not simply nonhierarchical. The new organizational forms are heterarchical not only because they have flattened reporting structures but also because they are the sites of heterogeneous systems of accounting for worth. A robust, lateral collaboration flattens hierarchy while promoting diversity of evaluative principles. Heterarchies are complex adaptive systems because they interweave a multiplicity of performance principles. They are heterarchies of worth.

Distributed authority implies not only that units will be accountable to each other but also that each will be held to accountings in multiple registers. The greater interdependence of increasingly autonomous work teams results in a proliferation of sometimes competing performance criteria. Heterarchies are organizations with multiple worldviews and belief systems such that products, processes, and properties carry multiple "tags" or interpretations.[59] Because resources are not fixed in one system of interpretation but can exist in several, heterarchies make assets of ambiguity.

---

[59] Andy Clark, "Leadership and Influence: The Manager as Coach, Nanny, and Artificial DNA," 1999; and John H. Clippinger, "Tags: The Power of Labels in Shaping Markets and Organizations," 1999.

Organizational ecologists have long held that adaptability is promoted by the diversity of organizations *within a population*.[60] I extend and, in the process, modify[61] this notion by considering the problem of diversity for adaptability *within an organization*. In making the shift from the societal to the organizational level, analysis moves from the ecologists' *diversity of organizations* to the heterarchical *organization of diversity*. The adaptive potential of organizational diversity may be most fully realized when diverse evaluative principles coexist in an active rivalry within the enterprise. By rivalry, I refer not to competing camps and factions but to coexisting logics and frames of action. The organization of diversity is an active and sustained engagement in which there is more than one way to organize, label, interpret, and evaluate the same or similar activities. It increases the possibilities of long-term adaptability by better search because the complexity that it promotes and the lack of simple coherence that it tolerates increase the diversity of options.

As it shifts from specific search routines to a situation in which search is generalized, the heterarchical firm is redrawing internal boundaries, regrouping assets, and perpetually reinventing itself. Under circumstances of rapid technological change and volatility of products and markets, it seems there is no single best solution. If one solution could be rationally chosen and resources devoted to it alone, the benefits of its fleeting superiority would not compensate for the costs of subsequent missed opportunities. Because managers hedge against these uncertainties, the outcomes are hybrid forms.[62] Good managers do not simply commit themselves to the array that keeps the most options open; instead, they create an organizational space open to the perpetual redefinition of what might constitute an option. Rather than a rational choice among a set of known options, we find practical action fluidly redefining what the options might be. Management becomes the art of facilitating organizations that can reorganize themselves.

The challenge of the modern firm is the challenge of building organizations that are capable of generating new knowledge. Flexibility requires an ability to redefine and recombine assets: in short, a pragmatic reflexivity. To do so, heterarchies maintain and support an active rivalry of evaluative principles. Rivalry is not competition among units based on the same

[60] "A system with greater organizational diversity has a higher probability of having in hand some solution that is satisfactory under changed environmental conditions." Michael T. Hannan, "Uncertainty, Diversity, and Organizational Change," 1986, p. 85.

[61] I elaborate my theoretical discussion of these issues in the section "From Diversity of Organizations to the Organization of Diversity" in chapter 5.

[62] Sabel, "Moebius-Strip Organizations"; and Charles F. Sabel and Jonathan Zeitlin, "Stories, Strategies, Structures: Rethinking Historical Alternatives to Mass Production," 1997.

principles of evaluation. Neither is it compartmentalization, in which different principles of worth map to separate departments or units, bounded and buffered from contamination. It is not a replicative redundancy or slack (more of the same) but a generative redundancy of difference.

I write of *organizing dissonance* because some forms of friction can be destructive. When personalized, differences can be petty as opposed to productive. To be constructive, rivalry must be principled, with the adherents of the contending frameworks offering reasoned justifications. Moreover, where multiple evaluative principles collide in heterarchical forms, the danger is that arguments displace action and nothing is accomplished. Success requires attention to the structure of temporal processes. I refer to a collective sense of rhythm and timing—of when to make temporary settlements to get the job done, with the knowledge that this is not a once-and-for-all resolution of the disagreements—as a *discursive pragmatism*. Heterarchy is neither harmony nor cacophony but an organized dissonance.

Dissonance occurs when diverse, even antagonistic, performance principles overlap. The manifest, or proximate, result of this rivalry is a noisy clash, as the proponents of different conceptions of value contend with each other. The latent consequence of this dissonance is that the diversity of value-frames generates new combinations of the firm's resources. Because there is not one best way or single metric but several mutually coevolving yet not converging paths, the organization is systemically unable to take its routines or its knowledge for granted. It is the friction at the interacting overlap of multiple performance criteria that generates productive recombinations by sustaining a pragmatic organizational reflexivity. Heterarchies create wealth by inviting more than one way of evaluating worth.

A Metaphor for Organization in the Twenty-first Century

From where have we found metaphors for organization? The manufacture of pins served as Adam Smith's metaphor for the division of labor. Clocks have been ever popular; for example, interrupted watchmakers served as Herbert Simon's parable for the "nearly decomposable" features of hierarchical systems.[63] Where organizations, whether as national economies or firms, were conceived as systems of planning, linear programming served both as method and as metaphor. More recently, organizational ecology

[63] Herbert Simon, *The Sciences of the Artificial*, 1969.

has looked to biological systems for metaphors of evolution, selection, population, births, and deaths.

But the dominant and long-lasting metaphor for organization, remarkably consistent over fifteen centuries, comes from religion. The term *hierarchy* was originally coined by Dionysius the Areopagite, a fifth-century medieval theologian, in two treatises on the celestial and ecclesiastical hierarchies, respectively.[64] In his *Celestial Hierarchy* we find all the elements of the metaphor fully elaborated: nine distinct levels organized in three tiers corresponding to senior executives, middle management, and lower-level functionaries, with the angels (closest to humans) at the bottom and the seraphim (closest to God) at the top. Each level supervises the level below and reports to the level above; beings can advance through promotion up the ordering; information cannot bypass the chain of command; and the structure is based on a strict hierarchy of knowledge, with the literally all-knowing boss at the top.

The term *heterarchy* is not of such heavenly provenance. It was coined at the beginning of the computer age, in 1945, by neurologist Warren McCulloch in an article published in the (appropriately hybrid) *Bulletin of Mathematical Biophysics*. McCulloch titled his elegant, five-page paper "A Heterarchy of Values Determined by the Topology of Nervous Nets."[65] In place of Dionysius the Areopagite's nine levels, McCulloch simulates a network of six neurons. Several years earlier, with Walter Pitts, McCulloch showed how to formalize the brain as a network of neurons viewed as logical processing elements.[66] In the "Heterarchy of Values" paper, he is simulating choice.

In his simulation, McCulloch first maps the neuron circuits on a plane with no diallels, or "crossovers." He observes that the resulting structure is a hierarchy: "The order is such that there is some end preferred to all others, and another such that all are preferred to it, and that of any three

---

[64] See especially Gunnar Hedlund, "Assumptions of Hierarchy and Heterarchy, with Applications to the Management of the Multinational Corporation," 1993.

[65] Warren S. McCulloch, "A Heterarchy of Values Determined by the Topology of Nervous Nets," [1945] 1965.

[66] Warren S. McCulloch and Walter H. Pitts, "A Logical Calculus of the Ideas Immanent in Nervous Activity," 1943. This work was critical in the definition of the classical computer architecture based on stored programs devised by John von Neumann. It also laid the basis for the new field of "automata theory." Another collaboration (Pitts and McCulloch, "How We Know Universals: The Perception of Auditory and Visual Forms," 1947) was a pioneering paper on neural networks for pattern recognition showing how visual input could control motor output through the distributed activity of a neural network without the intervention of executive control. McCulloch and Pitts later collaborated with Lettvin and Maturana on one of the classic papers on single-cell neurophysiology ("What the Frog's Eye Tells the Frog's Brain," 1959). For an overview, see Michael A. Arbib, "Warren McCulloch's Search for the Logic of the Nervous System," 2000.

if a first is preferred to a second and a second to a third, then the first is preferred to the third" (p. 43).

McCulloch explicitly notes the similarity of such a hierarchical system to "the sacerdotal structure of the church" and implicates the notion of a transitivity of values with "the notion of the sacred or holy." He points out that "to assert a hierarchy of values is to assert that values are magnitudes of some one kind. Summarily, if values were magnitudes of any one kind, the irreducible nervous net would map (without diallels) on a plane" (p. 43).

Aware that extant theories of value assume that values can be treated as magnitudes of some one kind, McCulloch argues to the contrary, stating explicitly that "for values there can be no common scale." The next step elegantly anticipates Kenneth Arrow's Impossibility Theorem on the intransitivity of preference orderings:

> Consider the case of three choices, A or B, B or C, and A or C in which A is preferred to B, B to C, and C to A. (p. 43)

To simulate intransitivity as the more realist problem in modeling choice, McCulloch presents two solutions: introduce a diallel, a crossover, in the network (if represented on a plane) or shift to the more complex topology of a torus. Either solution is nonhierarchical:

> An organism possessed of this nervous system—six neurons—is sufficiently endowed to be unpredictable from any theory founded on a scale of values. It has a heterarchy of values, and is thus interconnectively too rich to submit to a *summum bonum*. (p. 44)

McCulloch's highly original work led to the development of artificial networks as a new computing technology, which, in turn, fed back to the computational modeling of the brain.[67] His idea of redundant network ties was important for the conception of reliable organization built from unreliable parts, laid the basis for the new field of "automata theory," and contributed to the fertile concept of "self-organization."[68] "A Heterarchy of

[67] After publishing "A Heterarchy of Values," McCulloch chaired a series of ten meetings set up by the Macy Foundation to explore what biologists could teach computer scientists about signal processing, computation, and communication. The group involved biologists, technologists, and social scientists including John von Neumann, Norbert Wiener, Gregory Bateson, and Paul Lazarsfeld. Its inaugural meeting in New York, March 1946, was titled "Feedback Mechanisms and Circular Causal Systems in Biological and Social Systems." For summaries of the conferences and lists of participants see www.asccybernetics.org/foundations/history/MacySummary.htm. For a lively discussion of the Macy Conferences, see Jean-Pierre Dupuy, *The Mechanization of the Mind: On the Origins of Cognitive Science*, 2000.

[68] John von Neumann, "Probabilistic Logics and the Synthesis of Reliable Organizations from Unreliable Components," 1956; and Warren S. McCulloch, "The Reliability of Biological Systems," 1960.

Values" is cited as an inspiration for non-Turing, or non-Euclidean, computing, most recently in efforts to develop biology-based computing.

As one of the first efforts at network analysis—developed at the intersection of neurology, computer science, mathematics, biophysics, and linguistics[69]—McCulloch's pathbreaking paper is an appropriate source for a new metaphor for organization in the twenty-first century. Metaphors matter. The field of organization studies will be enriched if we adopt a concept that has applicability to the problem of "organization" inclusive of, but also of wider generality than, the study of formal collectivities of human agents.

Biologists, for example, have recently rediscovered the problem of organization (of which "the organism" is only the most apparent instance); levels of organization extend down to the cellular, even molecular, level, and outward to speciation and processes of coevolution.[70] Life is organization. Similarly, to speak of information or knowledge is to speak of organization. Work by colleagues in information science and the study of cognition and learning[71] suggests that hierarchy is not the only form of organization in these fields.

Most revealing are changes in our conception of code. Formerly, the term evoked procedures of *codification* in which elements were organized into a system of encompassing and mutually exclusive categories. With language as the exemplar of nonhierarchical structuring, code is now grasped in network terms. Researchers in genetic code, for example, see two structural properties as critical to the evolution of evolvability. The first is modularity, whereby elements retain their structure even as they are recombined with other modules in higher levels of organization. The second, no less important, is pleiotropy, whereby a sequence of genetic code is expressed in more than one subsystem.[72] In network terms, genetic code is tangled code. The term comes from computer science, referring to

[69] McCulloch was involved in the design of a (graphical) triadic logic and was very interested in Charles Sanders Peirce's experiments with a triadic logic (see Arbib, "McCulloch's Search"). Peirce, regarded as the founder of philosophic pragmatism, argued that all cognition is irreducibly triadic. His triadic theory of signs as icon, index, and symbol was a major contribution to modern linguistics.

[70] See especially Walter Fontana and Leo Buss, " 'The Arrival of the Fittest': Toward a Theory of Biological Organization," 1994; and Walter Fontana and Leo Buss, "The Barrier of Objects: From Dynamical Systems to Bounded Organizations," 1996.

[71] Geoffrey Bowker and Susan Leigh Star, "Knowledge and Infrastructure in International Information Management: Problems of Classification and Coding," 1994; and Luis M. Rocha, "Adaptive Webs for Heterarchies with Diverse Communities of Users," 2001.

[72] Gunter P. Wagner and Lee Altenberg, "Complex Adaptations and the Evolution of Evolvability," 1996; and Thomas F. Hansen, "Is Modularity Necessary for Evolvability? Remarks on the Relationship between Pleiotropy and Evolvability," 2003.

the bane of the programmer dealing with crisscrossing pieces of software. But where tangled code was to be avoided at all costs, work at the forefront of software engineering—for example, in the qualitative shift from object-oriented to aspect-oriented programming—is developing heterarchical software code in a field that was once seen as quintessentially hierarchical.

As a more general process, then, heterarchy refers to an organizational structure in which a given element—a statement, a deal, an identity, an organizational building block, a sequence of genetic code, a sequence of computer code, a sequence of legal code—is simultaneously expressed in multiple crosscutting networks. "A program which has a structure in which there is no single 'highest level,' or 'monitor,' is called a heterarchy."[73]

Thus, as a metaphor for organization in the twenty-first century, heterarchy has its provenance at the intersection of extraordinarily generative sciences. It also has potential for applicability across a wide set of domains including computer science, biology, and informatics as well as organizational analysis in the social sciences. It does have one drawback: it does not immediately trip off the tongue on first vocalization. But the terms "bureaucrat" and "bureaucracy"—as amalgams of bureau and aristocrat/aristocracy—also seemed peculiar when introduced to account for a new role and a new phenomenon. Despite this drawback, *heterarchy* has a distinct advantage because, as a member of a family of terms such as monarchy, anarchy, polyarchy, and hierarchy, the term immediately denotes a form of governance. Indeed, perhaps the first exemplar of heterarchical social organization was the U.S. Constitution, with its three branches of government, each based on a distinctive principle of legitimation, none of which is overarchingly superior.[74] As a form of governance, heterarchy organizes dissonance. But it is not a panacea. Just as the metaphor of heterarchy is not of heavenly provenance, so the problems that the implementation of heterarchy creates are all too human.

Worth in Contentious Situations

I follow John Dewey's insights on problems of inquiry, worth, and uncertainty; I also look to him for guidance on issues of methodology. In his *Theory of Valuation*, Dewey insists repeatedly on the need to study

[73] Douglas R. Hofstadter, *Gödel, Escher, Bach,* 1979.
[74] See László Bruszt, "Market Making as State Making: Constitutions and Economic Development in Postcommunist Eastern Europe," 2002; and Martin Landau, "Redundancy, Rationality, and the Problem of Duplication and Overlap," 1969.

processes of "actual valuation." His remarks from 1939 remain on target today:

> [T]he notion that an adequate theory of human behavior—including particularly the phenomena of desire and purpose—can be formed by considering individuals apart from the cultural setting in which they live, move, and have their being—a theory which may justly be called metaphysical individualism—has united with the metaphysical belief in a mentalist realm to keep valuation-phenomena in subjection to unexamined traditions, conventions, and institutionalized customs.[75]

The case studies presented here adopt Dewey's guidelines on both counts. First, following Dewey's injunction to study actual valuations in "cultural settings," I further specify the notion of setting, using ethnographic methods to study three very different kinds of workplaces. I study situated cognition *in situ*. In each case the ethnographic site is a single room—a factory workshop with about 100 manual workers, a former printing loft converted to an open-plan layout housing about 80 new-media employees in Manhattan's Silicon Alley, and the Wall Street trading room of a major international investment bank, similarly open plan, with about 160 traders.

Second, I follow Dewey's advice that practices of evaluation should not taken as "unexamined traditions, conventions, and institutionalized customs." Methodologically, the move is not simply to employ ethnography in specific settings but to shift from the analysis of *institutions* to the study of indeterminate *situations*.[76] As we shall see in the following chapters, unsettling situations are special moments in which the researcher discovers what is at stake because it is in such situations that the actors themselves become cognizant of what had previously been taken for granted. By studying cases involving the heterarchical rivalry of evaluative principles, we see that traditions, conventions, and institutionalized customs are not left unexamined. Indeed, they are opened up to reflective cognition by the actors themselves.

Because I examine situations in three distinctively different settings, the analytic lens for studying worth—evaluative practices—changes focus as we move from case to case. Correspondingly, the forms of indetermi-

---

[75] Dewey, *Theory of Valuation*, p. 64.

[76] On the rejection of both methodological collectivism *and* individualism in favor of "methodological situationalism," see Karin Knorr-Cetina, "Introduction: The Micro-sociological Challenge of Macro-sociology," 1981.

nate situations and the distinctive challenges of recognition are specified as analytically appropriate for each case.

In the case of the Hungarian factory, we meet 18 highly skilled workers, operating machine tools to build machine tools, who recognize an opportunity to win recognition of their self-proclaimed worth. The cultural setting is state-socialist Hungary with its central planning under one-party rule. More specifically, it is the exciting period of the mid- to late 1980s, after the upheavals of the rise and later suppression of Solidarity in Poland but before the collapse of communism in 1989. Yet more specifically, the machine shop of about 100 workers is part of Minotaur, one of the largest state-owned enterprises in Hungary, with more than 11,000 employees. The initial situations arise once Minotaur recognizes the legal right for its employees to form "partnerships," using the factory's equipment on the "off-hours," during which the members of the partnership are free to organize work on their own terms. If the routines of the shop floor had ever been "taken-for-granted," they certainly could be no longer. The parent company Minotaur exploits the partnership form as a way to earn hard-currency revenues; meanwhile the members of the partnership itself capitalize on the new form as a chance to demonstrate their worth. But their success creates new situations in which the toolmakers, however unified in their agreement that skill is the ultimate principle of value, face a series of perplexing challenges about how to measure its performance. In the process, they come to recognize new criteria of worth and new identities bound up with them. Later, with the collapse of communism after 1989 and the privatization of their factory, they confront new situations that challenge their worth, provoking them to articulate again their sense of justice.

The new-media employees in the second ethnography are also, in their own way, toolmakers building something—not operators of drills and lathes for cutting and boring costly metals but software programmers and interactive designers using new-media tools to build sophisticated online retail websites. The cultural setting is Manhattan, following the recession of 1993 that lowered rents and left programmers as well as artists and copywriters looking for work. More specifically, it is Silicon Alley at the end of the 1990s after the initial public offerings of Netscape and theGlobe .com but before the dot-com boom went bust. Yet more specifically, it is in NetKnowHow, a start-up company that grew from 15 to 150 employees during the several years we studied it. Here the relevant situations are in projects where business strategists, interactive designers, programmers, information architects, and merchandising specialists bring distinctive disciplinary identities. Projects are sites of contention, not primarily about the worth of the respective specialists but about the best criteria by which to evaluate the worth of the websites they are building. It is this rivalry of evaluative principles that allows the firm to never take its knowledge for granted. The collision of performance criteria yields a distributed cognition capable of the kind of search in which you don't know what you're looking for but will recognize it when you find it.

The arbitrage traders in the third ethnography would seem to be anything but toolmakers. But, as we shall see, each trader skillfully customizes his tools of the trade. The setting is Wall Street investment banking. More specifically, it is exactly at the turn of the century in the period after the emergence of quantitative finance but before the Enron scandal. Yet more specifically, it is the hedge fund of a firm we call International Securities, a major international investment bank whose traders are engaged in sophisticated arbitrage. Like the Hungarian toolmakers (uniformly highly skilled workers) and the new-media workers (almost uniformly young and culturally hip), the traders are culturally homogeneous. Even more than the Hungarian toolmakers, they share a common definition of how to measure the worth of a trader, in this case by "the value of his book" (the profitability—computed yearly, monthly, daily, hourly, literally minute by minute—of a given trader's deals). But this marked homogeneity belies a generative diversity, for although the traders share a metric for evaluating one another, they differ on the most salient dimension of their work: how to measure value in the games of arbitrage. As to situations, it might seem at first glance that a trading room is a site for responding to situations "out there" in the markets. But this is the nightly news version of markets with stories of crises, surges, and swings. The actual problem for these arbitrage traders is less how to respond to situations "out there" than how to recognize situations that their competitors have not seen. As we shall see, the trading room is organized as a cognitive ecology in which commitments to distinctive principles of arbitrage combine with interactions across these principles to produce a situated cognition that not only recognizes already-known kinds of opportunities but also *re*-cognizes situations as opportunities. In the epilogue to this chapter, I examine how the traders responded to a crisis situation, potentially a crisis of their identities, after their trading room was destroyed in the September 11 attack on the World Trade Center.

2

Work, Worth, and Justice in a Socialist Factory

with János Lukács

I have a tin can on my desk that I bought in Budapest at the end of 1989. It is considerably smaller than your standard tuna can and extremely light in weight. If you tap your fingernail on it, it gives a hollow ring. But the label, complete with a universal bar code, announces in bold letters that, in fact, it is not empty: Kommunizmus Utolsó Lehellete—The Last Breath of Communism.

If I were so inclined, I could take my tin can as a facile metaphor for the transition in Eastern Europe. In that case, the last breath of communism marketed by a clever entrepreneur would represent the irrepressible urge to truck and barter released by the fresh winds of the free market. Exhale communism, inhale capitalism.

But the conditions under which my tin can was actually manufactured suggest another story: it was not produced in the garage workshop of a petty entrepreneur but right in the heart of a state-owned enterprise by a work team that, since 1982, had been taking advantage of legislation allowing employees of socialist firms to form "intraenterprise partnerships." Like many thousands of such partnerships, this group of thirty workers in a large factory had been running factory equipment on the "off-hours" and on weekends, subcontracting to the parent enterprise and getting orders from outside firms. The limited-batch run of The Last Breath of Communism was a good joke, but the venture had been a serious one.

The internal subcontracting partnerships of the 1980s were a curious mixture of public property and private gain. As they blurred organizational boundaries, the partnerships were a form of organizational hedging: managers gained flexibility within the terms of state property, and workers gained higher incomes without losing the benefits of employment in the socialist sector. Within the subcontracting units, the partners allocated earnings and coordinated the production process through a mixture of evaluative principles from the logics of markets, redistribution, and reciprocity.[1] The work partnership arrangement allows us to examine

[1] Similar practices of organizational hedging, resulting in the blurring of public and private and the coexistence of multiple justificatory principles, characterize the bricolage of recombinant

evaluative practices in a situation in which a group of workers—using the same technology and in the same physical setting—are producing in two different forms of organization. The work partnership provides a fascinating laboratory for exploring the most basic element of any economy—the problem of comparing the value, the worth, the contribution, of the disparate activity of particular individuals when there is no naturally existing basis for making this comparison.

This chapter is the story of one such partnership, based on ethnographic research that I conducted with János Lukács during the summer of 1984, the winter/spring of 1985, and the early autumn of 1986. It is obvious, but nonetheless important to emphasize, that neither we, the researchers, nor the workers whom we were studying could know what would happen in 1989. Because this account would lose integrity if modified in light of subsequent developments, I present it here with only light editing of its original composition, drafted in Paris at the end of 1986 and revised in 1987.[2] As an implicit reminder that actors and researchers alike were operating in ignorance of the future, I adopt the convention of the ethnographic present.

The Partnership as Proof

"Come into my office," says István Farkas, gesturing toward his working space. Farkas is sitting at a small table near a cabinet alongside the complex horizontal boring machine that he operates. The space is tidy, but the wooden pallet floor one step up from the concrete slab of the factory floor is stained from years of grease and oil. Farkas's reference to his "office" is spoken with the same measure of humor and seriousness with which the other workers in the shop sometimes address him, saying "Professzor Ur" (Herr Professor) or "Professor Farkas."

Farkas is a highly skilled machinist. Five years from retirement, he has been working at this factory since the 1940s. He is also the elected representative of a group of workers who are members of an "enterprise work

---

processes that were a key feature of the early postsocialist period. The unopened tin can on my desk thus points to the emptiness of the toggle-switch theory of "market transition" that posits public ownership and state subsidies on one side and private property and markets on the other. And it signals a continuity of recombinatory practices in the repertoire of organizational innovation for actors at the enterprise level. See David Stark, "Recombinant Property in East European Capitalism," 1996.

[2] The study was published in French as "La valeur du travail et sa rétribution en Hongrie" in Pierre Bourdieu's journal *Actes de la Recherche en Sciences Sociales*, 1990. For this book, I have added an epilogue to briefly report on the fate of the partnership after 1989.

partnership," *vállalati gazdasági munkaközösség*, or VGM, organized as a semiautonomous subcontracting unit to build machine tools on their off-hours using factory equipment. Welcoming us into his office was our introduction to the partnership.[3]

Farkas's team works in a firm we shall call Minotaur, one of the ten largest enterprises in Hungary with over eleven thousand employees working in some eight factories, six of them contiguous in a Budapest location and two others in provincial cities. Minotaur primarily manufactures rubber products, such as many types of tires and rubber fittings, for the domestic market, on which it enjoys a virtual monopoly position. It also exports a sizable volume of its production (tires but also offshore-drilling pipeline and other products including machine tools) mostly to other socialist countries in the COMECON market. Since 1979, the firm has been under pressure to increase its hard currency sales on the capitalist market.

The partnership members work in a unit of Minotaur's Machine Factory, which produces equipment used in fabricating various rubber products both for the domestic market and, occasionally, for export. This unit employs approximately 120 workers and 15 engineers. The VGM partnership is composed of eighteen highly skilled workers—machinists working on large and often complex equipment (planing and milling tools, lathes and horizontal drills) and machine builders constructing and calibrating the finished machines from the pieces tooled by machinists. Fifteen of the VGM members are in skill grade 61, the highest designation for a manual worker. The remaining three are at skill grade 51, the next-highest designation. Most of the members are between thirty-five and forty-five years of age. Two of the members are about fifty-five; several are in their early thirties. At the time of its founding in January 1984, the group contained no managerial personnel and no engineers; only one worker in the group is a party member.

During regular hours, these skilled workers are paid a time wage—that is, they are not working in a piece-rate system. In addition to the regular eight-hour day, these workers also perform a considerable number of hours each month in obligatory and voluntary overtime (sometimes as much as sixty hours of overtime in a one-month period). They are occasionally

---

[3] Lukács and I had started studying the partnership form during the summer of 1983 and, in fact, had met with members of partnerships working in other operations of Minotaur. Over the course of several years, I studied eighteen partnerships located in eight different firms across a range of industries in manufacturing (electronics, steel, plastics, rubber, and paper) and services (engineering, architecture, and construction). Some of this field research was carried out with László Bruszt and László Neumann. The research with Lukács among the Minotaur toolmakers was the most extensive.

also compensated through various forms of "moving wages" (*mozgó bér*) and goal premiums, for example, bonuses in which the worker receives a fixed sum for performing a special task. Access to overtime and special bonuses is part of the shadow "selective bargaining" that is a distinguishing feature of shop-floor relations in a socialist enterprise.[4]

In its subcontractual arrangements with the parent firm, the toolmaking VGM in the machine shop at Minotaur makes contracts, bargained through its elected representative, to produce complete machines for which they are paid an "entrepreneurial fee" *as a group*. That is, in their VGM hours the members of the group are not working on tasks individually assigned by shop management. Having made a contract to produce a machine, the VGM members themselves decide on the organization of work and the distribution of the group's earnings among the participating members. In 1984, in addition to their regular, overtime, and moving wages, the members of this toolmaking group averaged a yearly net personal income of 49,250 forints from the VGM. In 1985, this figure fell to 35,850 forints. For a baseline comparison, the average yearly income of manual workers in Hungarian industry was approximately 60,000 forints in 1984. In other words, over and above their earnings from the main job, the partners added VGM incomes equal to about two-thirds of an average worker's income.

When he welcomed us into his "office," Farkas had been working on some technical drawings for a project on the regular hours. He explains that without these drawings it would be impossible for machinists to convert the specs on blueprints sent by the Technical Department into the actual cuts required to make a particular piece. This conversion involves computing some functions with the aid of a small calculator. ("I had to buy it myself," Farkas notes. "They promised to reimburse me, but they never did. So it's my investment.") Then a new drawing is produced, from which a machinist will know how to position the piece and the length and depth of the cuts. Even the most experienced machinist would run into trouble if he did not set up the tool correctly from the beginning. For most operations the blueprints themselves are sufficient, but for especially complicated tasks the standard blueprints should be accompanied by these additional calculations, prepared in advance by engineers in the Technical

---

[4] The ad hoc shadow bargaining of the socialist shop floor is "selective" both because certain issues are excluded from negotiations and because not all workers are included in its benefits. Whereas collective bargaining in market economies operates within a classificatory logic, selective bargaining in the socialist economy has an affiliative logic. See David Stark, "Rethinking Internal Labor Markets: New Insights from a Comparative Perspective," 1986.

Department. Pointing to the drawings, Farkas emphasizes again that this work is the responsibility of the engineers. He comments:

> Now and again, like this time, I do this kind of technical work for other people. If I had another mentality, I would say, "Why should I do that? It's not required for me to do this." But I have a different mentality. I could say to management, "Give it to the guy who is paid to do it." But that's not how I am.

Farkas's complaint here and in other, similar conversations is not that the job falls on him to do—for he clearly enjoys solving these technical problems—but that in the regular hours he is doing work that other people are being paid to do, and moreover that the knowledge required, which is his, is seen to reside elsewhere, in the Technical Department among the engineers, for whom Farkas has few words of praise:

> Two engineers were sent to Germany to buy a new machine. They stayed there for a couple of weeks while the Germans showed them how to run the machine. After they brought the machine back, one engineer was supposed to show a worker how to do it. He tried for three days. But he couldn't do it. He didn't know how to run it at all. Finally, he started shouting that he was done with it. So, the worker had to figure it out for himself.

Whether true or apocryphal, we can be certain that Farkas has told this story to any number of young workers in the shop.

For Farkas and the other members of the VGM, a major injustice in the shop is that the skilled manual workers do not receive the recognition and the pay that should accrue to them as the real backbone of the shop. If given the opportunity to reorganize the shop, he would redress this problem:

> Someone once asked me if I would be able and eager to run the shop as a VGM all the time. Yes, of course. I would reduce the rank and file down to 30 percent, advertise and seek on the street for good experts to build back up to 70 percent of the current staffing level. And this shop would be a gold mine. That would give more prestige to this knowledge.
>
> Three young lathe operators were here and they quit to go to the railroad station to unload coal wagons. There they could earn more. That's how valued our skill is now, you see? Without acknowledgment and without pay. To select good people at the gate would mean that I would have something to promise—ninety forints as the starting base wage rather than the ceiling like now. And with

that ninety I would be able to say, "we expect you to do this and this and this." It's like Henry Ford said: one has to pay for everything that is done but not one cent more. That's a good motto.

The conjunction of remaking the shop and giving more prestige to the toolmakers' knowledge is important for two reasons. First, for the machinists, the justification of higher earnings is not based on the discourse of formal qualifications and credentials but is grounded solidly in a logic of efficiency and production. Rewards should go to those who produce the greatest quantity and the highest quality of material goods. The question of how to increase the prestige of the machinists' knowledge is, thus, answered by reorganizing the shop so that it would be able to produce to its fullest potential. If so reorganized, it would then be a gold mine, in their view, and everybody whose opinion mattered could see that it was so. In such a case, in Farkas's logic, the real value of the toolmakers' knowledge would be undeniable. Increased production, *that* is what will increase the machinists' prestige.

But the conjunction of reorganization and increased prestige is also important for a second reason. In the toolmakers' view, it would be an injustice to receive higher earnings that were not backed by higher production. By the same token, it would also be an injustice if higher production were not matched by higher earnings. For this reason, Farkas's proposed reorganization would also entail a dismantling of the current system of enterprise wage regulation by the central authorities. The current ceiling would become the new floor—for only in those conditions could a manager be justified in telling a worker that he expects "this and this and this." Higher earnings are the precondition for better organization; and better organization would create the material basis to justify the higher earnings. It is in this light that Farkas's motto must be read backward and forward. It is unjustified to pay wages beyond the value of the work; but it is also an injustice to pay anything less than the value of the work. "One has to pay for everything that is done, but not one cent more. That's a good motto."

"The Good Money Comes Only for the Wrong Reasons"

Lest there be any misunderstanding, the toolmakers at Minotaur are not only highly skilled; they are also (by the standards of Hungarian manual workers) highly paid. The higher incomes of these toolmakers do not derive, however, from their classification as highly skilled workers but are the result of their location at key positions in the production process particular to this machine shop. Because the machinists and the machine builders who are the VGM members have the skills and abilities to operate a set of machines that are critical to the manufacture of the shop's most valuable products, they are called on to work overtime or to be paid through one of the "moving wage" forms. Moreover, because the operations they perform are often complex and nonroutine, management is not able to estimate with certainty the amount of time required for the tasks. The consequence is that the most demanding and most urgent tasks are often performed outside the basic wage formula. The combination of all these factors allows the toolmakers to claim that the true value (for the shop and for the shop management) of a critical operation cannot be measured simply by the time that it actually takes to perform the task. The machinists told numerous stories of earning the equivalent of an average worker's monthly salary for a weekend's work on an urgent task or of being given assignments for which management willingly paid a full weekend of overtime but that were completed by skillful operations in a matter of hours. (See interview materials in sidebars.)

These cases, Farkas argues, "show that how much time a task takes can't be evaluated. They can say that to do one piece 'costs' such and such. But exactly how much time one certain step or operation needs, that you can't tell. It could take three days, or it could take a half day. It depends on abilities, willingness, creativeness."

But the problem for the toolmakers is that "the good money comes only for the wrong reasons." Called on to exercise their autonomous skills too late, they are paid the best only when the situation is the worst. In their view, prior to the establishment of the partnership, the VGM members were most likely to earn wages at a rate corresponding to their self-evaluations in those circumstances when they were brought in to remedy a project that was already flawed. This situation—the haphazard coordination of work tasks, the substandard materials, the poor quality of the final product—is an affront to their craftsmen's sense of workmanship. And the fact that this is when they are well paid is a challenge to their identity, dignity, and honor. As a machinist who handles the final process of building the machine explains:

> "Here, you see, the good money comes only from the wrong reasons. I'll have to explain it. As a good skilled worker, I get extra pay if something is urgent at the last minute. If I see that something is going wrong—because of poor organization, because of some wrong decision or another—then it is inevitable that something will go wrong. In that situation I have two choices. The first one: if I see it but don't say anything about it, then I can be sure that a

"We Are Tolerated as the Fire-Extinguishing Brigade"

"Two years ago when there was no word on VGMs, the shop's products were of poor quality and not on deadline. It's often such that we beg, 'Don't deliver the tool, it has to be repaired,' and the simplest worker from the twentieth rank feels himself ashamed in the name of the factory that management delivers the tool."

"Let me put it briefly. When they get the documentation for an order, they sit on it for two months. They work up the blueprints according to Hungarian norms. I don't know what they do with it—maybe it is very complicated. Then they try to acquire the materials as fast as possible because already 50 percent of the time limit is up and the deadline is getting closer. The material comes in but only what's available and maybe not what is needed. We use, for example, a bigger piece and cut it in half. And then steps for the real work needed for the job. Only 20 percent of the time remains, counted from the time of the order, for the real work. And then there is the deadline and the quality isn't important—because of the deadline. We could tell such stories about deadlines that you would think were made up, that it's a joke. But unfortunately, it's true. But these eighteen people assured that they can solve difficult problems in time and in good quality.

"So, we are tolerated only because we are the fire-extinguishing brigade. We step in at the last minute and we can't produce a product of excellent quality because it is impossible at that point. But we can make an acceptable product. After it's all patched up, everybody else can keep his position, and everything goes along without any changes. If somebody isn't working properly, whether it's a manager or worker—there's no way to kick him out."

• • •

"These tasks are very serious ones. And if one proposes that three or four people should do it together—to do a good job—they just don't let it happen that way. In the end, the thing comes to us and we say to the boss, 'Sir, till now it's not a big success. We can't build a fort on it. What shall we do? Shall we deliver it like this, or not?' And then they say, 'Please do something.'"

"They didn't deal with who should have done this or that job at one point or another, and then they are surprised at why the piece can't be corrected after a certain point. Things are not organized properly and the technology doesn't look like what a real work technology should look like. And at that point all the money in the world that you wanted to pour into it wouldn't bring about success. We did our best."

"They Pour Bags of Money Into It"

Q. *What does it mean to "pour bags of money into it"?*

A. I earned that time thirty thousand forints. Our department leader came to me: "here's a model of the machine, what can be done?" At that point I was just back from vacation time. I saw that there were problems coming up and I took the holiday because I didn't want to step into that task. But I came back and the whole thing was thrown there waiting in front of me. "Please you have to do it." I said to myself, "At this point I can't be dainty. I'll have to get my hands in this dirty stuff, there's no choice." And I said, "Here and here and also here it's not similar to the blueprint." If there's need for welding in the tool, it can't be good. Because these are noble materials and if they weld them it can't be milled properly—only at reduced quality and a reduction in price.

At the first glance, it seemed quite good but the thickness was not good, and this came from the preparation. The tool had started on its way but at one point it ran into a foreman who didn't know what he was doing. Then everyone took a holiday from the shop. I calculated wrong and had to come back and do it.

Q. *In overtime or special bonus premium?*

A. Both, money came from all sides. They were willing to give anything to have it done. The best would have been to start all over again but that wouldn't have fit into the deadline. In the end it just got by. The Germans accepted it and didn't reduce the price. But I'll never do that again. I earned a lot from it. I don't want to complain. But if many people's work has to fit together and if there is no accurate idea at the beginning, the result is never good.

week later I will get the job to correct it. In that case management has to pay for its poor organization. The second choice is that I can mention something about it right away, be honest, say right away, 'sir, there's something wrong here.' In that case the mistake would be corrected right away. But I wouldn't get paid for saying what I know. What is rewarded is dishonesty. It's a shame. That's how it is.

"If I could wish for anything, I would not wish for more modern machines, more money, better conditions. But I would wish for a real honest management. Because if that would be the case, all the other things would come about."

For the toolmakers at Minotaur, the most grievous injustice in the regular conditions of the machine shop is that they are trapped in a moral double bind. To step in either direction is to jeopardize one's code of justice. To see something going wrong and not call it to attention is to fail to utilize the very knowledge on which the worker is making a claim to rewards. But to use that knowledge in every instance, even when "one is not paid for it," is to forfeit the opportunity for an adequate level of compensation—for it is when things go poorly that the worker will be well paid.

Acts of deliberate sabotage are not part of this dilemma but are a direct and total violation of the craftsman's code. Deliberate damage, or patently faulty workmanship, would place one outside the bounds of honorable behavior. In any case, when noticed by other skilled workers in later phases of production it might be indistinguishable from "sloppy work" and would lower one's position in the hierarchy of status based on skill. The problem is that of working to one's best abilities within conditions determined by management. In such cases, the worker withdraws from engaged participation in the work of coordination for which managerial or professional personnel, and not he, are being rewarded. Specifically, this involves behavior such as accepting an assignment and carrying it out to the best of one's abilities even though one knows that the sched-uled sequencing will result in avoidable complications during subse-quent operations; cutting exactly to prescribed tolerances even though pieces would fit better if slight adjustments were made and coordinated with similar departures from the blueprints for other parts; failing to call attention to errors in drawings or to mistakes made by others; and the like.

The essence of the toolmaker's moral double bind is succinctly ex-pressed in the phrase "What is rewarded is dishonesty." By establishing their work partnership, the toolmakers sought to escape this double bind. In the VGM, they would be able to work honestly, for honorable rewards. To be paid well *and for the right reasons* would establish a moral stability that could provide a basis for the stability of earnings. But if the VGM was to be an instrument for remaking a moral order, it would not be by alleviating workers' guilty conscience. Rather, insofar as the toolmakers wanted an organizational form in which they could work honestly, they also wanted a means for confronting what they saw as management's dishonesty in denying the true worth of their knowledge and skill. (The context of the "wish for a real honest management" is not a discussion of corruption but of the perceived structured injustice in workers' rewards.) Within this logic, in order to be released from the moral double bind and to bind management to honest behavior, the toolmakers needed a means to demonstrate their worth and thereby justify a restructuring of the terms of agreement governing their rewards by the enterprise.

Bringing the Second Economy inside the Socialist Firm

To understand how Farkas and his toolmaking colleagues had the opportunity to establish a venture to prove their worth, we must briefly move outside Minotaur to examine the dynamics of Hungary's mixed economy. Hungary had long been the leader in the socialist bloc in debating and exploring the possibilities of mixing planning with limited applications of marketlike mechanisms of coordination among firms in the socialist sector. It was the undisputed leader, moreover, in allowing the furthest development of a "second economy"[5] outside the direct control of state ownership. This shadow private sector had already started on state farms with the demise of Stalinism in the late 1950s, when peasants were allowed to raise animals and grow vegetables and fruit on so-called household plots. During the 1970s the second economy grew rapidly not only in agriculture but also in urban settings in private shops, restaurants, car and appliance repair, housing construction, and apartment renovation. Much of this activity was done "in the black" as families maintained employment in the socialist sector for access to stable if low incomes, health insurance, and other benefits while moonlighting "on the side" in the second economy.

Thus, by the early 1980s, in their daily lives millions of Hungarians were mixing experiences in a variety of economic forms: the engineer who worked for a socialist firm during the day and drove a private taxi at night, the worker who assembled motorcycles during the week and moonlighted plastering walls during the weekends, or the *kolholz* peasant who intensively cultivated strawberries for the West European market in the plastic-covered hothouse on his private plot were all part of the second economy where, according to official estimates, one-third of all labor time in the national economy was expended and three of every four households earned some additional income.

During the latter part of 1980 and early 1981, the Politburo of the Hungarian Socialist Workers Party (the ruling "Communist Party") held a series of extraordinary meetings, conferring with, among others, leading academic specialists on the second economy. The stimulus for these sessions was the recognition in Poland of the independent trade union

---

[5] The definitive statement on the tendential features of a socialist economy to produce a second economy is István Gábor's "The Second (Secondary) Economy," 1979.

"I Can't Grow Vegetables in a Bathtub"

The VGM form was a specific mechanism to supplement incomes for key workers, many of whom could not use their skills in the second economy. For although the informal sector had grown rapidly during the 1970s, it did not augment the incomes of all workers. If the washing-machine repairman in a state firm could gain clients and spare parts from his regular job for his off-hours "private practice" and if the peasant could intensively cultivate his own hectare of land, how was the furnace man in a steel mill or a machinist making sophisticated machine tools to use his special skills within the second economy? The VGM provided such an opportunity to gain additional income in the off-hours. As one young machine designer explained to me: "The VGM is a more civilized form than the second economy. I can earn extra money according to my skill and not on a lower level. If you do the work at your same level, you regard the extra money as less humiliating. Let's say, if I need the money, I don't have to wash little Aunt Mary's windows or unload wagons but I can do the work that I like and know well. There aren't too many possibilities to do design work in the black for enterprises. To design and make a tool can't be done in *schwartz*. But in the VGM, I continue my regular work and so it can bring about some professional development too."

Similarly an older machinist stated: "I can't grow vegetables in a bathtub. Those who live in the countryside have household plots and can earn some money from these, but we in the city don't have these. In the VGM, though, I can stay in the same place, use my same skills, and work with my same friends." Or, as a Central Committee member explained to me in an interview, "The VGMs are the household plots of industry."

Solidarity. From the perspective of the Communist leaders, skilled workers in manufacturing were the critical base of an independent labor movement. Determined to stave off any such developments in Hungary during a time of stagnating real wages, the political leadership looked for a means to increase the earnings of this segment of the working class. Such workers could, of course, partially "exit" in moonlighting jobs after hours. But, rather than open further opportunities in the second economy outside the socialist sector, why not bring the second economy directly inside the socialist firms? The VGM partnership form—an intermediate property form combining state ownership and private initiative—was the resulting organizational innovation. Because workers could gain extra income without taking their efforts entirely outside the socialist sector, state-owned firms could retain their core workers, have an additional element in the repertoire of selective bargaining to increase workers' revenues without increasing the wage bill,[6] gain from the extension of the working day, and reap through the subcontracting arrangement some of the benefits of the higher productivity of work performed in the partnership form.[7] By 1986, one out of ten blue-collar workers in Hungarian industry took part in this mixture of organizational forms—as wage laborer in the socialist enterprise and as participant in a self-governing partnership.

The Proof of Worth

One of the Minotaur toolmakers addresses the relationship of the VGM to the second economy,[8] notes that the organizational innovation is likely to be a short-lived experiment, and emphasizes that he regards it as an opportunity for "getting more recognition in the regular hours":

> For me it's not possible to take part in the second economy, because I have to be doing this skill and it can only be done at a big enterprise. There are no other possibilities. Our craft is not similar to the painters, the floor makers, to other service kinds of occupations that can be sold in different ways. I work on machines, I need machines. And big pieces of material. And because of that, it's important for us to know the VGM as a *tiszavirág életű* [an insect that comes out only one day a year, mates, and disappears], and with it we can make an effort for getting more recognition in the regular hours for our work.

---

[6] The budgets of socialist firms include three funds—for fixed capital, wages, and costs. The monies in these funds are not fungible. In fact, managers refer to three types of money: "investment forints," "wage forints," and "cost forints." Because they are counted as subcontracted work, payments to the VGMs are charged as costs and do not come out of a manager's wage bill.

[7] The simultaneous extension and intensification of work expressed some of the contradictions of late socialism. Extending the working day was a continuation of the typical logic of socialist production. Increasing productivity by decentralizing and reorganizing production was a departure. For the workers involved, the contradiction was acute: why extend the working day when work could be better organized during the regular hours?

[8] During our interviews and informal conversations from 1983 to 1986, Lukács and I made a point of asking everyone the following question: "Is the VGM part of the second economy?" What interested us was not whether yes or no, but the reasons why. The answers were almost as varied as the number of people we spoke with. Most interesting perhaps was the fact that among the literally dozens of workers we asked, only one (a young woman in her teens) was puzzled about the term "second economy." That is, within just a few years after its publication in Gábor's 1979 paper, the term had entered the popular vocabulary as designating a named place on the mental maps representing Hungarian society/social structure.

With the second economy ruled out as a setting for improving their situation, the toolmakers see a short-lived opportunity before them: they establish a VGM to get more "honor and appreciation" for their work. Farkas's description of how the Minotaur toolmakers formed themselves into a work partnership at the end of 1983 indicates that the process of creating the group was initiated by the members and not by management:

> I was the initiator, everybody wanted money. We didn't want to
> let the train pass by. We wanted to get on it. We are the cream of
> the rank and file and there was no reason why we should be left out
> of the possibility. So, I approached various people needed to do the
> machine building. Who would be essential? I asked three or four
> and suggested that he might ask others and whom they would sug-
> gest and, in turn, whom would they suggest.
>
> Every one of the eighteen—each is a skilled manual worker. Our
> aim was to have each skill. At least one from each. Each member
> doesn't have to be polyvalent. But at the one [skill] that he does
> have, he has to be very good, very expert.

Prior to the firm's formal recognition of the partnership was the mutual recognition by the members of each other. In the past, they had acted together as an informal network in their relationship to shop management. Constituting themselves as an explicit group expressed much more than ties of friendship and association, however, for the group's composition also reflected a strategic orientation: among the original thirteen founding members (later expanded to eighteen), there was at least one worker on each of the most complex machines in the shop. In this way the group would be self-sufficient and able to make subcontracts for the most demanding types of projects undertaken in the factory. Moreover, the group contained no managerial personnel and no engineers. In this way the VGM would show that a group composed only of workers could manufacture machines of better quality than those made under the direction of engineers and managers:

> We made it a question of prestige with these tools. We figured out
> who was best for each task. The enterprise isn't so successful. For
> our last task we didn't get any help, but we didn't want to accept any
> because we use quite different methods. We showed that without
> any help from the Technical Department we could do a very com-
> plex task.

The same view of this strategy is expressed by another member in slightly different terms. The context of the following exchange was a conversation about the VGMs as an "experiment"—a theme that appears prominently in public discussion of the partnership. (Communist Party chief János Kádár, for example, referred to the VGMs as a useful "social experiment" in his closing speech at the 1985 Party Congress.) The work partners are aware that they serve as the subject of an experiment, and they frequently use such phrases as, "the VGM? It's an experiment in unexplored territory. They want to see what's possible." Or, "The VGM is a satellite sent on a reconnaissance mission." In one such conversation in which a machine builder observed that the VGM was a test to see what was possible, I asked:

Q. *Was there any way in which you were testing them? In which you were using the VGM as a test?*

A. It was mainly not the test of what we are capable. We knew it before. What was important was to show to management that we could do it without them. We can. And so we did prove that all that extra organization is not necessary.

For the toolmakers, the VGM could be used as a test, a proof of the capabilities of which they were already cognizant but which were yet unrecognized. On weekends and in the late afternoon after the regular hours, the shop would be theirs, and they would turn it into a gold mine. The partnership would be proof of the justness of their claims. And, as such, it would be proof of the injustices in the regular hours—proof that the poor performance of the shop was not the fault of the workers, that the lack of recognition of their capabilities was unjustified, that clumsy bureaucracy was unnecessary, and that the inefficiency and poor organization of work (leading to less than optimal output and lower income for workers) was an injustice for the whole national economy.

By increasing the incomes of the toolmakers to a level above those of the managers and engineers employed in the shop, the VGM provides a more just payment in the workers' view, as the craftsmen's measure of social standing and the hierarchy of incomes in the shop would now be brought into the proper correspondence.

But, I must emphasize, the toolmakers do not view the higher incomes as a means to "correct an injustice" in the sense that higher earnings might serve as *compensation for damages*—as if each indignity in the lack of recognition of their skills could have a compensatory price. Neither, in the members' eyes, is recognition or honor in the abstract a substitute for higher earnings—as if there exists an algorithm in which a given unit of respect, as an "intrinsic reward," is substitutable for some unit of monetary reward. The goals of "making money" and "getting honor" are not two separate questions in the eyes of the VGM partners. For these machinists, honor and appreciation on the part of management are hollow and disingenuous if they are not also expressed in the currency of higher earnings. This was made obvious when two members of the toolmaking VGM who were designated as "excellent workers" by the factory did not show up to receive their medals at the award ceremony held after the regular hours, preferring instead to use the time to work in the VGM. It is in the VGM that the workers can make higher incomes through a means that at the same time proves, for them self-evidently, that such higher earnings are justified in the regular hours as well. The proof is not one of legal argument, not a proof of principles pure and abstract, not a proof of a "rational choice," but a proof in the idiom for them the most meaningful: "This fine machine we built proves the measure of our worth."

In their first steps to use the VGM as a "proof" to show what they could do, the toolmaking partners were demonstrably successful. After completing several routine projects for other factories in the enterprise (during which they worked out some new production methods), they placed a subcontractual bid to build a complicated machine tool for export to a West German customer. The previous export order by the shop had missed the contract deadline and only narrowly met the customer's performance standards. With this new opportunity, the toolmakers put themselves into their work, completed the project two weeks before the deadline, and shipped a tool that passed the most rigorous performance tests and was put into service immediately without modifications or adjustments. The toolmakers had scored a major victory in their industrial conflict with management.

"Payment According to Work"

After their success with the exported machine tool, the partners took on several other projects for the domestic market and wasted no opportunity in making public their excellent record. This led to some embarrassing moments for the shop and factory management when the Hungarian firms who were pleased with the VGM's product sent agents to Minotaur to make inquiries about future orders. When they came to the Machine Factory, Farkas, the VGM representative, made it clear that it was the partnership (not the regular shop) that had fulfilled the subcontract. Quickly circulated through the whole factory was Farkas's story that these customers had said they wished all their orders with the firm would be of such high quality.

But together with higher earnings, the VGM group began accumulating resentment against it from all sides. Managers and engineers in the unit were offended twice over—first, by the fact that the blue-collar VGM workers were earning much more than they, and second by the members' claims that the VGM could produce a better product without professional or managerial input. Alongside this animosity arose tensions between the VGM members and the nonmembers who provided auxiliary services (equipment transport, heat treating, tool sharpening, etc.) for the machinists. In its contracts with the firm the VGM was charged for these services (about 10 percent was subtracted from its "entrepreneurial fee"). But, as the members put it, to "avoid accidents" the VGM had to start allocating an additional 5–10 percent of its proceeds for illegal payments directly to auxiliary workers. These "pocket-to-pocket" payments only temporarily quieted the grumbling about the highly visible VGM incomes.

Thus, at exactly the time that the VGM members felt the most confident that they had demonstrated the justness of their claims, they confronted the growing criticism of high partnership earnings as "unjustified incomes." At all levels of society—from the shop floor to the Central Committee—one could hear workers, trade union officials, managers, and politicians discredit the partners' incomes as a "violation of the socialist principle of payment according to work." ("Two workers doing the same task at the same time, one in the second shift, one in the VGM. But the VGM man makes three times as much. This is an obvious departure from our socialist principles of payment according to work.") But the work partners respond with use of the same slogans: "I work just as hard in the regular hours as in the VGM but I make only half as much on official time. In the official hours I sell my time; in the VGM I sell my skills. You tell me where there's payment according to work."[9]

That the VGM toolmakers can refer to "socialist" slogans such as "payment according to work," however, is not evidence, as some might argue, that workers take seriously the legitimating ideologies of state socialism and thereby place constraints on the regime by forcing it to live up to its ideals. Eager to show that these regimes are trapped in their own rhetoric, such interpretations mistakenly assume that the meaning of words is fixed by the ideological packages in which they come officially wrapped. Phrases such as "private property" or "payment according to work" are used in different contexts and by different social groups with entirely different

---

[9] When using parts of official speech such as "payment according to work," the toolmakers' tone of voice often indicates that they are "quoting" others' words with an irony bordering on sarcasm.

meanings. Rather than conferring legitimacy to the slogans of authority, use of phrases from the official lexicon by workers can be a rhetorical device on the part of subordinates to make it more difficult for the authorities to delegitimize their speech. Subordinate social groups in state socialist societies do place limits on the power of state elites—not by embracing the official ideology but by taking their initiative into organizational forms not controlled by the state. The Minotaur toolmakers did not set up their partnership outside the regular hours to show that they were more capable of realizing ideals in the terms of socialism but to demonstrate their worth on their own terms.

Distributive Justice inside the Partnership

From Informal Group to Contractual Partners

When asked the question, "On what basis do you work out the internal distribution of the partnership's earnings?" many of the VGM members answer, "We try to do what's fair." This simple statement indicates an important aspect of the internal life of the VGM, for the question of fairness is essential to holding the group together. Failure to "do what's fair" could lead to so much disharmony that it would threaten the very existence of the group. Hence, from the perspective of any individual, unfair distribution would erode the possibility of earning this additional income, which, after all, depends on the existence of the group.[10]

For the VGM, integrally bound up with the process of exchanging its collective labor is the process of internally judging the value of the activity of its constitutive members. In reaching agreement among themselves, the VGM members have a variety of conceptual resources on which they can potentially draw. Among these, the most salient and ready at hand is the informal code of reciprocity that coordinates the relations among workers (and between workers and managers) on the floor.

---

[10] Recall that VGM participation is voluntary. "Extra" income, per se, does not depend on the existence of the group, since individual members could potentially exit the group to take on extra work outside the firm in the second economy or resort to the regular forms of overtime in the shop (exit to another VGM is not a realistic option). Anyone pursuing either of these individualistic strategies would have to consider the uncertainties involved in either case. In this light it is interesting to note that a successful VGM can have the effect of raising the level of the "moving wage" in the shop—thus cushioning the loss of VGM income to a member who quits the group. That is, a successful collective strategy can also produce the conditions that facilitate (or at least reduce the pressures against) individual exit from the group.

Each of the highly skilled machinists in this shop is an autonomous worker; each runs his own machine on an individual basis. But no worker, however skilled, can complete his tasks without some cooperation from other workers. Each skilled worker, especially if he is older and has been in the shop for many years, will have his own cache of special tools and fittings for his machine. Yet even the most experienced will sometimes need some new special fitting that will allow him to do a particular operation in less time. Acquiring these tools over the years will have required various informal exchanges with other machinists. Some workers, as we saw when we first met István Farkas, keep drawers of blueprints for tasks that were out of the ordinary (with drawings, figures, and calculations necessary to translate the design into the actual cutting depths, the positioning of the piece on the machine, and the most efficient sequencing of the detailed operations). Faced with a particularly unusual assignment, a machinist might consult with others to see if such a problem has been confronted before and to get useful tips on previous solutions. These and a host of other informal exchanges (relaying opportunities for making tools on the side for second-economy producers, etc.) bind the machinists together in a dense network of reciprocity. The ongoing series of favors is kept in motion because the various dyadic "accounts" are never exactly in balance.

The eighteen workers who constitute the toolmaking VGM know well the informal code of honorable behavior on the shop floor at Minotaur. That code regulates the informal exchanges of parts, tools, and information; it regulates behavior among older and younger, talented and less talented, practical jokers and quiet loners; and it designates those who should be treated with special respect because they embody an accumulated knowledge—whether it be the worker whose technical skills one can count on to give advice or sketch a practical solution to a difficult production problem, or another whose social skills and experience can be relied on to adjudicate a disagreement or deal with a supervisor who steps out of line. The shop-floor code can also guide the workers in their partnership. It serves as the basis for their coming together to form a group, as their mutually self-perceived standing ("the cream of the rank and file," "the most talented," etc.) set them apart from other workers. That same code also aids them in choosing a representative and provides the initial resources for collective self-organization of their work tasks ("they do it one way; *we* do it differently").

However, a problem arises when, inside the partnership, the informal code confronts a new and more formalized situation: the VGM is a distinct and officially recognized group, with relatively clear boundaries, distinct

Informal Code as Governing Code: Pirates of the Atlantic

Historian Marcus Rediker presents a fascinating account of how an informal code could become a governing code when sailors from the Royal Navy or the merchant marine took over sailing ships as pirates during the mid-eighteenth century. Although there are notable differences in the two cases, the parallel to the VGM work partners is telling along many dimensions. Rediker writes:

"Contemporaries who claimed that pirates had 'no regular command among themselves' mistook a different social order—different from the ordering of merchant, naval, and privateering vessels—for disorder. This new social order, articulated in the organization of the pirate ship, was conceived and deliberately constructed by the pirates themselves. Its hallmark was a rough, improvised, but effective egalitarianism that placed authority in the collective hands of the crew, which is to say that the core values of the broader culture of the common sailor were institutionalized aboard the pirate ship. It was a world turned upside down . . . in how pirates made decisions, how they designed and selected their leaders, and how they organized the distribution of plunder, food, and discipline—how, in short, they created and perpetuated their culture" (p. 61).

"Demanding someone both bold of temper and skilled in navigation, the men elected their leader. They wanted leadership by example, not leadership by ascribed status and hierarchy" (p. 65).

"To prevent the misuse of authority, pirates elected an officer called the quartermaster, whose powers counterbalanced those of the captain. . . . The quartermaster, who was considered not an officer in the merchant service but rather just a 'smart' (that is, knowledgeable, experienced) seaman, was elevated among the pirates to a supremely valued position of trust, authority, and power. . . . As the most trusted man on board the ship, the quartermaster was placed in charge of all booty, from its initial capture, to its transit and storage aboard the pirate ship, to its disbursement to the crew" (pp. 66–67).

"The distribution of plunder was regulated explicitly by the ship's articles, which allocated booty according to a crewman's skills and duties. The captain and the quartermaster received between one and a half and two shares; gunners, boatswains, mates, carpenters, and doctors, one and a quarter or one and a half; all the others got one share each. This pay system . . . leveled an elaborate hierarchy of pay ranks and decisively reduced the disparity between the top and the bottom of the scale. . . . If 'the pick of all seamen were pirates,' the equitable distribution of plunder and the conception of partnership may be understood as the work of men who valued and respected the skills of their comrades. . . . Rather than work for wages using the tools and machine (the ship) owned by a merchant capitalist, pirates commanded the ship as their own property and share equally in the risks of their common adventure" (p. 70).

All passages from Marcus Rediker, *Villains of All Nations: Atlantic Pirates in the Golden Age*, Boston: Beacon Press, 2004.

contractual obligations, and organizational tasks such as allocating monetary rewards. As we shall see, the VGM story illustrates the limits of the informal. Informality can be drawn on where formal organization fails; its flexibility can counter formal rigidities; it can provide unseen avenues for the powerful and can offer limited protection to the subordinated. Informality can coexist with formality, but it cannot be directly translated into the formal or stand without difficulty as a substitute for formal organization entirely.

It is decisions about an internal payment system[11] that pose special problems for the workers' informal code. For in the regular hours of the shop floor, however much the informal code could prescribe standards of fair payment and provide the resources for informal bargaining to attempt to match actual payments with these standards, it remains the case that it is the bosses who pay the workers and not the workers themselves who make the final decision. If discrepancies exist between payments ideally prescribed by the workers' shop-floor culture and those actually made by the firm—if, for example, managers and engineers (who stand lower in that culture's hierarchy of social stature) receive higher incomes than those of the most highly skilled workers (who stand at the top of the scale), or if some workers receive more or less than would rightly be their reward within the informal code—this injustice (from the standard of the shop-floor culture) does not call into question the code itself. Discrepancies, injustices, can be explained because the bargaining partner (management) has not, or cannot be, constrained to pay according to workers' rules.

Within the VGM, however, the relationship between principles and payments is much more direct because there is no possibility for interference by any outside party. The negotiated price of a particular subcontractual order can be lower than what the workers desire, but the distribution of that fee among themselves rests on an agreement independent of any actions by management. Disputes about payment inside the VGM, therefore, make the unwritten rules of workers' shop-floor culture an object of explicit reflection.

Moreover, disputes among workers about payment are much more likely within the VGM than during the regular hours. In the regular hours, of course, workers are paid individually. If one worker receives more, it is not generally perceived that another will get less. In fact, successful individual bargaining can rebound to the later advantage of others to the extent that it can be invoked as a precedent in subsequent bargaining. In

---

[11] For theoretical reflections on payment systems as an object of sociological analysis, see Viviana Zelizer, "Payments and Social Ties," 1996. In subsequent work, Zelizer conceptualizes payment systems—like that of the Minotaur toolmakers—as part of a broader social process she refers to as "circuits of commerce." See especially Zelizer, "Circuits of Commerce," 2004.

the VGM, the fact that the subcontractual fee is a finite sum to be distributed among the members makes the ratios of individual earnings within a particular subcontract more of a zero-sum game. This increases the likelihood of disputes. The fact that the VGM has prospects of repeated subcontractual orders, of course, mitigates the zero-sum nature of the game (cooperation across time is a prerequisite for being able to play the game at all). But the need to hold the group together so it can make future subcontracts also means that disputes about payment within the VGM cannot simply be ignored.

What Is My Work Worth?

For an internal payment system to be fair—not, of course, according to some external and arbitrary standard but according to the logic of the VGM members themselves—it must correct the perceived injustices of the system operating in the regular hours. The problem of the moral double bind, recall, was that the toolmakers argued that the official system did not reward workers for honest and conscientious application of their full set of skills, knowledge, and capabilities. The VGM system, by rewarding a group for its collective endeavors, held the hope of correcting this dilemma: because the group would be paid a fee for its total efforts, there would be a collective incentive for the group to reward each member for using that knowledge (including the work of coordination), which was, in their view, punished in the regular hours. Farkas links these ideas to an internal payment system:

> What would be justice for the whole economy, would be spending on working places only the amount necessary for production—not for all the extra nonproduction and nonproductive. In a situation where not only the socially necessary work is done, then people who are the ones who are really necessary can't be paid enough.

Q. *And what about the VGM?*

A. In this group there are the best skilled. They are not the tail of the comet but the head of the comet. You have to see that in regular hours there are a lot of people who can't do their job properly. But they still get paid. And there are those who get money without even showing up to work. In the VGM only the head of the comet is in. They are able to work properly. The best, in terms of justice, would be for everyone to work as hard as he can and get money according to the hours worked.

In a group composed exclusively of highly skilled workers, the differences between a system of paying "according to hours" and that of paying "according to skill" are not irreconcilable—provided, of course, that "everyone works as hard as he can" and is honest about the time it takes to do the job. But, as we shall see, this proviso was easier to state in principle than it was to achieve in practice. Some of the tensions within the group sprang from problems inherent in any payment system operating under conditions of a combination of group and individual incentives. Others were amplified by problems in the relationship between the partnership and the firm.

At the beginning, the group used a system of pay based on the number of hours that each worker reported to have actually worked for his assignments for a given project, and the rate of payment was the same for all workers. Everything worked smoothly at first—perhaps because of the initial commitment of each member to make the group work, perhaps as well because the initial payments exceeded almost everyone's expectations. In this first period, it seems, the sudden possibility of a higher standard of living meant that the relevant point of comparison was to each member's *own previous earnings* in the regular hours. As this initial period of exuberance began to fade, some workers started to complain that other members were not working as hard as they could. Somewhat later, and after much informal conversation on the shop floor, the group addressed the generally perceived problem of overreporting hours.

The revised system of payment was based on estimates of the hours for each task prior to undertaking a collective project. Thus, after blueprints were preliminarily examined to see whether it would be worthwhile for the VGM to make a subcontractual offer, internal "negotiations" began in earnest. Each member made an estimate for the hours that it would take to complete his operations for the project. This was not a formal bidding system in one meeting of the whole group but was conducted informally in those frequent situations during the regular hours when members (either individually with Farkas acting as intermediary, or in small groups) could meet to discuss the subcontract. Through this iterative process of revising estimates, an agreement was reached about the relative proportions for the distributive "hours" for the project.

Meanwhile, the group through its representative was negotiating with management about the subcontractual price for the machine tool. When the final "entrepreneurial fee" was determined and the anticipated proceeds calculated, the group could earmark 20 percent for its "reserve fund" (to pay charges and to cover the pocket-to-pocket payments), set aside an additional percentage for the representative (originally set at 10 percent

> **"One's Security Can Be Increased Only at the Expense of Others"**
>
> **Q.** *How do you work out your estimates among each other?*
> **A.** We sit down and come to an agreement [does not use alku, "bargaining"]. "That's too much for you." "Give a little here." "I'll reduce my estimate there." And so on.
>
> **Q.** *What is it like?*
> **A.** Quite hard. [He shows a piece of paper with six names or so down one column and figures down the other column. The smallest figures remain unchanged, but the larger figures have all been written over at least once.] Everyone says how much. Some might overstate by 1,000. And then we start talking it over. I say, for example, "I reduce mine by 150." Someone else says the same. One time, I estimated that my task would take 900 (hours). But during the discussion I reduced it to 750. In the end the job took me 950 hours. I had to take a big loss on that.
>
> • • •
>
> Suppose a project with 1,000 hours. Everyone tells how much his task needs. If I know that my task, say like this one here [at the workbench] would be worth 8 hours, I say 12 because I know that then that will ensure enough time. If the time limit is too narrow you can be in trouble. Sometimes people play with their estimates. One's security can be increased only at the expense of others'.

and later reduced to 5 percent), and each member would then know in advance what sum he would receive for his work on the project, regardless of whether he accomplished it slowly or quickly.

By eliminating complaints and tensions about overreporting hours, the new system restored mutual confidence and stimulated production inside the group. But, in time, it too gave rise to new tensions. The system of prior estimates worked especially smoothly in those circumstances where the projects called for more routine operations, in which the members could assess the required time and the relative weights with some precision. But it proved much more difficult to make accurate estimates for the more complicated projects—precisely the type on which the group had staked its "prestige"—especially for the complex export orders, where room for making mistakes in estimates was much more narrow.

The smaller margin of error for the export projects was due, in part, to their greater complexity but also to the fact that (within the system of pricing

"Even an Experienced Man Might Not Be Able to Say in Advance How Long It Will Take."

Q. *What would be fair?*

A. People have different views. Mine is that capability should be the thing. Pay according to skill and not hours. Once Laszlo Berki said that a piece would take 140 hours—I knew that he could do it in only four days. But it really was worth 140 hours.

• • •

"In the VGM, the money should be divided evenly but the work shouldn't be divided evenly. The two people with the same type of a skill but one can do the job quicker than the other—they should get the same amount, but one of them will be able to make it in less time. In the VGM there is not such a system like 'I'm a better lathe operator than you and so I should earn more than you.' But [instead a system] that "I get the same money for less work."

• • •

Q. *Are there ever conflicts about how people work?*

A. It's complicated—because the group is composed from several skills and there is a human habit that people tend to underestimate the others' work and to regard their own as more useful. That is a difficult thing. . . . In the last price offer the representative was talking with each craftsman about how much he would need to get to agree to do the task, how much time is needed.

I also sit down and with my ten years experience I can define, with a certain risk, the time. But there is a risk too, for the whole group. Because if someone underestimates his time, then it can throw off everything for everybody else. This is teamwork, no one can cross fingers against anyone [crossing fingers is wishing bad luck on someone], because we have a common interest. Once it happened that a colleague underestimated his time and that was his fault and his misfortune, but at the end of the year he was compensated from the common profit.

• • •

"The men in the shop have a very specialized skill. A grinder could work on any grinding machine, a driller on any drill, et cetera. But a grinder couldn't run the drill, or the driller the lathe, et cetera. With maybe about a half a year on another type of machine someone could work well enough on that specialty. But that's not where the problem lies exactly."

"The problem is that every task, every new order, is unique. Even if someone knew all the skills and could run all the machines, he wouldn't be able to say exactly how much time and effort would be required to do a particular job. Even the most experienced man on his own machine might not be able to say in advance exactly how long it will take."

orders in the shop) export jobs appear on the books as normed more tightly than the domestic orders. Minotaur's enterprise managers (and its factory directors and its unit managers, in turn) are under pressure to generate hard currency earnings by the sale of products to Western firms. These sales must show a profit. That is, when economic authorities audit the company, the records of time, wages, costs, et cetera for an export project must show that profits were earned. In fact, however, many of the export projects undertaken in the regular hours are not profitable; that is, the resources expended are greater than the hard currency earnings. One means by which management masks this unprofitability at the level of the factory and shop is that the hourly accounting of wages paid for the export projects undertaken in the regular hours is shifted to the records for orders of Minotaur's domestic customers.[12] Over time, this accounting practice shows hours worked on the export orders artificially low and those for domestic orders artificially high. The consequence is that the norms for the domestic orders are extremely loose while those for the export orders are very tight. These norms form the basis for the subcontractual price setting between the VGM and Minotaur.

In its first year of operation, the toolmaking VGM was able to take advantage of this disparity on the side of domestic orders. In negotiating contracts for machine tools for other parts of the enterprise or for the domestic market, it was able to place bids that were 30 percent below those of the regular shop and still clear enough profits for the members to be making over 200 forints per hour (about four times their regular hourly rate). The problems set in after the partnership's first major achievement, the export order to West Germany. Once factory and enterprise management saw that the VGM could fulfill export orders that would bring real, and not simply fictional, profits, they wanted the VGM to be doing the most complex export projects all the time.

This situation led to the first major showdown between the VGM and factory management of 1985. In a dispute over subcontracts for four expensive machine tools for another West German customer, negotiations between Minotaur and the toolmakers broke down for almost four months. In the end, the VGM partners won the subcontracts, largely on their own terms. But the costs of this victory were high. The four-month dispute had fueled the tempers of members, and their winning three of

---

[12] As one manager noted: "We make the Hungarian firms pay very well. We can make fools of them." This example of practices in an economy of shortage with soft-budget constraints has its parallel in the defense industry in the United States. Directors at General Dynamics were recently slapped on the wrist when it was revealed that the company was charging the Defense Department for wages that were actually spent on orders from the private sector.

the four export orders heightened the hostility of shop management and the nonmembers. Moreover, because it was especially difficult to estimate times in advance for the complex operations, some members who had been "burned" by underestimating on one project tried to protect themselves by overestimating on the subsequent projects. So long as everyone was equally overestimating, the system could be stable. But there was no way to be entirely sure that someone was overestimating or underestimating. Each of the members was a highly skilled worker, but most of them worked on different kinds of machines. Each valued his own skill a bit above those of the others and thought he could second-guess the others' estimates. But some of the tasks were so complex that not even the most experienced worker could make predictions accurately even for his own tasks on his own machine. Over time, "counted hours" came to depart more and more from hours actually worked.

Most members felt that the tensions could be remedied if the group could bid for the less complex tasks (that is, if it could, like the shop, mix export and domestic orders in the hope that the "easy money" would allow more internal room for maneuver). But enterprise management was happy with giving the VGM the export orders, and shop management (happy for its own reasons to prolong conflicts inside the group) was opposed to giving the VGM the less complicated orders for the domestic market. Moreover, the VGM had committed itself to justifying its higher earnings on the basis of complexity, quality, and skill. If the price was right, how could its members legitimately refuse a complex task, and how could they justify doing the simpler projects if these could be done just as competently by less-skilled non-VGM members in the regular hours?

Meanwhile another VGM was formed in the shop. In the view of our toolmakers these workers were "less talented." But without taking on the complicated orders, this second group was making more money than the first VGM: "Those in the other VGM who are much less talented laugh at us. We're doing these complicated projects but with lots of risks. They are doing really simple things and making good money." Moreover, the existence of the VGM helped to increase the bargaining power of some of its members in the regular hours. Because of their higher earnings in the VGM they were able to refuse extra overtime and to reject the individual offers of the special premiums and other "moving wage" forms. The consequence was that shop management was forced to increase the level of earnings that were available through these channels. At the same time, new taxes and other charges on the VGM that were introduced in 1985 and again in 1986 reduced the real earnings in the VGM. These measures combined to narrow the gap between the rates of earnings in the VGM and the rates that were sometimes available through the moving wage.

The toolmakers had formed their group to show that their claims to higher incomes were justified on the basis of their more effective and efficient performance when free to organize the work themselves. The VGM's work on the most complicated tasks was to be proof. In so doing, they faced a set of risks. Some of these were known in advance—the personal risks of poor health and the risks to marriages and families owing to the long hours of extra work (which I have not covered here, but which figure prominently in their conversations) as well as the collective risk that they might fail in these endeavors. But the risk that they did not anticipate was that they would succeed all too well and now be called on to "prove themselves" in every situation—situations, moreover, in which they would run the personal risk of miscalculating their possible earnings and the collective risk of becoming the laughingstock of their less ambitious fellows. Having dispelled any uncertainties about their capabilities, the toolmakers now found that management was shifting uncertainties from the shop over to the VGM. This burden led to problems inside the group and raised questions about the basis for future strategy:

> We showed that without any help from the Technology Department we could do a very complex task. Now the firm wants us to do only the complex. But these are from the West Germans who can be hard bargainers because of the economic difficulties of the whole economy.
>
> In the regular hours, if you underestimate for one job, it can be taken over by another. In the regular hours, with special premium, if you underestimate, it can work out. But you don't have much room for mistakes in the VGM work. If these other opportunities weren't here, or if we could get some other, less complicated orders, it would be worth it to solve these tensions.
>
> When the VGM was formed, we were very enthusiastic, proud to show what we can do as a group. Now, we've already shown that, so it's not important to do it all the time. Now it is not worth enough. If the prestige question drops out of the picture, it's not worth it.

As we have seen, the terms of agreement for evaluating worth were not fixed within the partnership. In fact, the very units to be compared changed with the changing bases for making the group. Something so basic as "skill," for example, shifted its meaning and its place in the systems of payment. In its early phase, VGM partners were faced with the task of forming as a group, and the payment system emphasized skill as the *shared trait* of the group. "Skill" was the marker of collective difference distinguishing the members (on their terms) both from engineers and from other workers; its sole measure was membership in the group, and, insofar as the partners were involved in a collective proof, skill was a property of the group itself. The toolmakers emphasized this commonality by remunerating all members at the same rate according to the hours each reported. In the later period, "skill" became the marker of difference within the group, and the earlier payment system was condemned as violating the very principle of rewarding skill that its members had set out to prove.

The general consensus within the group identified the source of the problem as individual shirking, pinpointed the proximate culprit as the system of paying by the hour, and adopted the corrective of payment by task. The fundamental sources of the problem, however, were grounded in the ways in which the partnership form altered the experience of work and worth.

First, the more the toolmakers were involved in collective subcontractual negotiations about the entrepreneurial fee for the complete tool that was cut, assembled, and calibrated by the team as a recognized group, the more they thought about the value of their labor in terms of the market value of the completed product. In this bargaining the toolmakers, "for the first time," as they said, did some research to discover the market price of the exported equipment and the hard currency earnings that would accrue to the firm. In the selective bargaining over their regular-hours work prior to the establishment of the VGM, the toolmakers had sought to get the best prices for their *time*; in establishing the partnership they sought the best price for their *skills*; but as they bargained for a subcontractual fee they sought the best price for the *product of their labor*. At the level of the individual member this had the effect of attenuating still further the relationship between the expenditure of time and the value of one's contribution.

Second, the more the work partners were involved in *collective* decision making about rewards, the more they experienced the *singular* individuality of their labor inputs. The more that each attempted to evaluate the relative contribution of the others, under their simultaneous and mutual scrutiny, and the more that each experienced the difficulty of estimating with precision the time required for complex tasks on his own machine, the more each was struck by the idiosyncrasy of his contribution. This was not simply a danger that one might underestimate the time required for a certain operation. The experience of one's contribution as singular and unique and the difficulty of making a comparison of relative contribution heightened the sense of danger that *one's worth might be undervalued in one's own estimation*. If you are the only able judge of your value, then by your own hand will you suffer the injustice of being misjudged. Thus, it was not greed nor opportunistic taking advantage of others but fear of being taken advantage by oneself that caused the periodic inflation in estimates of worth in the partnership.

Maneuvering across Economies

Exclusion from all but the most complex export orders not only amplified tensions among the VGM members but also eroded relations between the group and Farkas, its representative. Farkas's actions exacerbated rather than mitigated these problems, and eventually the work partners asked him to resign his post as representative.

The story of Farkas's replacement begins with the revised payment system of estimating tasks in advance, which could entail some risk that the actual time to complete the operation might exceed the estimate. It was in such circumstances that Farkas acted on his own, and without consulting the members, to correct what he perceived to be an unfair decision by the other members:

> The crisis started when I broke my hand. A guy who usually works on another machine had to do the operations that I would normally have done for the VGM on my machine. If I had been able to do that job, it would have taken me about 150 hours. But it took him 400 to do it. The others said that the estimate of 150 hours had already been made and they didn't want to pay the guy for all that "extra" time. They didn't want it to come from their earnings. So, I paid him from the common fund.

This payment from the common fund did not, however, remain an isolated incident. Struggling to reduce the tensions about the payment system and to hold the group together, Farkas unilaterally made adjustments in cases where workers had underestimated their tasks. This money was taken from the VGM's reserve or "common" fund, which existed for the purpose of making the "pocket-to-pocket" payments to the auxiliary workers as well as for the various overhead charges to the firm.

As the representative, Farkas would normally receive every month from the enterprise a statement or bill for the charges that the VGM must pay to the enterprise. After the group won its protracted struggle with the enterprise over the three export orders to West Germany, Farkas claims, the enterprise did not send him these bills. This period during the summer and fall of 1985 was precisely the period in which the group's internal tensions were at their height. In the midst of that critical period, the enterprise suddenly notified Farkas that the VGM owed the firm over 80,000 forints. Rather than pay it, Farkas continued to use the common fund to compensate workers in the partnership. His explanation of these actions was that the firm had deliberately misled him about the bill. Responding within the norms of the code of the shop floor regulating relations between skilled workers and managers—quid pro quo, tit for tat—Farkas set out to repay "blow for blow":

> Management tricked me by not telling me about the charges. I figured: they tricked me, I'll trick them. We'll continue to pay the workers from the common fund and if management insists on the charges, we won't pay it. They have to eat the frog.

Within the code of the shop floor, Farkas's actions obeyed a certain logic; but within the new conditions, they were a breach of the contractual relationship between the VGM and the enterprise. Similarly, Farkas's unilateral steps, taken without consulting the group, would make sense if he saw himself as a "big man" in the shop-floor culture. But these same actions were seen by the members as violating his role as a *representative* of the VGM who should be acting only with the consensus of the formally constituted partnership. On one side, management insisted that the VGM meet its contractual obligations and pay the charges; on the other, the members (still supporting Farkas to the world outside the group) were privately angry that he had broken their trust.

This situation reached a crisis several months later when the VGM, for the first time, failed to meet a contract deadline. That failure resulted from a lack of cooperation if not outright sabotage by the resentful auxiliary workers, deliberate efforts by the shop management to hinder their work, and dissension within the group itself. At the point that it became obvious that the VGM would miss the deadline, Farkas went to see the factory director. He tried to "reach an agreement," pointing to the good record of the VGM in the past. When the factory director threatened to disband the VGM, pointing to the "founding contract," which specified that all orders must be fulfilled according to the deadline, Farkas argued that the group's "good credit should count for something." But this appeal to the logic of reciprocity gave him no leverage with a director who chose to invoke the most narrow interpretation of the letter of the contract.

Informed of that discussion, the members demanded that the factory director meet with the entire partnership. At that meeting, they demanded that the VGM be granted permission to make contracts directly with other Hungarian firms. If they could escape the subordinated subcontracting position, avoid Minotaur as an intermediary, and go "on the open market" (at least for some orders), they hoped to gain direct access to the less difficult, yet more lucrative, types of projects. The factory director refused even to discuss the matter.

Farkas's position as the group's representative was not raised in this meeting. But within a few weeks, the group replaced him with a new representative. The problem was not that Farkas had "confused" the terms of contract for the terms of reciprocity. Rather, his abilities to exploit the ambiguities of a situation in which multiple frames of evaluation were contending had reached their limits. His efforts to maneuver through the informal codes of the shop floor and the codes of the managerial ranks became ineffective.

Within the culture of the shop floor Farkas had been recognized indisputably as a "big man." On the shop floor, the network of reciprocity operates in such a way that some individuals, over the course of many years, build up such a stock of "credit" that the return of favors to them still leaves the group "indebted" to them. Not unlike the "big men" who dominate the system of reciprocal exchange in Melanesian communities, such workers are "big men." In fact, the discourse of the Hungarian shop floor is not so markedly different from that of the Melanesians: workers use the language of "weight"—referring to those who are "lighter" or "heavier" as a way of indicating position within the informal hierarchy. In the culture of the shop floor, Farkas's status rested on his technical knowledge, experience, and bargaining skills, as well as on the many favors that he had done for younger workers over the years. With the creation of the VGM, Farkas sought to gain recognition for another set of talents: his ability to lead and manage a group.

For Farkas, the VGM not only demonstrated the group's capacity for profitable performance. It also proved his managerial talents. Farkas held these managerial skills in high regard and believed that the demonstration of these abilities led to his undoing by prompting resentments on the part of long-time rivals in the machine shop:

> As the representative, I was a scapegoat in the conflict with management. Management cooperated with some people in the group to push me in a position where I couldn't defend myself. The reason is because of Róka [the unit manager]. He and I have the same degree. We're both technicians. [Farkas and the current unit manager, Róka, started working at the factory in the same year at the end of World War II. Róka was promoted through the ranks to become the unit manager. Farkas stayed at his machine.]

The former shop superintendent always told me that if someone should be a group leader, I should be the one. But Róka never put me in that. I don't mean to say that I would like to be a manager. I would never. But from the unit manager's side there was always a fear that somehow I am competing with him.

Through the VGM it was proven that my managerial capabilities are good. That strengthened Róka's hatred toward me. There was one occasion when for another unit we did a project with a completely different method than in the regular hours. Earlier there would be all kinds of problems with the functioning of that machine when it was built in the main hours. With ours there were no problems. It worked beautifully. And when that factory director [for whom the machine was prepared] came to get the tool, the shop manager here said, "Look at the this tool that we made for you. What do you think of it?" And the other guy, knowing that the VGM made it, said: "It would be nice if it were like that every time. That's what we would like." You see, it turned out that we, and especially I, can organize things better than in the regular hours.

Whether or not the unit manager "feared" that Farkas "was competing with him," the VGM members began to feel that Farkas should settle his long-standing personal scores through other means, and they began to voice their reservations aloud that Farkas was claiming some of the group's achievements as his own accomplishments:

Farkas is a self-regarded, self-created genius. He does think that he knows everything. He was proud of such things that were accomplished by others. It's the machine builders who have to lead, coordinate. Farkas took credit for it. He did some managerial work but not he alone. He was responsible for the contract making and in many cases it turned out that he didn't bargain strongly enough. Sometimes he accepted their offers without pressing harder.

The members also began to wonder whether Farkas's goal of rising from a big man in the shop to a big man in the factory was in the best interest of the VGM. In numerous instances they worried:

Farkas was not diplomatic enough, he was too proud, he made it too clear what the group made. He overemphasized what we had done. Good quality, short time. . . . His style was too tough in the bargaining. He regarded himself as equal with the managers. And they really hate it when some worker does that.

Most importantly, they became convinced that Farkas had miscalculated the situation:

> Once Farkas told a department leader of the factory that he had to talk to him as to the manager of an independent enterprise—not as a subordinate. It made that guy furious. Farkas should have realized that we aren't on an open market. If we get a job or not depends on their signature. So even if you know your real stature, you have to keep in mind your situation.

Evaluating the Situation

In forming a partnership to increase and justify their continued higher incomes, each of the toolmakers, to some degree, linked his identity to that of the group. But in Farkas's case this linkage was special because the identity of the partnership as a group was linked to his person. Farkas was the representative, the individual who represented the group to others; in fact, many outsiders referred to the VGM as "Farkas's group." It also differed because Farkas was making a move even more daring than the VGM's collective proof by attempting a double conversion of his capital: first, from his position as a big man, a "heavyweight," in the informal culture of the shop floor to a position of prominence in the VGM, and then a second conversion, from representative of the VGM to a position of prominence in the "managerial ranks."[13]

These moves were not implausible. Farkas was well situated, and the situation was well disposed for him to attempt this gliding back and forth from one frame to another. The conjuncture of Farkas's interests and those of the group provided the resources necessary to give it a try. In the first year of the group's operation, when the members were intent on demonstrating their superior performance, Farkas's predilection for loudly and widely broadcasting the VGM's accomplishments did not immedi-

---

[13] It is important to note that this conversion was not a case of simply increasing the total "volume" of Farkas's capital but of converting it from one form, or from one frame, to another. Within the discursive frame of the shop floor Farkas had enormous capital. That specific capital would not increase if he were recognized as a "manager"; in fact, such recognition might come into conflict with his role as a "big man." Farkas's case is important because it shows that the concept of capital adopted here should not be taken too literally. As the case illustrates, there is not some universal standard through which the various forms of capital—and their corresponding frames of social standing—can be expressed. Different forms of capital are specific to the different and diverse frames of affiliation and evaluation in society and are not like currencies that can be exchanged with each other through a simple formula. Their conversion requires not the exactitude of formulaic equivalence but the unconscious skills to exploit those instances where there is ambiguity about which frames are operative.

ately transgress the aims of the partners. And his insistence that he not be treated as a subordinate was justified with the same appeals to efficiency and performance as those made by the group.

But Farkas's gliding back and forth among the social standings of big man, representative, and manager was not free of resistance from the group. As we have seen, the members of the VGM held managerial abilities in low regard. Skill, talents, and abilities—*defined in their own terms as craftsmen*—were the criteria for distributing persons in a hierarchy of status. Yet here, too, Farkas was not entirely without resources. He could claim with all sincerity that he "never wanted to be a manager and never would want to" and quite rightfully point to the fact that he had no managerial title and was, after all, just a worker like everybody else. At the same time, he could use his title as a representative (a "nonmanagerial" title when it came to his fellow workers) to support his claims to the outside that he should be treated as if he were the director of an independent enterprise. And the ambiguous legal status of the VGM as a semiautonomous subcontracting unit provided support for both claims. But to be treated as a "manager" of sorts, of a size equal to that of a department leader, Farkas had to behave and to talk like a manager at least some of the time. The more he did so (the more he emphasized that "it turned out that *especially I* could organize things better"), the more he came into conflict with VGM members.

At first glance, one might argue that it is obvious why Farkas's project was defeated—by presenting himself as an equal to a department leader or factory manager he had touched the most sensitive nerve, he had confronted "power," he had challenged bureaucracy. In such a view, Farkas's attempt was futile from the very beginning; there was no hope of success. He should have known that he could never get away with such a feat in a state-socialist society. But this perspective is wrong because it requires that we assume without a test that Farkas's project was senseless, that we view him as a Don Quixote, a misplaced person who did not understand the principles of operation in the society in which he lived.

On the contrary, Farkas proceeded not as a romantic or tragic figure but pragmatically, acting rationally like most of us in ambiguous situations where no one can calculate with perfect information the chances of success—because ambiguities are not about information, perfect or imperfect. Farkas was living, practically, in the ambiguities of the situation with some skills but not unlimited resources to exploit those ambiguities. If his efforts were ultimately defeated, it was not because they were foolhardy. Given the situation, a reasonable person might decide that it was worthwhile to see if the possibilities could be put to a test, to play his cards, to see if he would win or lose. It would depend on how you evaluated the situation.

Evaluating the situation entails not only "sizing up the situation" in advance (as when figuring out the relevant value[s] that can be brought to the situation, for not every form of worth can be made to apply, not every capital or asset is in a form mobilizable for the situation) but also actively shaping the process of evaluation (as when maneuvering to use scales that measure some types of worth and not others or making one's account the standard accounting procedure). Evaluating the situation means assessing which frameworks of evaluation for determining worth are actually or potentially in operation and acting to validate some modes or to discredit others.

In identifying the institutional frameworks across which Farkas was maneuvering, we draw on Karl Polanyi's conceptualization of three "modes of economic coordination": reciprocity, market, and redistribution. By a *redistributive* mode of economic coordination Polanyi referred to those economies, such as the early empires of Central America, in which resources were appropriated by some central agency and reallocated back to society. This concept has recently been elaborated to characterize modern economies in which resources are allocated through centralized *budgetary* mechanisms. The concept is especially useful in analyzing contemporary state-socialist economies because it allows us to specify (with much more rigor than in this brief summary)[14] fundamental processes that are not adequately captured with the more inclusive label "bureaucratic."

With reference to Farkas's problems and prospects, a manager's social standing would be measured, in a redistributive model, by the size of his budget. Together with this single measure other factors (such as the size of the labor force of his/her industrial branch, enterprise, subdivision, factory, or shop; the perceived and politically constructed strategic importance of his unit's activity for the economy; his contacts, connections, and access to privileged information; and so forth) would be correlated. But basically, to the extent that his/her budget was larger, a given manager could claim a larger social size than (and be more highly valued by) other managers. A redistributive logic calculates managers' standing as a function not of outputs but of inputs. A manager's relative "weight" is not determined by producing more, nor by producing more efficiently, but by being responsible for reallocating a larger share of economic resources than some other manager. Criteria such as profitability (from a market discourse) are outside, and not strictly relevant to, a redistributive logic.

If the Hungarian economy in the mid-1980s was purely or uncontestedly regulated by a redistributive logic, Farkas's efforts could reasonably

---

[14] See János Kornai, *Economics of Shortage*, 1980; and George Konrad and Ivan Szelenyi, *The Intellectuals on the Road to Class Power*, 1979.

be seen as having virtually no chance of success. In fact, however, each of Polanyi's three modes of economic coordination were operating in Hungary: redistribution (predominant in the socialist sector), market (predominant in the second economy), and reciprocity (as we have seen operating among workers on the shop floor but also in such activities as home building). Moreover, since 1968 and especially during the 1980s, elements of a market discourse were appearing within the socialist sector. Redistribution had not lost its dominance within the socialist sector, but actors were beginning to make claims based on market principles to argue that their activities should be highly valued. At the time of this research, for example, an interesting debate emerged (which one could read and hear almost daily in newspapers and on television) about the new "small enterprises"—of which the VGM was one such form.[15] In this debate, proponents of the "small enterprises" were reversing the traditional correlation between the size of the firm and the social stature of its directors. In so doing, these managers were using a different standard to measure worth—not the size of the budget, nor the volume of production, but the rate of profit as the criterion for evaluating a manager's performance. When measured by this standard, the "entrepreneurial managers" of many small enterprises are "bigger" (they are more valuable, they claim) than the "redistributive managers" of the largest and most powerful firms.

In the light of such competing claims about economic rationality, Farkas's project appears much less irrational. Like the directors of small enterprises he was reading about in the paper, he decided that this was an opportune time to test the situation. Farkas failed in this test because his evaluation of the situation differed too radically from that of the other toolmakers in the partnership. First, in their view, Farkas had misread the situation, confusing his "real stature" in the market framework for the actual situation inside the enterprise. In their assessment, the standing of redistributive managers could not be directly challenged with the discourse of profitability.

Second, and most importantly, whereas Farkas saw the VGM as the proof of his *individual* skills, the other toolmakers saw the *partnership as the entrepreneurial unit* that could exploit the situation. The partners were

---

[15] The Minotaur toolmakers subscribed to two business periodicals championing these ideas, *Vállalat és vállalkozás* (Enterprise and Entrepreneurship) and *Heti Világ Gazdaság* (*HVG*, Weekly World Economy), and were particularly avid readers of the latter, explicitly modeled after the *Economist*. Not unlike journals during the French Revolution, some journals in Hungary during the 1980s sponsored clubs, or had clubs formed around them by their readers, especially in provincial cities. At *HVG* clubs, people could meet with reporters and editors of the journal as well as with other like-minded citizens.

not simply unwilling to challenge the socialist managers; in fact, they were entirely uninterested in such a challenge. They were not resigned to a subordinate status as registered in the senior manager/middle manager/supervisor/worker hierarchy. This they could tolerate because, in fact, they had in mind a status in a different social register.

As we shall see in the next section, the Minotaur toolmakers were reevaluating the situation. Although they had formed the partnership as a way to confirm that they were the "cream of the working class," its activities were leading to new identities not in the managerial ranks but as part of a new class in another economy. Medals were for heroes of socialist labor; bigger budgets for the bureaucrat; profits for the private producer. If trade union announcements were on the bulletin boards of the shop, the newspapers on their "desks" were the journals of the "small entrepreneurs." Sizing up the situation, they realized that they could stay in the socialist factory *and* exit to the second economy.

Exit

After the crisis with Farkas and after learning that management was penalizing them for failing to meet a deadline and refusing to allow them to make their own independent, outside contracts, the toolmakers decided that they needed to choose a new representative from outside their group. They looked for someone "careerist enough to have good connections" to senior management. They found their man in Szabó, a young engineer employed in the factory unit. ("I think of my own career. I have to think of my long-term interests in my regular job.") Somewhat mollified by the perceived sacrifice of Farkas and eager to support the young engineer in his (perceived) new leadership role, senior management conceded that the group should be awarded subcontracts for domestic orders.

The VGM had come a long way from its earliest phase, when the toolmakers had expressed their "groupness" by excluding managers and engineers. But the work partners had not lost a sense of group identity. In fact, they deliberately chose an outside engineer *in order to be able to act effectively as a group of workers*. Their plan was to refuse to pay the back charges and to refuse all but the most lucrative projects. If the strong posture invited retaliation, it would have to be directed at the entire group:

> Q. *When you looked for a new representative, why not someone from already inside the group? Why weren't you [one of the machine builders] the new representative?*

A. We were asked, but that would make it very difficult for us, personally and for the group. Because I'm in an employer–subordinate employee relation to the management. And if I don't behave the way they expect, they can pay it back against me. There are many ways.

If this engineer, an outsider, is the representative, and he says the group doesn't want to make that and that, he can't be punished—because he is an outsider. If they press him to accept a task, and everyone doesn't take it, well, that's a fact and everyone has to accept it for that. But if I were the representative, it would be much more difficult for me to say that I'm not able to convince the members. They [management] wouldn't believe it. And if I said I'm not willing, then personally I'm in trouble. Now, with the outsider we can make policy in an impersonal way. The group is responsible, not individuals.

The ability to resist pressure to accept less than adequate terms for their work did not rest simply on the (seemingly paradoxical) fact that an outside representative facilitated group solidarity. It was also grounded in a fundamental shift in the toolmakers' activity: although the VGM continued to do some subcontracts through Minotaur, for the most part it had become a shell for "*szisztematikus fusizás*"—systematically working in the black after the regular hours to build machines directly for private producers in the second economy. The technical requirements for these machines were much less demanding than for the machines that the partners had made for export to West Germany, but the profits from them were much higher. If the enterprise would not allow the VGM to make contracts directly with other Hungarian state firms, then the group would escape the subcontracting relation it had with Minotaur by going instead to a market that was wide open. The partners were still working in the state's factory, but they were exiting the state-socialist economy.

In this new situation, the young engineer held the title of "representative," but he had little authority: technical coordination was being overseen by the four machine builders, and the "weight" of the group had shifted to the three members who commuted to Budapest from a nearby village, for it was through them that the group was getting many of its private customers. Farkas had been a *representative* of the group; the young engineer was an *employee* of the partnership.

This distinction well illustrates the change in orientation of the Minotaur toolmakers. So long as they saw the VGM as a proof, they needed a representative in the *emblematic* sense of a figure whose identity embodied the group. Farkas, as the worker representing a group that deliberately excluded supervisory personnel, could perform this emblematic function as the part that stood for the whole. In time, the emblem ceased to be an interpreted figure and (as emblematic representation often can) began to interpret the meaning of the group. The problem was not simply that Farkas had interpreted the meaning of the group's "proof" to be the proof of his own worthiness (for in this he was merely emblematic) but that he had claimed a proof of value (in managerial ranks) that the members did not evaluate as worthy.

So long as they were operating within the political field of the socialist enterprise, the Minotaur toolmakers also needed a representative in the *political* sense of an officially authorized delegate. Farkas had filled this function. But, in his case, the emblematic and delegatory dimensions came into conflict. In the case of his replacement, however, the two dimensions could not be confused, for there was no possibility that anyone would see the careerist engineer as an organic emblem of the group of machinists. But we should not mistakenly conclude, on that account, that the group's rejection of the former sense of representation was for the purpose of more fully realizing the latter. As the emblem comes to interpret meanings, so the delegate comes to interpret interests. When the Communist Party claims to represent the Hungarian working class, it does so on the grounds that it is uniquely qualified to interpret their interests (justified, no less, by scientific knowledge of the laws of motion of history). The toolmakers are certainly not interested in lending legitimacy to such a system of representation but rather in negotiating through it to maintain the minimum recognition necessary to keep the VGM on the books. With decades of experience in a regime of representation, the toolmakers reason: Let the Party exist if it must, but its truth claims are irrelevant and fall on deaf ears. If there must be a delegate, if someone must occupy the position, let it be this young engineer so there will be no confusion. If we authorize him to speak in our name, we do not authorize him to interpret our interests.

Most importantly, to the extent that they are now taking most of their energies outside the socialist firm and into the second economy, the partners feel no need for a representative in either an emblematic or a delegatory sense. When they finalize the sale of a machine they built for a private producer, the transaction is not about delegatory claims but about profit, not about interpreting the proof of their autonomous skills but about being autonomous. In moving into the second economy, the Minotaur toolmakers, together with much of Hungarian society, are distrustful of interpretation and representation. As in the difference between Poland's

Solidarity and Hungary's second economy, the toolmakers are looking less to politics than to an alternative economy. Whether this will be a civil society without a civic sense (built on kin ties and the cash nexus) or some new commonwealth of producers (in which small cooperatives like the partnerships are linked in new associational networks neither market nor redistributive) will be decided by the ongoing contests over worth within and across Hungary's mixed economies.

Epilogue

In 1993, several years after I bought the tin can with which I introduced this chapter, a friend in Budapest told me about a board game he had played as a child during the early Communist period. Prior to the Second World War, Hungarians had played Monopoly, known there as Kapitaly. But the competitive game of capitalism was banned by Communist authorities, who substituted another board game, *Gazdálkodj okosan!* (Economize Wisely!). In this goulash communist version of political correctness the goal was to get a job, open a savings account, and acquire and furnish an apartment. My friend was too young to have a Kapitaly board, but his older cousins from another part of the country knew the banned game and taught him the basic rules. You did not need to be a nine-year-old dissident to see that Monopoly was the more exciting game. And so they turned over the socialist board game, drew out the Kapitaly playing field from Start to Boardwalk on the reverse side, and began to play Monopoly—using the cards and pieces from Economize Wisely. But with the details of the rules unclear and with the memories of the older cousins fading, the bricolaged game developed its own dynamics, stimulated by the cards and pieces from the "other side." Why, for example, be satisfied with simple houses and hotels when you could have furniture as well? And under what configurations of play would a Prize of Socialist Labor be grounds for releasing you from or sending you to Jail?[16]

The notion of playing capitalism with communist pieces strikes me as an apt metaphor for the postsocialist condition.[17] The political upheavals

---

[16] The story itself was related while we watched my children playing their own hybrid version: having left the houses and hotels of their Monopoly set at a friend's house, they had started to use Lego building blocks (much preferred to the Monopoly pieces even after returned) to construct ever more elaborate structures in a game whose rules evolved away from bankrupting one's opponents and toward attracting customers to the plastic skyscrapers that towered over the Monopoly plain.

[17] In East Central Europe (and especially Hungary), proximity to West European markets, more familiarity with democratic institutions, prior experience with market culture (a subtext of

of 1989 in Eastern Europe and 1991 in Russia turned the world upside down. Misled by an apparent tabula rasa, the IMF and Western advisers issued instructions for the new "rules of the game," but it was played with the institutional remnants of the past, which, by limiting some moves and facilitating other strategies, gave rise to multiple systems of accounting. Postsocialism was not built on the ruins of communism but with the ruins of communism.[18] The toolmaking workshop at Minotaur was no exception.

The toolmakers' partnership ended in January 1988, when a decree by Minotaur's general director dissolved all VGMs operating in the company. Lukács and I returned to the machine factory in 1990, 1992, and 1993 to keep in touch with developments there. The first questions we asked were about the demise of the VGM. The response:

> When the VGM was dissolved, we gave a sigh of relief and took a deep breath after all the pressure and tension. We would have died if we had continued. It was a question of honesty. If we agreed to make something, we would do it. So there was a lot of stress to meet the quality and the deadlines. That stress was too much—it required so much energy and time. Now that pressure is off.

If the pressure was off the toolmakers, the pressure was intensified, however, for Minotaur's managers. Following the events of 1989 and the free election of a new government in the spring of 1990, Minotaur entered a new period of political and economic turbulence. Its monopoly on domestic markets for tires and other rubber products no longer assured, it quickly faced competition from foreign imports. With the abandonment of the COMECON trading agreements following the collapse of the Soviet Union, it then lost its once-guaranteed markets (as well as many of its suppliers) to the East. The machine factory, with its reasonably strong contacts with clients in Germany, thus stood as one of the few remaining parts of the company with potential for profitability.

The center-right government that took office in 1990 set out on a course to eliminate socialist planning, dismantle state ownership, and establish a market economy in Hungary. Its tasks included new legislation regulating

---

my friend's story), and much higher levels of direct foreign investment have operated to channel the recombinant strategies along recognizably capitalist, though distinctively East European, lines. More challenging, politically and analytically, are developments in the former Soviet Union, where some of the pieces from the communist past are the firearms of the now criminalized parts of these economies that are very far from child's play.

[18] Stark, "Recombinant Property"; and David Stark and László Bruszt, *Postsocialist Pathways: Transforming Politics and Property in East Central Europe*, 1998.

accounting, banking, trade, labor codes, and corporate governance. But none was more daunting than the problem of privatization. More than 90 percent of the productive assets of the economy were in the form of large state-owned enterprises. Creation of a market economy would require the privatization of these assets.[19]

Who should be the new owners, and how should they be determined? The situation was challenging because the aggregate book value of all of the state-owned enterprises greatly exceeded the collective savings of the Hungarian population. In a curious sense, the demand for owners exceeded the supply. Moreover, because these assets were not simply to be given away, how would one determine the "fair price" value of the assets to be sold? The old socialist principles of accounting were clearly inadequate, yet the new Western standards were not yet established. The typical answers from mainstream economists, that "the firm is worth whatever someone is willing to pay for it" or "let the market decide," were problematic where there was not yet a market—and where, in fact, the explicit motive for the sales was to create a market. Eventually, the new government established a State Property Agency to oversee the privatization process; after some false starts at centralized, administrative control, it settled on a course of more decentralized management.[20]

Many enterprise managers, however, did not wait for the dust to settle. Instead, they began the process of property change by transforming their companies from the state-owned enterprise form into other property forms that, although legal, occupied an ambiguous property status that was neither state nor private. This was the situation at Minotaur.

Senior management at Minotaur divided the firm into dozens of limited liability companies, *korlátolt felelősségű társaság* (KFT). The legal basis for the KFTs rested on an 1848 statute establishing limited liability, suppressed under socialism but resurrected in 1988 as one of the last major economic policy changes of the final Communist government. The various KFTs at Minotaur were joined in a complex web of holdings in which the parent company typically held a controlling interest in each unit and the units themselves were frequently linked through ties of cross-ownership. The factory workshop in which the toolmakers operated was one such KFT. Each KFT was governed by an enterprise council in which employees had 50 percent of the votes. But because "employees" included mid- and lower-level management personnel, it was a simple matter for senior management to gain a voting majority.

---

[19] David Stark, "Privatization in Hungary: From Plan to Market or from Plan to Clan?" 1990.
[20] David Stark, "Path Dependence and Privatization Strategies in East Central Europe," 1992.

Despite these odds, the toolmakers used every opportunity to voice their views in the enterprise council. "It's a new form. Why not try it?" they told us. For example, they defiantly criticized management for mishandling a World Bank loan to finance technical upgrading to new computerized, numerically controlled (CNC) machinery. Factory management, in the toolmakers' view, had failed to order the necessary auxiliary equipment. Without proper investment, bottlenecks persisted, and management continued to "throw money," in the form of overtime and special bonuses, to solve the problems. One toolmaker spoke mockingly of factory management: "When they were opening the new installation, they were pinning medals to each other, praising each other that 'now we've met world standards.' But now it's been a year and a half and they have nothing to show for it." Indeed, the loan was so mismanaged that the workshop's books reported record losses and the leased machines were transferred back to Minotaur. The toolmakers: "In America, if a firm went broke, the manager would jump out of an eighteen-story building. Here, when it goes broke, they throw millions for management training." The toolmakers' perspective on America was faulty, from the height of the building to the lack of understanding of corporate practice, but the derisive tone about their managers came through clearly.

The toolmakers also used the enterprise council to voice a recommendation that Szabó, the "young engineer" whom they had elected as their VGM representative, should be selected as the new factory manager. When this failed, they argued that the workshop should be sold to a foreign buyer:

> If a foreign capitalist comes in, brings his money, looks around, and
> sees the constraints, then he would see the kind of manager that
> would be needed. Now, as it is, the "friendly relations" hold things
> in place. A foreign owner would change all that. . . . Between the
> management style now and the capitalist management, neither of
> them is really attractive. But the latter is a bit preferable because the
> manager interested in profits should be able to see what's going on
> in production and make the changes. We wouldn't be happy with
> the ownership change as the solution—but we would accept it as
> the only way to make the changes [in the organization of work].

Finally, and perhaps most interestingly, the toolmakers argued strenuously that, upon privatization, they, as workers, should receive shares in the privatized venture. The toolmakers were unlikely to have read John Locke, but their theory of property was a clear and concise articulation of that view:

For thirty years we invested our skills and efforts in building this economy and this company. We should get some stock, or share, for that, shouldn't we? Of course.

Their proposals were dismissed:

At the enterprise council we raised the view that the employees should get some share. But that was swept away immediately by the general director who said there's no legal way to do that. Employees can't get a part of the property on the basis of that thirty years of work. What's going on now is like taking away the land from the peasants. Up to now we were told that we were the owners of the company. It was ours. But it changed from one day to the next. We lost the property rights overnight. In fact, there were never any real property rights but we had the feeling we could have them. But now even that illusion is evaporated.

The political context of the toolmakers' claims for workers' shares in companies was that the Smallholders Party, one of the parties in the new governing coalition, had campaigned in 1990 on a promise of restitution to peasants whose land had been seized by Communist collectivization in the late 1940s and early 1950s. Through legislation in the early 1990s, families who could show that their agricultural property had been appropriated were granted vouchers that they could invest in a designated set of privatized firms whose shares traded on the newly established Budapest Stock Exchange. Surveying the political landscape, the toolmakers found no party that was a comparable advocate for their interests:

I'm most familiar with the SzDSz [the social liberal, Free Democrats] program. During the referendum campaign, I would hear them in subway stations. I talked with them once at a stand. The issues around the working class, I told him, aren't picked up by any party including SzDSz. The guy told me—"the working class is a fiction." I can't accept that view, because there is a wide part of the population relying only on the products of their hands. If someone makes a tool worth 100,000 deutsche marks, he's not a fiction.

In the end, the machine factory was privatized. The new owner was Róka, the factory manager and the nemesis of Farkas, both of whom had entered Minotaur in the same postwar cohort. Róka was joined in his new ownership venture by a silent partner, a former Communist official who landed safely in the new capitalist economy, referred to by the toolmakers as a "parachutist." About conditions in the privatized firm, the toolmakers told us: "According to a new fashion, the label of the firm is changing, but the substance stays the same."

> Privatization for the few, and a miserable safety net for the poor
> and unemployed. This is the government's line. To be uncertain
> about who was the owner—that was the past. Now it's certain.
> We're not. What was ambiguous is now clear-cut. It's obvious. We're
> the losers.

Szabó, the young engineer, left Minotaur to lead a new start-up venture with six skilled employees, among whom he works at a cutting tool, producing machine parts. Renting a workshop in a district of small manufacturers, he was steadily building up a client base. "I won't rule out being a big business, but it will be step by step. Even if I would win the lottery, I'd still take it up gradually." Unlike Róka, who leased a Mercedes, Szabó drove a modest car.

Having worked at Minotaur for more than forty years, Farkas had retired shortly after being removed as the representative of the VGM. Despondent, less than a year later he died of a heart attack.

3

Creative Friction in a New-Media Start-Up

with Monique Girard

Throughout the 1990s, construction sites in Manhattan grew in number; this growth accelerated to a peak in the spring of 2000. But although these new construction sites had subcontractors, they had no cement; they had architects, but no steel; they had engineers and designers who built for retail firms, financial services, museums, government, and cultural institutions, but no one ever set foot into their constructions. These architects were information architects, the engineers were software and systems engineers, the designers were interactive designers, and the builders were site builders—all working in the Internet consulting firms that were the construction companies for the digital real estate boom that marked the turn of the millennium. Whereas the Hungarian toolmakers built tools with alloyed steel, the toolmakers of the start-up companies in Manhattan's "Silicon Alley" were building the digital tools of the new economy.

From the spring of 1999 through the spring of 2000, with follow-up visits through mid-2001, Monique Girard and I were fortunate to be able to observe one of these start-up firms and watch its website construction projects, not through a Plexiglas peephole, but close-up as ethnographic researchers. What we found, in almost every aspect, was a project perpetually "under construction." At the same time that the software engineers and interactive designers were constructing websites, they were also constructing the firm and the project form. And this relentless redesign of the organization was occurring simultaneously with the construction, emergence, consolidation, dissipation, and reconfiguration of the industry itself.

"What is New Media?" This was the question we encountered numerous times scribbled on whiteboards in brainstorming sessions during or just prior to our meetings in various interactive companies. Or, as one of our informants posed the question, "People are always trying to come up with a metaphor for a website. Is it a magazine, a newspaper, a TV commercial, a community? Is it a store? You know, it's none of these . . . and it's all of these and others, in many variations and combinations. So, there's endless debate." Of one thing you could be certain: if you were sure you knew the answer, the pace of organizational innovation to make new business models, the pace of technological innovation to make new afford-ances, and the pace of genre innovation to make new conceptualizations had likely combined to make your answer already obsolete.

What is a new-media firm? In answering the question, the start-ups did not start from scratch. The form of the firm and the shape of projects were borrowed from prior, existing models. Many were shaped around the consulting firm model; others adopted the model of an architectural firm, an advertising agency, a film or television studio, a software engineering or systems integration company, a design studio, a venture capital firm, or the editorial model of a magazine.[1] Forming the basic template, these models were repurposed for new functionalities as well as recombined for new purposes (e.g., consulting model + systems integrator, media produc-tion studio + venture capital model, etc.).

But whatever the choice of model (and note that, with few exceptions, most firms studiously avoided a "construction company" moniker), every new-media firm that was in the business of constructing websites had to cope with the same two problems: not only that the field was in flux, but also that every successful innovation in carving a niche, creating a new product, defining a new business model, or introducing a new technology could be replicated by competitors. Unlike other high-tech firms in fields such as biotechnology where patents could protect intellectual property, in the new-media field innovations were not likely to yield a stream of rents. Under circumstances of low barriers to entry (because innovations—in genre, technology, and organization—could be easily assimilated), firms were forced to be relentlessly innovative.

Thus, firms could not prosper simply by learning from their construc-tion projects. It was not enough to master the project form, to codify, to make routine, or even to perfect what they had been doing. If you locked in to what you had done previously, you would be locked out of markets that were changing rapidly, regardless of how much you improved per-formance by your existing criterion. On the other side, if you spent all your organizational resources searching for new products and processes, always and everywhere exploring for new opportunities, you would never

---

[1] These models are frequently made explicit in the names of firms and echoed in their de-cor—for example, *Plumb Design* (architecture), *Agency.com* (ad agency), *RG/A Studios* (design studio), *Concrete Media* (magazine + construction company), and so on. The decor of the offices of Pseudo in New York and Razorfish in NYC and San Francisco might seem to break out of any model, except that resembling a trendy nightclub is part of a branding strategy: shocking the corporate client can be a source of reassurance that the product will be unquestionably hip.

be able to exploit your existing knowledge. For the new-media companies, James March's problem of "exploration versus exploitation"[2] could be rephrased as the problem of staying ahead of the curve without getting behind on your deadlines.

When coping with complex foresight horizons,[3] where dislocations can be anticipated in general but are unpredictable in their specific contours, firms must be perpetually poised to pursue innovation. To do so they build organizations that are not only capable of learning but also capable of suspending accepted knowledge and established procedures to redraw cognitive categories and reconfigure relational boundaries—both at the level of the products and services produced by the firm and at the level of the working practices and production processes within the firm. These organizations innovate in ways that allow them to recognize, redefine, recombine, and redeploy resources for further innovation. That is, alongside technological innovation, they also engage in organizational innovation by creating organizational forms that allow for easy reconfiguration and hence minimize the costs of reorganization. Such capacities for organizational innovation go beyond the discovery of new means to carry out existing functions more effectively and efficiently. Under conditions of radical uncertainty, organizations that simply improve their *adaptive fit* to the current environment risk sacrificing *adaptability* in subsequent dislocations.

We explore these themes by examining the collaborative interactions among the multidisciplinary project teams working in a Silicon Alley new-media firm. First, we establish the highly uncertain environment within which new-media firms operate, with the paramount uncertainty being the shifting content, parameters, and value of the new-media industry itself. What is the meaning and where is the value of new media?

We then explore how a new-media start-up adopted a heterarchical organizational form to reassess the shifting terrain and deftly adjust its positioning and strategy.

After describing the project form and the web of social relations that comprise it, we address the process of collaborative engineering in which intelligence is distributed in forms of lateral accountability. The scaling back of administrative hierarchy is matched by prominence given to the competing evaluative and performance criteria specific to the multiple disciplines that must collaborate in website construction. In place of directives, the multiple disciplines engage in a discursive pragmatics in

---

[2] James G. March, "Exploration and Exploitation in Organizational Learning," 1991.
[3] David Lane and Robert Maxfield, "Strategy under Complexity," 1996.

which the disciplined judgment needed to do a good job is balanced with compromise needed to get the job done. Sharing the responsibility for getting the work done, one fights to promote the values of one's discipline, but one yields out of allegiance to the project and the firm. By distributing authority, the firm yields control of disciplined argument but wins the competitive edge that results by cultivating a diversity of options in the face of uncertainty.

An Ecology of Value

Silicon Alley: New Firms in an Uncertain Environment

During two years of intense ethnographic research, we observed organizational features and evaluative frames in practice at NetKnowHow, a pseudonymous new-media start-up in Silicon Alley navigating uncharted Internet territory. Before getting more specific about NetKnowHow, I shall first introduce Silicon Alley, the thriving socioeconomic scene at the center of the emerging new-media industry.

Silicon Alley was a (post)industrial district that can be thought of first as a *place*, running south of Forty-first Street along Broadway through the Flatiron District and SoHo into Chelsea and down to Wall Street. But it was also, and just as importantly, a *social space* linking the financial district on Wall Street to the traditional big advertising firms and the traditional big media companies in broadcast and publishing in Midtown.[4] By 1999, new media was one of New York's fastest growing sectors with almost 100,000 full-time equivalent employees in Manhattan alone (that is, more than the city's traditional publishing and traditional advertising industries combined) and with an estimated 8,500 new-media companies in the larger New York City area.[5] In that same year, the New York new-media industry produced revenues of $16.8 billion and generated $1.5 billion in venture capital funding and $3.5 billion in IPO (initial public offering) funding.

Bolstered by industry associations, promoted by government officials, and exuberantly championed by the trade publications, these new-media

---

[4] Gina Neff, "Organizing Uncertainty: Individual, Organizational and Institutional Risk in New York's Internet Industry, 1995–2003," 2004.

[5] All figures in this paragraph are from the *3rd New York New Media Industry Survey*, 2000, sponsored by the New York New Media Association and conducted by PriceWaterhouse Coopers. Numbers of jobs listed are full-time jobs plus the full-time equivalent of part-time jobs and freelancers.

companies showed, on their public face, a brash self-confidence. But they were acutely aware that they were operating in a highly uncertain environment. Their statements to the Securities and Exchange Commission (SEC) upon filing for an initial public offering provide a litany of this uncertainty. (All statements in bold or italics are quotations from SEC filings by Silicon Alley new-media firms.)

Among the risk factors reported by these new-media firms are some standard items commonly found in almost all SEC filings. More interesting are those factors common to early-stage companies in which the elapsed time from start-up to IPO is brief, as reflected in these statements to the SEC:

1. **We have an extremely limited operating history and may face difficulties encountered by early stage companies in new and rapidly evolving markets.**

2. **Our recent growth has strained our managerial and operational resources.** *Our recent acquisitions have created financial and other challenges, which, if not addressed or resolved, could have an adverse effect on our business. We acquired five businesses during 1998 and completed our merger with* [another new-media firm] *in January 1999. We are experiencing certain financial, operational and managerial challenges in integrating these acquired companies. This process of integration. . . . will require the dedication of management and other resources, which may distract management's attention from our other operations.*

For some new-media firms, the liabilities of newness are extreme, as in this case where almost all the senior personnel are newcomers to the company:

3. **Several members of senior management have only recently joined the company.** *Several members of our senior management joined us in 1998 and 1999* [this from a March 1999 filing], *including our Chief Financial Officer, Chief Operating Officer, Senior Vice President for Sponsorship, General Counsel, Vice President for Finance, Controller and Chief Accounting Officer, Senior Vice President for Human Resources, and the Chief Technology Officer. These individuals have not previously worked together and are becoming integrated as a management team.*

In a tight labor market, loss of "old hands" is a real threat and, in this knowledge-based industry, would spell a loss of the company's primary assets, especially where contacts to clients are contacts through personnel:

4. The loss of our professionals would make it difficult to complete existing projects and bid for new projects, which could adversely affect our business and results of operations.

Moreover, assets are not contained within the boundaries of the firm but are distributed across a network of interdependent firms. In choosing partners, alliances, and technologies, winners cannot be known in advance:

5. We may not be able to deliver various services if third parties fail to provide reliable software, systems, and related services to us. *We are dependent on various third parties for software, systems and related services. For example, we rely on* [another Internet company's] *software for the placement of advertisements and* [another Internet company] *for personal home pages and e-mail. Several of the third parties that provide software and services to us have a limited operating history, have relatively immature technology and are themselves dependent on reliable delivery of services from others.*

6. Our market is characterized by rapidly changing technologies, frequent new product and service introductions, evolving industry standards, and changing customer demands. The recent growth of the Internet and intense competition in our industry exacerbate these market characteristics.

In a newly emerging field, measuring assets is also complicated by the absence of industry standards and by uncertain government regulations:

7. The market for Internet advertising is uncertain. *There are currently no standards for the measurement of the effectiveness of Internet advertising, and the industry may need to develop standard measurements to support and promote Internet advertising as a significant advertising medium.*

8. Government regulation and legal uncertainties could add additional costs to doing business on the Internet.

Being a front-runner in an emerging field is only a temporary advantage where there are few barriers to entry, no patentable rents, and larger and more established firms ready to exploit the profitable activities revealed by the trials and errors of the pioneering start-ups:

9. We compete in a new and highly competitive market that has low barriers to entry.

10. We do not own any patented technology that precludes or inhibits competitors from entering the information technology services market.

11. We expect competition to intensify as the market evolves. We compete with: Internet service firms; technology consulting firms; technology integrators; strategic consulting firms; and in-house information technology, marketing and design departments of our potential clients.

12. Many of our competitors have longer operating histories, larger client bases, longer relationships with clients, greater brand or name recognition and significantly greater financial, technical, marketing and public relations resources than we have.

Above all, will e-commerce prove viable? Will the Internet as we know it be sustainable? Will it continue to grow? And might it mutate into unpredictable forms?

13. Our business may be indirectly impacted if the number of users on the Internet does not increase or if commerce over the Internet does not become more accepted and widespread.

14. If the Internet is rendered obsolete or less important by faster, more efficient technologies, we must be prepared to offer non-Internet-based solutions or risk losing current and potential clients. In addition, to the extent that mobile phones, pagers, personal digital assistants or other devices become important aspects of digital communications solutions, we need to have the technological expertise to incorporate them into our solutions.

Hence, at the height of exuberance during the Internet bubble, the following sober assessment:

15. We anticipate continued losses and we may never be profitable.

Searching for Value in an Evolving Ecology

Our litany of risk factors in the Silicon Alley IPO filing statements points to the difficulties of evaluating Internet stocks.[6] But over and above the problem of the market figuring out what these firms are worth is an even more interesting uncertainty: How do the firms themselves figure out what is *the basis of their worth*? To be clear, the problem is not in establishing the level of their market capitalization, which in any case is set by the

---

[6] Daniel Beunza and Raghu Garud, "Calculator, Lemmings, or Frame-Makers? The Intermediary Role of Securities Analysts," 2007.

market, but in surveying their actual and potential activities to discover what they are doing (or could be doing) that is of value.

Many of the Silicon Alley new-media firms that were formed during the initial expansion of the Web around 1995 began their operations designing websites. Suddenly every corporation, it seemed, needed a website. This surge in demand for the skills of designers and programmers created a sizable niche, with relatively few players, and a yawning knowledge gap between producers and clients. The folk history of the industry is strewn with stories by the start-up entrepreneurs who tell of their early experiences with midlevel corporate managers who had never surfed the Web but who had been instructed by senior executives of major corporations to "get us a website!"

Many of the twentysomething new-media pioneers were rebounding from a string of marginal jobs, having graduated from college after the 1987 stock market crash and the following recession that devastated the New York City economy. With the sudden expansion of the Web, their generational position, which had seemed such a liability, now became an asset: having grown up in the computer age, they were quick to grasp the implications of the Web. Equipped with a couple of PCs, an Internet connection, and the rudiments of HTML, they could make some kind of living, doing something they enjoyed, while making up the rules as they went along. Here was an opportunity to prove their worth—in circumstances where their marginality to the corporate world could be recast into a source of authority as legitimate interpreters of an alternative medium. With nothing to lose and with little or no experience in the corporate world, they met corporate executives who had little or no experience in the emerging field of new media. Frequently negotiated in their apartments-qua-offices, the six-figure contracts they landed for building websites were instant proof (sometimes surprising in magnitude) of their value.

If the corporate world was not only paying attention but also willing to pay, what was it paying for? In these early days, the corporate clients of the new-media pioneers were anxious to establish a presence on the Web, imagining websites as little more than billboards alongside the information superhighway. But, as the new-media entrepreneurs were introduced to the business operations of the firms, their interactions with various units yielded new insights about the capabilities of interactive websites as innovative corporate tools. Looking inside marketing departments, they realized that the Web could provide new kinds of information about customers; in interactions with production departments, they learned that the Web could establish new kinds of relationships to suppliers; and probing technology departments, they recognized how the Web could exponentially extended the network of information transfer well beyond the task of integrating proprietary data.

Although they were being paid for design work, the new entrepreneurs concluded that the real value they brought to the deal and to the client was as consultants. And so they adjusted their positioning. As "Web shops" they were like construction companies, building in a digital medium, to be sure, but nonetheless basically working to the specifications of the client. Reconfigured as "Web developers," they were in the business of advising clients about how to develop an overall strategy on and for the Web. The new mottos and redesigned logos on their own websites told the story: "Interactive Strategy," for example, and "digital.change.management."

The new management consulting/Web design hybrid took the Web developers more deeply and more intensively inside the organizations of their corporate clients (as the price of a well-designed corporate website rose into seven figures). And this increased interaction brought them into new fields with yet different identities. Their increased interaction with marketing departments, for example, resulted in "interactive advertising" and brought them onto the domain of the Midtown advertising agencies. As they began to design intranets and virtual offices for flexible communication within the corporation, the Web developers learned that their programming skills in graphic design had to be augmented with programming skills for the "information architecture" of knowledge management. And with the development of e-commerce, the front end of the website (the interface with the customer) quickly became more integrated with the entire organization and its "legacy systems" working on older operating platforms in production, purchasing, billing, and data archiving. To deliver a comprehensive product that linked the user interface to the "back end," the graphic designers, thus, also found themselves moving onto the terrain of the system integrators.

And so from graphic designers the Web developers had evolved into a composite: interactive designers, management consultants, advertising agencies, information architects, system integrators. Some of them were now being approached by a new kind of client—not simply major corporations who needed a website to augment their brick-and-mortar facilities but also start-up entrepreneurs with no physical plant and equipment but ideas to build click-and-order operations. Whereas the midlevel executives of the earlier period had come with a corporate charge to "build me a website," the exclusively e-commerce entrepreneurs now came with venture capital backing to "build me a company." The entrepreneurs for galoshes.com, soapsudsonline, YouNameIt.com brought financing, contacts with suppliers, and usually some modicum of marketing experience in a specific line of goods; but everything else from server farms to user interfaces, from e-carts to returns policies, from supplier interfaces to knowledge of online consumer buying practices rested in the knowledge base of the Web developer.

After creating one or two such virtual companies for fees, the Web developers were confronted yet again with the problem of value: Why simply charge a fee for a professional service when so much of the value of the virtual company resulted from the Web developers' efforts? The answer: Acquire some of the created value as well, that is, in addition to charging a fee for service, acquire partial equity in the new online companies. But things were usually not so additive, and the resulting deals often involved trading off some part of fees for equity. So, to protect their "investments" in deferred fees, some Web developers began incubating their client companies, working closely with the managers of the start-up ventures to guide them to the online market. In doing so, the Web developers acquired yet a new set of skills. In taking on a new project, it was no longer enough to assess whether a new client could pay its bill. As equity holders, the Web designers could see that the value of their own new-media firms now rested in part on their ability to evaluate the potential of new ventures, the profitability and/or marketability of the companies they were building. The more they began to think of their product as building a company, the more they had to consider the built company as a product—that is, the likelihood that it could be sold, whether through an IPO or to another round of investors. As such, in addition to all their other new identities, these Web developers were taking on some of the roles of venture capitalists. Whereas the Silicon Alley new-media firms were once digital construction companies, now they joined the venerable New York City tradition of real estate developers—developing properties on the digital landscape.

But as the Web developers evolved in a zigzag course of learning where the value was, other actors, of course, were doing the same. The major Midtown ad agencies, for example, established interactive units or spun off their own dedicated interactive agencies; the big consulting firms did not leave the field of interactive management to the new-media startups but moved aggressively into the field; and the big systems integrators developed their own e-commerce units and launched new initiatives in the lucrative business-to-business (B2B) Web development field. From a scarcely populated niche, the field of new-media services had mushroomed into a whole new world; its wide-open territory was now being filled with more-established competitors, coming to it from multiple starting points.

Meanwhile, the nascent industry was faced with new waves of technological innovation disrupting its emerging digital ecologies. On one side, players in the field were anticipating major breakthroughs in the development of broadband technologies that promised the convergence in one device of the various functionalities now parceled out across your television, your computer monitor, your stereo, your CD or DVD player, and your telephone. But just when one might have thought that this hailed a new "single appliance" era, we began to see, on the other side, the proliferation of myriad electronic devices (e.g., wireless PalmPilots and the like) through which we could receive and transmit digital information in a mobile environment.

These simultaneous processes of convergence and divergence would have two consequences. First, the joint appearance of broadband technologies, on one side, and multiappliance mobile interactivity, on the other, would have important consequences for the website genre form. That is, just at the point that the website genre seemed to be stabilizing, that moment of stabilization was revealed as a tiny moment in the history of the medium. Second, as bandwidth was expanding to broadband proportions, another set of actors entered the field—cable companies, network broadcasters, recording companies, and telecommunications firms. Sony, NBC, AT&T, and Telefonica (the Spanish telecommunications firm), for example, were among the major corporations who moved most aggressively. They were joined, with the arrival of mobile interactivity (from *Wired* to the "wireless revolution"), by new hardware manufacturers such as Nokia, Ericsson, and Palm, Inc. (as well as rapidly growing companies such as Symbol Technologies, makers of handheld bar-code-reading devices).

Companies striving to make headway amid such dizzying impermanence were in constant search of that "sweet spot" which consisted of finding the right temporary permanence to commit to—the winning clients, technology, marketing strategy—which would position them favorably for the next imminent shift of course. The challenge for these companies was not only to have the operational flexibility needed to change direction quickly; they needed to maximize their capacity to recognize opportunities and realize their promise, not only by exploiting their immediate benefits but also by exploring them as openings to new opportunities. To attend to these challenges, new-media start-up NetKnowHow adopted the heterarchical features of distributing intelligence and organizing diversity.

The Firm and the Project Form

NetKnowHow was a full-service Internet consulting firm. It was founded in 1995 by two young entrepreneurs, each with experience in the large

corporate sector (traditional consulting and traditional media). In its formative years it was a software development company, but it quickly moved
into the new-media field, producing intranets and websites for corporate
and university clients. NetKnowHow acquired a reputation for excellence
in retail e-commerce after its website for a famous department store won
a prize for an outstanding e-commerce site. In 1999, while continuing to
build retail e-commerce sites for nationally recognized corporate clients,
it also built sites for start-up dot-coms (striking partnerships with several
of these) and merged with another smaller start-up in the field of digital
kiosks. In 2000, it stopped taking on dot-com clients, focusing instead
on consulting for "click and mortar" operations that combined physical
and digital retailing while experimenting on the side in developing applications for the wireless interface. Like the overwhelming majority of
new-media start-ups in Silicon Alley, it had no venture capital funding;
and, also like the majority of new-media firms during the period prior to
the industry's downward spiral beginning in April 2000,[7] it was a profitable company. When we began our ethnographic research in the spring of
1999, NetKnowHow had about fifteen employees. Within eighteen months
it had grown to over a hundred employees.

The physical setting of our research was in the Flatiron District, at the
core of Silicon Alley. At the point of its maximum growth, NetKnowHow
occupied three workplaces several blocks apart, in addition to a small
business office that it briefly held in the prestigious Flatiron Building. The
three workplaces were lofts converted from displaced printing operations
with as many as thirty computer workstations in an open room where no
walls, dividers, or cubicles separated the programmers, designers, information architects, and business strategists. The plan of these workplaces
was not just open but so closely packed that almost anyone could reach out
and literally touch someone. And, like construction sites, they were places
in movement. Although there were periods, typically midmorning and
midafternoon, when it seemed that everyone was still, each concentrating
on his or her own monitor, for much of the time the rooms seemed in motion with dozens of micromeetings in twos or threes, some sitting, others
standing, leaning over shoulders to point at lines of code or graphics on
their monitors, some lasting thirty minutes, many only thirty seconds.
Some formal project meetings took place around large tables in the official
conference rooms, but just as often a project team would claim a part of
the open room by wheeling chairs toward it and sitting on tables around

---

[7] New York New Media Association (NYNMA) 1999 survey. April 14, 2000, marked the first
dramatic drop in Internet stocks.

"We Are Looking for . . . What You Could Bring to NetKnowHow's Table"

NetKnowHow, Inc. seeks Cold Fusion/ASP/MS SiteBuilder (or CGI/Perl) programmers with proven experience developing a wide range of leading-edge Internet systems. The ideal candidate will have experience in database design and development (Oracle/SQLServer) and strong HTML and JavaScript skills. *Team players must be able to juggle multiple projects, prioritize to meet client needs and established deadlines.* Requirements include one year solid experience programming in Cold Fusion or equivalent language, as well as familiarity with database systems (MS Access, MS SQL Server, Informix and Oracle). *We are looking for quality people who take pride in their work and enjoy working in an eclectic, hard-working and creative environment.* If you're interested in beginning a career with a cutting edge new media company, drop us a line. NetKnowHow's *flat organizational structure permits self-starters to thrive.* Benefits include medical, dental, 401-k and gym membership. If you have something special to contribute, submit your résumé and a cover letter describing your work experience and *what you think you could bring to NetKnowHow's table,* to recruiting@NetKnowHow .com. [emphasis added]

several workstations. For the most intense discussions, people could go to one of the "private conference rooms" in the stairways and on the fire escape, where smokers congregated.

The social setting of our ethnography, like the de rigueur hardwood floors, was Silicon Alley standard: the workforce of NetKnowHow was tightly grouped around its median age of twenty-seven. But its demographics departed from the typical new-media start-up with a higher proportion of women and a broader ethnic and racial mix. The job listing in the first sidebar of this chapter indicates the qualities that NetKnowHow was seeking in its employees. For this programmer position, beyond the obvious technical qualifications, it wanted "team players" who could "take pride in their work" and thrive in its "flat organizational structure."

Job categories at NetKnowHow, like those in other Silicon Alley firms,[8] were loosely defined and were sometimes unconventional. The job title on the business card of one young programmer, for example, read "Technology Evangelist." "My job," Yuval told us, "is to scout for new developments in the field and then spread the word within the company and to our clients." All employees were expected to take initiative. We saw this in action

[8] On job categories and career structures in Silicon Alley, see Amanda Damarin, "Fit, Flexibility, and Connection: Organizing Employment in Emerging Web Labor Markets," 2004.

when NetKnowHow hired a programmer with more than ten years of experience working for IBM. Over the course of his first days at the start-up we had several opportunities to talk with him as he filled out some forms with the Human Resources specialist, was assigned to a workstation, and met other programmers at adjacent desks. On Wednesday I asked him how things were going. "It's great here, so much better than my job at IBM, where they controlled even the stuff you put up in your cubicle. But there's one thing I don't understand. Nobody's told me what to do." By Friday, when he still hadn't figured out that it was his job to find out how he could best fit in, he was let go.

Reflecting the casual work environment, NetKnowHow's refrigerators were well stocked with soda, juice, and beer. And like a construction site, the place was frequently noisy—not from crane engines and jackhammers but from the music that provided a nonstop umbrella of sound over the low hum of many conversations. In this setting, the counterpart of a hard hat was a headset wired to one's own music as some protection against the din and as a signal "not to be interrupted." Although the work atmosphere was casual, the actual work was intense and the hours long. Both hours and intensity increased with the approach of a project deadline and reached manic levels each autumn, when the hardwood floors were littered with futons and mattresses as NetKnowHow's employees worked literally day and night to build e-commerce sites that could be launched for the holiday buying season. Like preindustrial work rhythms[9] with bouts of work followed by relative idleness, rush work to meet deadlines could be followed by less intense, typically short, periods "between projects."[10] But if the rhythms of work were preindustrial, there was nothing preindustrial about the overall experience of temporality. In the new-media field, there was no sense of a "passage of time." Instead, time was compressed; like a time warp it was something that you were being shot through.

The Web of a Web Project

The process of designing and building a website at NetKnowHow, as in new-media firms generally, took the organizational form of a project. A project was not a permanent construct but a temporary ensemble whose

---

[9] E. P. Thompson, "Time, Work-Discipline, and Industrial Capitalism," 1982.

[10] These periods of relative "downtime" between projects were not simply relaxation but provided opportunities to pick up new skills by monitoring the activities of others going about their work. Grabher refers to this process as "learning by watching." Gernot Grabher, "Ecologies of Creativity: The Village, the Group, and the Heterarchic Organisation of the British Advertising Industry," 2001.

players had been working on other projects before and would move to other projects after its conclusion.[11] Together with every new-media firm we encountered in Silicon Alley, NetKnowHow devoted considerable energy not simply to monitoring projects ("building accountability of the project and in the project") but also to monitoring the project process ("codifying our practice," "institutionalizing our process," etc.)—in part as marketing strategy (e.g., "The Razorfish 5 Step Process"), in part because the project form is a critical component of the core competence of these firms.

Some projects lasted no more than a month. Some, whether because of their innate complexity or because of indecision or insolvency on the client side, lasted five or six months. The typically sophisticated project ran sixty to ninety days, and this extraordinarily compressed time to market was an important factor in project dynamics. Projects could bring earnings to the firm ranging from several hundred thousand to nearly a million dollars. Project fee structures could vary: NetKnowHow sometimes contracted fixed fees, sometimes adopted a retainer model, and sometimes took equity in lieu of partly defrayed or deferred fees. More typically, it negotiated overall price estimates based on material expenses plus billable hours.

The participants in a project included business strategists, interactive designers, programmers and other technologists, information architects (IA), and merchandising specialists. Each project had a project manager; most projects included a designated design lead and technology lead, and larger projects would designate a lead information architect as well as a lead business strategist. While they were temporarily the "members" of a project, personnel remained part of an ongoing functional unit (e.g., design, programming, IA, strategy, etc.) variously referred to as a "community," "discipline," or "guild" but most frequently called a "team" or "groups" (e.g., "the design team," "the technology group," etc.).

Although everyone at NetKnowHow would have preferred that people be assigned to only one project at any given time, the exigencies of this poorly capitalized firm (and its billable-hours revenue structure) frequently required that personnel work on multiple projects simultaneously. This fact created time-allocation problems (and the need for cross-project coordination) among project managers. Moreover, it repeatedly short-circuited the ongoing discussion about the principles guiding

---

[11] On the project as an organizational form, see Gernot Grabher, "Cool Projects, Boring Institutions, and Temporary Collaboration in Social Context," 2002; and Jörg Sydow, Lars Lindkvist, and Robert DeFillippi, "Project-Based Organizations, Embeddedness and Repositories of Knowledge," 2004.

the physical layout of the firm, specifically, whether personnel should be spatially grouped by project or by team.

A project, of course, was a project *for* a particular client. To an important extent it was also a project *with* a client. In some cases, representatives of the client were a part *of* the project. Project managers and members at NetKnowHow were aware that "the client" was itself a complex entity in which different parties had different, and even conflicting, interests. When working with a large retail chain, for example, the proximate client might be a new online unit that was itself involved in turf wars and budget battles inside its own organization. Similarly, the marketing department, financial services, warehousing, and production units that were typically a part of the client could have different stakes in the (definitions of) success or failure of the venture. Thus, when NetKnowHow's project members (and not simply project managers) telephoned, e-mailed, or instant-messaged their counterparts in the client organization for technical information (for example, when a programmer got in touch with a database manager of the client's "legacy" system, or a merchandizing specialist called a marketing manager), such contacts could also be opportunities for intelligence gathering.[12]

Motivated in part by the recognition of these complexities, some clients began hiring independent contractors who specialized in the role of interface between the corporation and the Web-development project. Thus, just at the time that NetKnowHow and its competitors were acquiring the skills of "managing the client," their corporate clients were hiring a new type of professional whose skills were to manage the representations of the client (on the one side) and to manage the project managers (on the other). From the vantage point of Internet companies such as NetKnowHow, such developments were a mixed blessing. The injunction that only one person spoke definitively for the client (and a corporate outsider at that) was potentially positive because nothing could be more disastrous for a project than to operate with erroneous or conflicting ideas of the intentions of the client firm. But, at the same time, as "the client" was likely to have multiple (and even competing) objectives, the reduction to a single channel could result in messages that were difficult to decipher in the absence of multiple sources of information, which are often needed to make real interpretation possible. That is, mixed messages are likely, whether from one source or many. The challenge for the project

---

[12] Even when the client is not located in New York City, programmers (or other specialized skill groups) are in networks—school ties, special interest groups, immigrant communities, Listservs, instant-message buddy lists, bulletin boards, chat rooms—that make it relatively easy to open direct lines of communication with counterparts in the client's organization.

was to construct from these mixed messages a relatively robust picture of the client, with enough depth of focus to commit resources and yet fuzzy enough to anticipate potential changes in direction or to facilitate quick adaptation to the unanticipated.

These kinds of interactions, whether tactically technical or strategically organizational, are part of the web of a Web project. A more complete elaboration of the network of a Web project would include technology "partners" (licensing and other arrangements through which the Web developer can offer access and support for new technologies); hardware and network affiliations through which the Web developer offers server space, maintenance, and network security; venture capitalists, whether brought from the side of the client or brought to the client by the Web developer; other Web-development firms (when different parts of a project are distributed among different firms or when the firm elects to subcontract parts of the project to other firms); vendors to the client (whose information systems must be reconciled with the categories and the functionalities of the site); order fulfillment firms, credit services, and so on. Intelligence is distributed across this web.

We turn now to the knowledge networks within the firm characterized by ties of lateral accountability across organizational units. To signal the difference from conventional *sequential engineering*, in which a project is hierarchically designed with central subsystems setting the boundary conditions for the design of lower-ranking components, we refer to this process of mutual monitoring as *collaborative engineering*.

Distributing Intelligence

The life cycle of a Web project typically has a preformative, "preproject," stage of matching firm and client, followed by stages of identifying the project personnel, a formal "kickoff," planning and site design, production, testing, soft launch, and a celebration at hard launch. Figure 3.1 presents a diagram of a typical project life cycle at NetKnowHow.

From the idealized representation in figure 3.1, it might seem that building a website is a matter of sequential engineering: in principle, all design and engineering should be completed before production begins. The diagram shows distinct moments of parallel engineering, for example, during weeks 2–5, when the information architects, technical architects, and graphic designers work in parallel to draw up their plans for the site, which are then "handed off" to the site builders. In the actual process, however, engineering was more simultaneous than sequential.

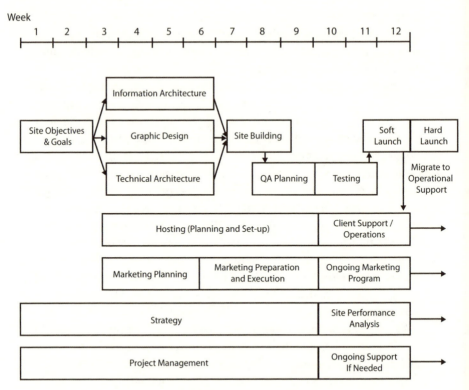

Figure 3.1 NetKnowHow Project Management Guide

At NetKnowHow, website construction was a process of collaborative engineering.

An industry in which there can be extraordinary first-mover advantages creates strong pressures to be quick to market. The results are excruciatingly tight project deadlines that force production to begin before design is completed. Typically, the database managers and other programmers begin construction just as soon as they hear initial ideas about the project. Of course, they are not literally writing each of the many thousands of lines of code from scratch but are looking to previous work to find promising templates for the various functionalities that are likely to be adopted for the project. At the same time that they are searching through their existing stock of code, they are also searching for solutions to the new functionalities that were discussed in the kickoff meeting (as well as those that were not even mentioned there but which they are literally overhearing in the close quarters of the open workplace). If they were to start programming only after the information architect presented them with the finished "wire frame"[13] (a kind of blueprint specifying each part of the website and their interrelations), the project could never be completed on deadline. Similarly, the information architect is consulting with the programmers about the code that they are already preparing, hearing their proposals about new solutions to old problems, and picking up new ideas that could be adopted in the site. Without such iteration, she might draw up an exquisite wire frame—but one that could not be completed on time and on budget. In short, production workers participate in design as a process that involves bricolage.[14]

If production begins before design is completed, it is also the case that design is ongoing, continuing almost to the point that production is completed. First, even with the best efforts to manage the client's expectations and even within a project cycle as short as ninety days, it is nearly impossible to prevent project creep—the ratcheting up of project specifications. Because clients learn during the process of building the site, they will demand new functionalities. Some can be resisted ("that's not in the project specifications"). But they cannot all be deflected, especially when the firm has promised a "cutting edge" website and the client now sees a competitor's site with new features that "have to be adopted." From a narrow business logic, new functionalities can be incorporated with a corresponding increase in price ("yes, but it will increase the programming costs dramatically"). But from a design perspective, introducing new features can have enormous implications that ramify throughout the site. Seemingly simple changes in the order of steps within "checkout," for example, might require major restructuring of the database.

But there is a second, more important, reason why design—as the work of figuring out the whole—continues well through the production process, even when no additional functionalities are introduced after the initial stages. Because of the rapid pace of organizational, technological, and genre innovations, website construction at NetKnowHow was almost always a process of engineering something they had not built before. Even when the project could benefit from utilizing existing templates, the particular combinations were likely to be novel, and likely to incorporate novel elements as well. Moreover, at NetKnowHow, learning was by doing. That is, instead of understanding a technology and then adopting it, one came

---

[13] The wire frame is an example of a "boundary object" stable enough to circulate, ambiguous enough to be an object of multiple meanings. See Susan Leigh Star and James Griesemer, "Institutional Ecology, Translations, and Boundary Objects: Amateurs and Professionals in Berkeley's Museum of Vertebrate Zoology, 1907–1939," 1989.

[14] Raghu Garud and Peter Karnoe, "Bricolage versus Breakthrough: Distributed and Embedded Agency in Technological Entrepreneurship," 2003.

> ### "A Puzzle That Keeps Changing as You Put It Together"
>
> Early on in the project you have a kickoff meeting and you do have an understanding of the project up front. You have a sense of what the project is, the size of it, the scope of it, and everything else. But as soon as that kickoff meeting is over, that whole concept just . . . [throws up his hands]. It's like a puzzle—you see the cover of the box, you know what the puzzle is supposed to look like, you have a really good idea of what you need to do, but then you open the box, you just see all those pieces, and then you have to start putting all those pieces together.
>
> In trying to figure out how the puzzle pieces might fit together, the wire frames are not much help because the projects are always so fluid and there are always so many changes you have to go through, regardless. Every client wants changes; every project leader encounters some complexity that requires a change; so the deeper you go into changes, the farther you get from the realization. You'll have the puzzle pieces, and then someone will dump a whole other fifty or hundred pieces into your lap. And when they dump the additional pieces in your lap, you also don't know how those fifty pieces relate to the cover on the box, you don't know if it's the bottom, on the side, on the top, or the left. But you do know that what you're going to end up with is not like the initial picture you started with at the kickoff meeting, because you change so much.
>
> No matter how many new changes come across, for every new change you can tie up and get your arms around, get a resolution to, and get it implemented, then that actually serves to be a greater step towards the realization than just figuring out how the two pieces you had in the beginning fit together the way that you thought they would, because it's now more like you're getting these undefined pieces and you're able to define them and that sort of leapfrogs you toward that realization. At some point when you get all of those changes done and a good portion of the rest of it done and at that point, that's usually when I have that realization that YES! I see what it is that we're doing now. I have a good understanding of the whole thing and what it's going to end up looking like. For me it usually happens toward the end.

to understand a technology by using it. As a result, the process of figuring out how all the pieces fit together did not take place in the initial "design" phase but, instead, occurred during and through the process of constructing the site. "It's like a puzzle," explained Aaron, age twenty-seven, one of the firm's two most senior project leads, "but it's peculiar because the picture on the cover keeps changing as you put it together." The passage from our conversation is quoted verbatim in the above sidebar.

In these observations, Aaron is expressing a view that design is an emergent process, distributed across many actors in a highly interactive way. And, like design, innovation is not a moment that occurs at a particular stage in the Web development process. At NetKnowHow, innovation was not an activity confined to an R & D department. Every unit, indeed everyone, was involved in the process of innovation as an immensely pragmatic activity of collaborating to "figure out how it fits together." In short, instead of the conventional view of innovation by design, in these website construction projects we find design by innovation. As a self-organized, emergent process, it was not engineered from above.

To understand the complexities of "figuring out how it fits together," we need to go beyond the simple "front end/back end" dichotomy that figures so prominently in discussions of websites. The distinction exists in the folk categories of the Web: the "front end" is what you, the end user, experience when you go to a website, but it is like the tip of the iceberg; the "back end" is everything you do not see below the waterline, but which makes it work. The distinction is meaningful but misleading—especially if it connotes website construction as parallel processes that have to be made to converge or leads to metaphors in which the "front end" people (designers and such) are building a bridge from one side, the "back end" people (programmers) are building from another side, and they have to meet in the middle. Their interdependencies, we found, are much greater.

In the simple version of the front/back end model, there are two computers and one interface: the server where the code of the website resides, your PC, and the graphical user interface (GUI) through which you experience the site. But sophisticated e-commerce sites involve many computers and multiple interfaces—yours, the servers leased by the client of the Web developer, the mainframes on which the client's multiple databases are operating, as well as the computers of the client's suppliers and vendors, the computers of the order fulfillment service, credit card companies, and so on. Your click as end user can initiate a purchase, create a delivery form, enter a credit card payment, provide feedback to marketing, and route an order directly to a supplier. Some sophisticated e-commerce sites reach deeply into the production and inventory systems of multiple suppliers and use algorithms (with weights for the suppliers' price, location, level of inventory, opening or closing phases of production runs, and even the quality of the suppliers' data) to determine which supplier will fill a particular customer's online purchase.

The challenge for the website developers is to build a site in which the activities of the end user are seamlessly linked to the various other computers to which the site is interfaced. The performance of the website critically depends on the performance of an actor—the user—whose actions might be anticipated but cannot be controlled. It is this interdependence between website and user that most dramatically increases the interdependencies among the website construction crew. A programmer can design a beautiful interface between the website and the suppliers, but she needs to make sure that it does not interfere with how the information architect is thinking about navigational issues for the interface to the user. The more the site is truly interactive, the more the various parts of the team must interact. A change in the categories of the database, for example, can change parameters for the graphic designers, and vice versa. The more the intelligence of the site is distributed—including, most critically, the user's intelligence—the more the construction site must use a distributed intelligence among the team in collective problem solving. When graphic designers and database programmers speak, the phrase "being on the same page" can refer to an injunction to focus on the same problem, a request to consider how an action will have consequences in another sphere, an opportunity to bring each other up-to-date on new methods, applications, functions, and reporting systems, as well as quite literally being on the same page of code.

The distributed intelligence of collaborative engineering does more than flatten reporting structures; it laterally extends them. Nor could we simply say that the heterarchical firm has radically decentralized decision making. The term decentralization might imply that autonomous units are making *independent* decisions. In fact, the complex *interdependencies* among the parts require dense communication for coordinating production and recalibrating strategic action as the parameters of any given unit's activities are shifting in midcourse.

The more the project members must take into account how their actions will shape the parameters of others, the more they must increase the lines of lateral accountability. As a young programmer explained to us in an apt epigram for collaborative engineering: "In this company, I'm accountable to everybody who counts on me."

Organizing Dissonance

Multiple Performance Criteria

The directionality of accountabilities in heterarchical organizations such as NetKnowHow is lateral. But these accountabilities are not of a singular logic. These are organizations where evaluative principles operate in multiple registers. If collaborative engineering involves the pragmatic activity of figuring out how everything fits together, it also involves the discursive activity of evaluating how it performs.

You build a website that works. But, as more websites get built, you cannot make a distinction between yours and others' simply on the grounds that yours works. You say that yours performs better. But then immediately you must begin to articulate your performance criteria.[15] You cannot silence the talk about evaluative principles and point to a purely pragmatic frame, since your claim that you are making a valuable product raises the question not only of what is its value but why.

Questions of value—the value of work and the value of the product of work—are central to a Web project. At NetKnowHow, some criteria of worth were shared across all communities. Formal credentials were unimportant; actual skills were critical. Not surprisingly, in this project-based organization, an ability to work well with others was highly valued. This trait has several components: First, an ability to get along with others in an extraordinarily stressful and fast-paced environment.[16] Knowing the subtle cues for when and how you can interrupt is one of the skills relevant in this area. Second, an ability to convey knowledge (whether explicit or tacit) to others. Finally, and most ubiquitous, an ability to figure things out quickly. As important as (and for some even more important than) one's absolute or relative knowledge is the rate of acquiring new skills and knowledge as well as being able to rethink a problem so that it can be solved. "Picking things up quickly" is highly valued by one's co-workers, both within and across communities of practice.[17]

However, not all criteria of worth are shared. The different communities of practice at NetKnowHow differed in their conceptions of value and in their measures of performance. In our summaries of the principles of four such logics, italicized terms indicate words that appear frequently in employees' written evaluations of their coworkers and in our field notes made from conversations with them.

The logic of programming. A good programmer is above all *logical*, and a good website must be judged by the same criterion. When she performs

---

[15] For a fascinating analysis of performance criteria in the field of popular music, see Antoine Hennion, "Baroque and Rock: Music, Mediators and Musical Taste," 1997.

[16] As academics we might think about this as a collegial respect, but that would miss the physical dimension of working in such close proximity. Imagine five people all working together in a space the size of your office; if you have a big office imagine ten, and then you will get the idea.

[17] In 2000 NetKnowHow initiated a formal evaluation process for all employees. Each employee was able to choose five coworkers to write evaluations. "Picking things up quickly" was one of the most frequently mentioned positive traits. The summary statements below draw from these evaluations, as well as from our field interviews and observations.

well, she does so with *speed, efficiency,* and *accuracy;* and a good website must do the same. A good programmer can *translate*—express a functionality in the language of a computer code that is *categorical* and *hierarchical.* A good programmer understands the deep structure as well as the quirks and idiosyncrasies of the program. When she speaks, it is not simply on behalf of other programmers but on behalf of the program. The legitimate tests and proofs of worth are Quality Assurance tests and other instruments that measure the speed, efficiency, security, and reliability of the site.

The logic of design. A valuable designer must be knowledgeable about processes of *perception,* and a good website must use graphic cues that conform to these processes. When he performs well, he does so with *creativity,* and the results will be *exciting* and *stimulating.* A good designer is also a *translator*—into a language that is *visual, intuitive,* and *interactive.* At work he engages in a visual dialogue with other designers, the client, and users. When this work of translation is successful it makes links to the *imagination* because both the client and the user live not only in a real world and a virtual world but also in *imaginary* worlds. The designer's translation creates multiple links among all these—in the process, making connections between the self-image of the client and that of the user. Exploiting interactive as well as visual features, he creates the overall "look and feel" through which the site achieves the desired *effects/affects* and conveys a branding *experience.* If necessary, he has authority to argue with the client provided he speaks as an advocate of the brand. Winning clients, winning audiences, and winning competitions are legitimate proofs of worth.

The logic of information architecture. A good information architect must be knowledgeable about principles of *cognition.* A site that successfully applies these principles will be characterized by *clarity, ease,* and above all *usability.* A good website conveys information by creating navigable pathways that conform to cognitive pathways. An information architect's activities are valuable because they are based on *studies* that use *statistics* to understand user *behavior.* In discussions with other members of the project, including the client, the information architect is an advocate of the *user.* The user lives in a world of *information* that is accessed through *tools,* some of which are more and some of which are less *appropriate* for the *tasks* that the user attempts to perform. "Conversion rates" and other statistical metrics of user activities are legitimate tests of a website's performance.

The logic of merchandising. A good website is one that moves product. To do so, a good online merchandiser exploits powers of *suggestion.* Because the *shopper* lives in a world of *desire,* she is open to suggestion. *Playfulness* takes precedence over information, surprise takes precedence over search, product *placement* takes precedence over navigation, and *pleasurability* takes precedence over usability. Proofs of value are metrics that measure how product is moving in relation to inventories.

The various communities of practice at NetKnowHow were articulate and adamant about their respective performance criteria. "We yell and scream" was a repeated refrain in conversations when we talked about this friendly rivalry. Discussions could be heated, especially when proofs of worth[18] were not immediately recognized outside the frames that made them seem so obvious to their proponents. The statistical studies on user behavior produced by the leading information architect, for example, were characterized by a leading designer as "arbitrary," provoking the counter-charge that this was yet another instance in which he, the designer, was being "irrational."

Despite occasional flare-ups, the temperature stayed cool since the dominant mode was persuasion rather than denunciation. Because every community of practice was a minority view, each attempted to enlist or enroll others in recognizing the legitimacy of its performance criteria. In this process of ongoing realignment[19] people spoke openly about seeking allies.

We saw this process at work, for example, in a dispute over competing claims about who could speak on behalf of "the user" that raged for many months at NetKnowHow and was still ongoing when we concluded our fieldwork. This development was triggered by the information architects, who thought that they had a special claim on knowledge about the user. Their hope was that every group would start focusing on the user's performance and that, by maintaining their special definition, they could raise their own performance criteria to a special status to which all groups gave credence. The information architects' strategy was initially successful: as references to "the user" indeed circulated through the company, we could hear this theme more and more frequently in discussions, formal and informal.

But the strategy also had consequences unintended by the information architects: instead of deferring to the information architects, each of the disciplines began to articulate its own definition of the user consistent with that discipline's value system and metrics of performance. That is, each community developed its own distinctive claims to represent the

---

[18] Luc Boltanski and Laurent Thévenot, *On Justification: The Economies of Worth*, 2006.
[19] See Bruno Latour, "Powers of Association," 1986.

user. The merchandizing specialists, who had previously seemed to be speaking on behalf of the merchandiser, offered seminars in which they presented their view of the user as "shopper" and mobilized an alternative set of findings. Similarly, the firm's leading designer, who was genuinely most attentive to the studies of the information architects, came to the defense of the designer who had derided them as "arbitrary," pointing out that these statistical studies were conducted at a particular stage of the development of the Web. In a variety of settings, he suggested new directions in the evolution of the Web that could make these findings obsolete. And, more quietly but quite forcefully in their individual interactions with the other communities, even the programmers began to articulate their own representation of the user.

Disputes such as this were vital for firms like NetKnowHow. If the firm locked in to a single performance criterion, it would not be positioned to move with flexibility as the industry changed and the Web evolved. Thus, even the principle we have not yet mentioned—profitability—was not itself an evaluative principle that trumped all others, since continuing profitability was itself based on the ability to anticipate new developments and re-cognize new performance criteria for evaluating well-designed and well-functioning websites. Tolerating, even encouraging, such friendly rivalry was a source of innovation to navigate the search for value within the young industry.

To Build a Site, Make Settlements

Collaborative engineering is a discursive pragmatics. It is, at once, an ongoing conversation and an intensely practical activity. I present to you accounts of my work so that you can take my problems and goals into account in yours. We do what works to make it work. We need to talk to do the job well, but to get the job done we need to stop talking and get to work. We give reasons, we explain the rationale, but we use different rationalities. We do not end disputation so much as suspend it. To build sites, we make settlements.

Settlement of the Web and settlement in Web projects share some common features, not least because the two dynamics are recursive. As a frontier, the Web is going through a process of settlement.[20] It is not simply that sites are built but that they are built in settlements. Landscapes are reshaped, and structures are recognizable by their contours. We can dis-

---

[20] On settlement, see the extraordinarily rich and insightful analysis of online newspapers by Pablo Boczkowski, *Digitizing the News: Innovation in Online Newspapers*, 2004.

tinguish an e-commerce site from a portal site from an informational site. Things get settled.

For the members of Web projects, the process of building websites has the result that things also get settled. From a very low division of labor, some professional boundaries develop. It is possible to distinguish a graphic designer from a business strategist from an information architect. Things settle down, people settle in. They work out ways of dividing tasks and managing the relationships across their professional boundaries. On many issues they reach agreement.

But you cannot settle back in your ergonomic chair too long—because, unlike settlements on physical landscapes, things do not stay settled on the Web. The built structures on the digital landscape lack the permanence of physical structures. An abandoned warehouse is a boarded-up blight on the landscape until it is destroyed or gentrified into luxury apartments. An abandoned website is a Code 404, "File Not Found." Websites can be destroyed with ease and new ones created. Repurposing takes more work,[21] but in general the process of recombining forms takes place with marked rapidity when working in the digital medium.[22] Thus, just when we thought we could easily recognize the difference between e-commerce sites, portal sites, and information sites, fusions arose that confused the distinctions. AOL's mall of affiliated storefronts began to double as a portal, the Yahoo portal adopted e-commerce features, and we can go to the dominant e-commerce site, Amazon, for information and for its affiliated shops. Things might be settling down, but they are not settled once and for all.

Life in Web projects is much the same. Sometimes the parties actually come to agree. But frequently, instead of reaching an agreement, they reach a settlement. Like the term itself, with its connotations of law and locality, our informants at NetKnowHow reached settlements (1) by judicious appeals to other actors who were outside the dispute, and (2) through their highly localized practices. When the incommensurable systems of value came into conflict in a project they were sometimes settled by contingent compromises (often through appeals to the project lead) and by

---

[21] The analogy to physical buildings and landscapes has merit when we move from destruction (almost without cost in the digital case) to repurposing. Sites like Yahoo, Amazon, and other major online retailers can be rebuilt only with considerable investment. Like newsmagazines, they can be cosmetically redesigned with some frequency; but changing their *form and functionality* is a major operation that is fraught with difficulties. Witness the calamity at Deja.com.

[22] Even in the digital environment, relative stabilizations occur because of investment in forms. Genre forms are malleable but not infinitely so. On investment in forms, see Laurent Thévenot, "Rules and Implements: Investment in Forms," 1984.

"relativization" (through appeals to the client). In relativization,[23] the parties to the disagreement can maintain their principled position; they merely agree to accede to whatever outcome is chosen by the "outsider." "So, it's settled, right?" The highly localized practices of the project, so confined in space and time, further contribute to temporary settlements. Working in such tight quarters creates a forced intimacy and a heightened tolerance. Where everything is overheard and everyone is monitoring not only what is said but also the tone of voice, project team members are on the alert for a pitch of voice that signals an unproductive impasse. "Ok, let's settle this and get back to work." Deadlines have a way of settling disagreements. Not surprisingly, like those on the landscape of the Web, these settlements are more provisional than permanent. Limited in time, localized in space, a project is a provisional settlement.

Discursive Pragmatism and Bountiful Friction

The provisional character of project settlements is an expression of discursive pragmatism. Pragmatic, because provisional settlements make it possible to get the job done. Discursive, because provisional settlements are open to reinterpretation when the project is concluded and the next begun.

Our understanding of collaboration in heterarchical organizations is thus more complex than coordination *within a project*. A frictionless coordination, in which everyone shared the same performance criteria, might make life smooth for project managers; but it would lose the creative abrasions[24] that are the source of ongoing vitality. Although settlements facilitate coordination within projects, the unsettling activity of ongoing disputation makes it possible to adapt to the changing topography of the Web *across projects in time*.

For conventional organizational analysis, one of the major challenges of project-based work is how to preserve the knowledge that is learned within a project for future projects. When the project is the basic unit of production, how does the firm keep its knowledge in forms that can be transferred from project to project? What we learned from our observations at NetKnowHow is that the practices of discursive pragmatics address a different but equally challenging problem: for organizations in

[23] See Boltanski and Thévenot, *On Justification,* 2006.

[24] John Seely Brown and Paul Duguid, "Organizing Knowledge," 1998; see also John Hagel III and John Seely Brown, "Productive Friction: How Difficult Business Partnerships Can Accelerate Innovation," 2005.

highly uncertain and rapidly changing environments the key challenge is not how to keep your knowledge intact and transferable but how to develop practices so that you will not take your knowledge for granted. For such firms, knowledge is valuable if it can be recombined, for it is through practices of recombination that new knowledge is created. Well-defined problems can be solved with the firm's accumulated knowledge, but the real challenge of innovation is less to solve already identified problems than to anticipate and generate new problems. The friction of competing performance principles, never entirely settled and therefore recursively resurgent periodically within the life of the organization, does not keep knowledge intact. Instead, the friction of multiple evaluative frames challenges the taken-for-granted and takes knowledge apart so it can be creatively recombined. The evaluation of performance from divergent perspectives promotes organizational reflexivity not at some specialized or privileged location but throughout the organization.

This type of complex coordination through a discursive pragmatics differs, therefore, from the silent coordination of circulating boundary objects.[25] Star and Griesemer developed the concept of "boundary object" to explain coordination among very heterogeneous actors. In a study of a natural history museum, they found that coordination was achieved because objects—such as maps, forms, and specimens—circulated among the disparate participants. What Star and Griesemer make clear is that the different communities did not share a common set of attributions in regard to these objects. Instead, the objects were recognized by the different communities in distinctively different ways. Although Star and Griesemer do not use the term, we can think about their study as making a positive case for misunderstanding in organizational settings. The silently circulating boundary objects could help with the work of coordination precisely because actors did not share an understanding about them.[26]

How were things similar and different at NetKnowHow? Different, first because there was nothing silent about what was happening there. Coordination was overtly discursive; people argued, and not simply about peripheral matters but from principles; they gave reasons and provided justifications as they attempted to persuade others about the things they valued. Similar, because a deeper coordination among the heterogeneous

---

[25] Star and Griesemer, "Institutional Ecology."

[26] See also especially Peter Galison, who shows that the dynamism of microphysics is shaped by the lack of agreement across the cultures of instrumentation, experimentation, and theory. (Peter L. Galison, *Image and Logic: A Material Culture of Microphysics*, 1997.) I elaborate these issues of the creative role of misunderstanding in chapter 5.

participants at NetKnowHow was facilitated by misunderstanding and lack of agreement.

Sociologists (and it is my discipline that I speak of here) are inclined to assume that whereas disagreements make for conflict, shared understandings make for cooperation and coordination. The programmers, information architects, interactive designers, and merchandising specialists at NetKnowHow taught us something different. True, as we have shown, they needed to settle their differences to meet their project deadlines. But, as we have also shown, these settlements were provisional, beneath which were profound disagreements and misunderstandings that would come to the fore once again in the next project. The programmers, interactive designers, business strategists, information architects, and merchandising specialists never agreed once and for all to "iron out their differences." If the reporting structure at the firm was flat, there was nothing flattened about the topography of competing value frames at NetKnowHow. To be sure, cooperation rested in part on shared understandings, but the more complex coordination required for adaptability was produced by the rivalry of value frames that were neither shared nor commonly understood.

NetKnowHow was a vibrant social space because its employees did not speak with one voice. Although everyone spoke English, we can even say that the respective disciplines did not always speak the same language. Multivocality was a characteristic feature of the organization. Our observations at NetKnowHow thus resonate with the study of the multivocality of Cosimo de Medici in Renaissance Florence by John Padgett and Christopher Ansell.[27] Cosimo, they argue, had a distinctive position in the network structure of Florence as the only actor who linked otherwise disconnected social communities. Because of this position, Cosimo could make utterances to which different communities made differing attributions. That is, the same statement was not understood in the same way, and thus, not unlike Star and Griesemer's boundary objects, it could circulate (and Cosimo as entrepreneur could reap benefits) precisely because it was selectively misunderstood.

At NetKnowHow we saw multivocality operating in a different way, not as the property of a position that was structurally privileged by its location as a unique intersection of multiple networks, but as a property of the organization. Entrepreneurship is not brokering difference between otherwise disconnected identities but instead occurs at sites where identi-

---

[27] John F. Padgett and Christopher K. Ansell, "Robust Action and the Rise of the Medici," 1993.

ties and their competing orders of worth are densely interacting. Friction can be bountiful because complex coordination is a function not only of the values we share or of the language we have in common but also of our creative misunderstandings.

Epilogue

The latter part of millennium year 2000 was not kind to Silicon Alley. The glamorous new-media firms that had scored quick successes by tapping into the Internet gold rush with an early IPO and had pegged their worth according to their soaring stock values (from $12 to $120 in months or even weeks) now found (with their shares trading in pennies) that allowing the market to be the measure of their worth could just as easily undervalue as overvalue a company's actual performance. Those who had turned away clients in 1998 and 1999 because "our cultures just don't fit" now found themselves making pitches in the most improbable places. And those who hoped that their reputations—as capable professionals who delivered value on deadline—would help them weather the storm now found themselves competing for clients that were not only fewer in number but also temporarily more cautious about allocating resources for Internet services.

NetKnowHow, like almost all the other thousands of Silicon Alley start-ups, did not survive the meltdown that followed the massive stock market devaluations of the publicly traded dot-com companies.[28] Although it managed to stay in business, through a series of painful layoffs, longer than many other larger and better-financed companies, and for a while seemed that it would be one of the very few New York new-media firms that would outlive the crisis, in the end the company was sold to a firm that itself, some months later, declared bankruptcy.

Ironically, the beginning of the end was in the early spring of 2000, when the two owners of the company announced their intention to launch an IPO. With support from an outside venture capitalist (VC), they planned to take the company public. The news was announced at a Friday afternoon party where the VC was introduced, the stages of the rollout were

---

[28] Were heterarchical firms in Silicon Alley more or less likely to fail? Even if one could distinguish heterarchical firms from more conventional firms, one could not answer the question in a meaningful way, because there is too little variance on the dependent variable. That is, among the thousands of New York new-media firms, almost all of them failed. In all likelihood, "creative destruction" of such tidal wave proportions eliminated not only bad firms but also firms with good records of performance and strong potential for future growth.

presented, and the policies for employee stock options were elaborated. Champagne was uncorked and the volume of the music was pumped up, but the mood, especially among the core group of employees who had been working at NetKnowHow the longest, was far from festive.

Although it might seem that an IPO, with its promise of stock options, was every new-media worker's dream, the "older" employees were clearly unhappy. The timing was completely wrong, for one thing. But the major complaint was that NetKnowHow's owners, who had been working alongside them from the time the firm was founded up until just months before, had always promised that they would never take the company public. That promise had been part of the interview process when they were hired and had been repeated during retention negotiations when they had offers from other firms. And the new-media employees, in turn, had woven that promise into the narrative they told about "the culture of NetKnowHow" when talking with new hires. Now this promise was being broken, and the core employees—precisely the ones who would benefit most from the rules for stock option vesting, based on the number of months they had been working for the company—were rethinking the terms of their relationship to NetKnowHow.

To understand this disappointment, indeed bitterness, we must examine the nature of the difficulties and sacrifices of working in a company like NetKnowHow. To say that the work was demanding would be an understatement. The hours were long, especially during the rush work at the end of project cycles, and the additional perks—for example, when the company paid for a professional masseuse to come in to give programmers back rubs or called a limo to take an interactive designer home at 2:00 a.m.—were small compensation. The subject of long and demanding hours came up often in our conversations. Take, for example, Meg, a young business strategist who sat down with us once as Monique and I were looking at our calendars to coordinate meetings with our children's teachers. "You mean an actual parent-teacher meeting?" Meg inquired. Yes, we said. Meg, after a long exhale: "I'm *so* not there right now." Meg's emphatic statement was more than an expression of a generational difference. She was twenty-eight, an age when many people were starting families or, in similar professional roles, were at least seriously thinking about it. Meg explained that such considerations were simply out of the question for her at this point in her life. Faced with long working hours on top of supposedly nonwork time in which "recreation" frequently meant another kind of work attending new-media parties or club hopping where "networking" took place, many NetKnowHow employees such as Meg were putting their personal lives "on hold."

Employees at NetKnowHow were aware of these costs. Most interesting to us was that these young professionals were most likely to voice their concerns when they were talking about others. "Get a life" was a common parting shot, spoken in jest. But, almost just as common, we also heard expressions of genuine concern. "You're working too hard." "You've gotta give it a rest, take some time off." And each of us observed occasions when a coworker told another employee working with him on a project that she had to stop work, turn off her monitor, and "get out of here for a while." When we asked the coworker about his insistence in these cases, he told us that it was not because of sloppy work or tensions on the project but out of personal concern: "Katie gets so committed to a project that she would work day and night. It's like she's not got an internal regulator that tells her she can quit. We have to look out for each other."

This "looking out for each other" was mutual and generalized. That is, with few exceptions, everyone had tendencies, like Katie, to work without limits. One could push oneself hard, very hard, knowing that others were watching out for one's well-being.

Heterarchical forms, as regimes of flexibility,[29] thus, give new meaning to the problems of "self-management." Worker self-management had long been a goal of some portions of the socialist labor movement. Although discredited by its ideological role in the Yugoslav variant of nondemocratic socialism, the idea that workers could manage their own firms remained an active vision for many on the left. It is curious, then, that the actual forms of extremely flattened hierarchy and lateral accountability should develop within high-technology sectors of the most advanced capitalist economies. To be clear, it is unlikely that anyone in Silicon Alley ever voiced the term *self-management*, but the themes were there, though expressed in a different rhetoric.

The problem is that lateral accountability is emotionally demanding. The absence of clear-cut lines of vertical authority involves trade-offs—for you are now accountable to many. And because you are also accountable in many crosscutting, even conflicting registers, you are ultimately accountable to yourself. Not unlike the Hungarian toolmakers of the previous chapter who, in the trials and errors of the internal payment systems within their own form of self-managed group, came to the realization that in the end judgments about skill and effort ultimately rested on self-assessments, so the new-media workers came to realize that questions of commitment and effort were highly personal—only you yourself can know if you are working to your best abilities. Self-management thus

---

[29] See especially Luc Boltanski and Ève Chiapello, *The New Spirit of Capitalism*, 2005.

becomes the management of self. When work and play are not separated, your very personality becomes an object to be managed.[30]

Because this task is difficult and can become paralyzing if left in a solipsistic loop, you turn over some of these responsibilities to the people around you, looking to them to monitor the process, even to take control when they sense the dangers of exhaustion and burnout. In this way, the flexibility of heterarchical forms becomes attached to highly personalized engagements. "We have to look out for each other."

The announcement of the IPO put these emotional costs and personal attachments in new relief. These costs were worth it—but only up to a point. If their efforts were now to be registered on the price quotes of a stock ticker, the core employees would now rethink their investment. They always knew that they did not "own" the company, but in some palpable sense they felt it was theirs. And so, when the owners announced new reporting requirements and proposed other supervisory changes as part of the first stage of the IPO rollout, the core employees voiced their objections to these efforts to introduce more hierarchical forms. Over the course of several months in spring 2000, the two young owners and the new VC attempted to lure key employees with promises of lucrative stock options, but they were refused. Even if it meant forgoing higher incomes, the NetKnowHow employees were not willing "to give up what we had worked so hard to build."

The promised/threatened IPO never materialized. It evaporated during the summer of 2000 when the air burst out of the failing dot-com bubble. With that, too, went some of NetKnowHow's clients, as investors were reluctant to fund new online retail ventures. Because it had a strong mix of clients, including established retailers who were bringing their products online, NetKnowHow was able to stay in operation by cutting back its workforce. But, as more and more client firms brought new-media production in-house, even this strategy became untenable, and the company effectively dissolved.

How have the NetKnowHow new-media workers fared in the years since the company's demise? Fortunately it has not been difficult to stay in touch with, and follow the whereabouts of, many of them. It helped that we hired two of them to work at our research center, one temporarily and another on a longer-term basis. The Web itself also helped. By googling the names on a list of NetKnowHow employees, we could easily locate a good number of them, many of whom, not surprisingly, maintain lively

---

[30] Andrew Ross, *No Collar: The Humane Workplace and Its Hidden Costs*, 2003; see also Gideon Kunda, *Engineering Culture: Control and Commitment in a High Tech Corporation*, 1993.

blogs in the fields of technology and design. But the main reason it has been so easy to follow their trajectories is because the networks among the employees themselves have remained so strongly intact.

As NetKnowHow disintegrated as a company, at least four teams started their own consulting firms/Web production outfits. Legally distinct, the teams were nonetheless organizationally integrated through their close network ties. A group composed predominantly of designers, for example, would subcontract software development to another group of mainly programmers, and vice versa. In this way, each group could pitch projects of a scale larger than its own limited capacity.

Just as ties of attachment were important for the interlinked small ventures, so the strong network connections among the former NetKnowHow employees were important for those who took jobs at in-house new-media operations, whether those of former clients or in other firms. Again and again, we heard stories of one former NetKnowHow employee landing a job and then finding a position at the new company for a former coworker in the NetKnowHow network. Flows of information were facilitated first by a "NetKnowHow Group" on Yahoo, later replaced by linking to each other on Friendster, and most recently the more professionally oriented LinkedIn. Aaron, the project manager whom we quoted about a website as a morphing puzzle, for example, recently looked at his LinkedIn connections. Among his "inner circle" of approximately one hundred contacts, he counted more than thirty former NetKnowHow employees—this more than six years after leaving the company. Such ties, moreover, are more than professional. In our telephone conversations and e-mail exchanges, the new-media workers told us about regular poker games and other frequent socializing. Several mentioned that a former coworker was best man or maid of honor at their wedding.

For the most part, former NetKnowHow employees have remained in the new-media field, now redefined. Some pursued graduate degrees or got new training in related fields after the company folded. All three of the project team leaders, for example, got MBAs and continue to do work in project management. Many who did not start their own small companies took positions with former NetKnowHow clients, working first on projects that were directly or closely related to projects that had been developed at NetKnowHow and later starting new projects developed in-house in the new-media units of the former clients. By the end, Silicon Alley was no longer a glittering thoroughfare. But as the lights were turned out there, new media was transformed from a localized setting to become diffused throughout the business landscape. And as its employees migrated, they took their experiences in new organizational forms with them into corporate settings of finance, advertising, and marketing. Their debates about "the user" were quickly revived as fresh opportunities for experimentation developed in the new social networking sites.

One of the more interesting aspects of the "death of the new economy" was the rapidity with which pundits on both the right and the left rushed in to celebrate its demise. Always suspicious of the freewheeling culture of new-economy firms such as the new-media start-ups, op-eds in newspapers like the *Wall Street Journal* almost chuckled that "real value" and more sober business practices had triumphed. The playful start-ups had had their day, but now the grown-ups were back in charge. It was only several months later, of course, that the scandals of the big boys' corporate boardrooms at Enron and on Wall Street would be revealed. But the Left had also been suspicious, perhaps even a bit worried, that talk like "all the rules are changed, you either get it or you don't" was encroaching on its discursive domain. And so the Left's periodicals almost cackled that the new-media faux revolutionaries had got their comeuppance. Whether the economy was old or new, it was capitalism after all, and the only thing that counts in capitalism is the bottom line.

Where Left and Right agree, and even for the same reason, seems to me to be an indicator that there is something worth investigating. My point is not that I mourn a loss that others celebrate, but that something more interesting is happening than can be captured in the language of "death" or "return to business as usual." Did new media die with the exhaustion of the Internet land rush? The dot-com bubble collapsed, to be sure, but new media has thrived. The difference is that whereas at the cusp of the twenty-first century new media was a separate line of business, today it is synonymous with business itself.

While studying NetKnowHow, one of the problems I had to consider (because it was frequently asked of me at seminars where I presented this research) was whether our observations were of limited value because we were studying an industry in its early, immature stage. Would organizational structures and processes look different once things settled down and became institutionalized as new media developed into a traditional industry? The fact that we cannot answer this question seems to me the interesting outcome. That is, new media did not mature as a separate industry, traditional or otherwise. Instead, the industry, as such, disappeared from specific focus because it appeared everywhere. The sociotechnologies of interactive media are now a part of nearly every branch or sector of the economy—education, government, newspapers, advertising, hospitals, transportation, catering, cinema, real estate, finance, engineering, architecture, the military, heavy and light industry. Your local convenience store or gas station may not have a website, but your electrician or plumber might; and your likelihood of going to a particular restaurant might be increased if you can check out the menu or decor ahead of time online. Websites, moreover, are but the most obvious ubiquity. Even more vital are the ways in which interactive technologies have become an important part of the production process—in aircraft assembly, in surgeries, in electoral campaigns, and on the battlefield.[31]

It is too early to know whether the fate of new media—emphatically not a demise when we see it arise nearly everywhere—is a harbinger of new, more general trends. But there are reasons to expect that our inherited notions of the life cycle of an industry—experimentation, growth, maturation, stabilization, decline—might need to be reconsidered. Development of new technologies is less likely to take a straightforward path of improvement and refinement so much as branching and splintering as innovations occur through recombinations with other technologies.[32] Crisp boundaries of industrial codification are likely to be most difficult to discern in the newly recombinant fields where genetic code, software code, linguistic code, and legal code become increasingly tangled code. If so, new media will not have been an exceptional outlier but a precursor of new patterns of development.

Thus, whether the new economy is alive or dead, the analytic problems survive. Valuation of knowledge-based activities where the effective unit of organization is a network of entities and not isolated firms will continue to be a challenge when available metrics all revolve around corporately bounded balance sheets. The heterarchical structures of lateral coordination will continue to operate in an uneasy coexistence with corporate hierarchies. The goal of workplace democracy will continue to be troubled by the realization that being accountable to one's peers is extraordinarily demanding and that workers' self-management might involve management of the self. The emergence of new communication technologies will continue to destabilize established routines. Collaborative organization will continue to coevolve with interactive technologies. And competing and coexisting evaluative principles will continue to make their productively noisy clash.

[31] Across a range of settings, Timothy Lenoir has been doing exciting work on these topics. See, for example, "The Virtual Surgeon," 2002; "All but War Is Simulation: The Military-Entertainment Complex," 2000; and "Programming Theaters of War: Gamemakers as Soldiers," 2003.
[32] Brian W. Arthur, "The Structure of Invention," 2007.

4

The Cognitive Ecology of an Arbitrage Trading Room

with Daniel Beunza

What counts? Faced with an avalanche of information from many and varied sources, we need to select the information we will take into account in going about our business. Nowhere is this question more demanding than when faced by securities traders in the era of quantitative finance. With unprecedented earnings fueling access to enormous databases expanding both in volume as well as in diversity, and with unprecedented risk exposure propelling demand for yet more and better sources of data, securities traders are immersed in a virtual flood of information. Faced with such information overload, the real challenge for traders is not faster, higher, stronger—as if the problem of the volume of data could be solved by gathering yet more—but selecting what counts and making sense of the selection. The more information is available to many simultaneously, the more advantage shifts to those with superior means of interpretation. How then is a trading room organized for making sense of what is to be taken into account?

A trading room, as we shall see, is a kind of laboratory in which traders are engaged in a process of search, discovery, and experimentation. The object of their search—value—seems straightforward, but it is exactly what is contentiously at issue. One might say that the problem is simple: securities traders are searching for profit opportunities. But that immediately raises the more general question: How does someone recognize an opportunity? More specifically, how do you recognize an opportunity that your competitors have not already identified? At the extreme, therefore, traders are searching for something that is not yet named and categorized. The problem they confront, in that respect, is a problem fundamental to innovation in any setting: How do you search when you do not know what you are looking for but will recognize it when you find it? How then is a trading room organized to engage in the search to recognize opportunities?

What counts? This question also expresses most succinctly a challenge for economic sociology. As we study the twinned problems of what counts—interpretation of information and judgments about value—what organizational features should we foreground in our accounts of these processes? In answering this question, our analysis starts with the fundamental theme that network analysis shares with other schools of economic sociology: the conception that markets are social.[1] But we extend and deepen that perspective by arguing that social network analysis should not be limited to studying ties among persons. Because the social consists of humans and their nonhuman artifacts, in place of studying "society" we must construct a science of associations—an analysis that examines not only links among persons but also among persons and instruments.[2] What counts? Tools count. Instrumentation must be brought into the accounts of economic sociologists. Calculation, as we shall see, is not simply embedded in social relations. Calculative practices are distributed across persons and instruments. In saying that tools count, we overstate for purposes of emphasis. Tools count insofar as they are a part of situated sociocognitive and sociotechnical networks.[3]

To explore the sociocognitive, sociotechnical practices of a distinctive type of securities trading known as arbitrage, Daniel Beunza and I conducted ethnographic field research in the Wall Street trading room[4] of a major international investment bank. International Securities (a pseudonym) is a global bank with headquarters outside the United States. It has a large office in New York, located in the World Financial Center. Almost an entire floor of this skyscraper houses International Securities' equities trading room with approximately 160 arbitrage traders, as well as other support staff. It was here that we observed trading and interviewed traders from 1999 to 2001. Like the Hungarian toolmakers and the Silicon

---

[1] Mark S. Granovetter, "Economic Action and Social Structure: The Problem of Embeddedness," 1985; Neil Fligstein, *The Transformation of Corporate Control*, 1990; and Brian Uzzi, "Social Structure and Competition in Interfirm Networks: The Paradox of Embeddedness," 1997.

[2] Bruno Latour, "Powers of Association," 1986; Edwin Hutchins, *Cognition in the Wild*, 1995; and Michel Callon and Fabian Muniesa, "Economic Markets as Calculative Collective Devices," 2005.

[3] These hybrid terms are admittedly clumsy, and they should not imply that tools are technical while organization is social. Tools are a part of the social, and there is no human organization that is not also somehow technical. Similarly, cognition is not simply a mentalist operation that takes place within the brain. Because cognition is social, the sociocognitive embraces instrumentation while never being reduced to it.

[4] A trading *room* differs from a trading *floor*. Many readers are likely familiar with a trading floor (such as that of the New York Stock Exchange or of the trading pits of the Chicago Board of Trade) from images on the evening news. Whereas a trading floor brings together traders or brokers representing many different trading houses, a trading room typically involves traders from a single firm as a base of operation for trades that are executed on exchanges. For a large-sample approach to the organization of trading rooms, see Srilata Zaheer and Elaine Mosakowski, "The Dynamics of the Liability of Foreigners: A Global Study of Survival in Financial Services," 1997.

Alley new-media workers, these Wall Street traders were very engaging as they reflected on the nature of their work and were correspondingly generous with their time. During the course of sixty half-day visits across more than two years, we conducted detailed observations at three of the room's ten trading desks, following trades as they unfolded. In the final year of our investigation, Daniel was more formally integrated into the trading room—provided with a computer, a telephone, and a place at a desk from which to roam to other parts of the room. Periodically throughout the research, we complemented direct observations with in-depth interviews.

Our discussion begins by pointing to the insights and limitations of the leading analytic strategies used by sociologists studying the quantitative revolution in finance. In the subsequent section, we propose a sociology of arbitrage, making the case that arbitrage constitutes a distinctive trading strategy that operates by making associations among securities. In contrast to value and momentum investing, we argue, arbitrage involves an art of association—the construction of equivalence (comparability) of properties across different assets. In place of essential or relational characteristics, the peculiar valuation that takes place in arbitrage is based on an operation that makes something the measure of something else—associating securities to each other. Stated polemically, at the epitome of high-tech capitalist finance is a sensibility so postmodern that it would make your colleagues in comparative literature blush. Subsequent sections analyze how the trading room is organized to recognize opportunities. We first observe how the spatial organization of the room facilitates general sociability among traders. Second, we examine how these traders are grouped into specialized desks, each deploying distinctive financial instruments and evaluative metrics for pattern recognition. Next, we examine the trading room as an ensemble of multiple desks, exploring how this ecology of diverse evaluative principles facilitates practices of recognition; and, finally, we examine the room as an assemblage of instrumentation, exploring how the sociocognitive and the sociotechnical are intertwined.

Studying Quantitative Finance

Whereas István Farkas welcomed us onto the grease-stained floor of his "office," and the new-media workers welcomed us on the hardwood floors of their crowded workspace to the loud strains of the latest indie band, the manager of the trading room at International Securities welcomed us into a space that resembled, in its muted colors and hushed tones, the lobby of a luxury hotel. The architecture and the ambiance of this trading room would have been unfamiliar to someone who retired from trading several decades ago. To appreciate the changes, consider the following description of a typical Wall Street trading room in the 1980s, given by Tom Wolfe in *Bonfire of the Vanities*:

> No sooner did you pass the fake fireplace than you heard an ungodly roar, like the roar of a mob . . . the bond trading room of Pierce & Pierce. It was a vast space, perhaps sixty by eighty feet, but with the same eight-foot ceiling bearing down on your head. It was an oppressive space with a ferocious glare, writhing silhouettes . . . the arms and torsos of young men . . . moving in an agitated manner and sweating early in the morning and shouting, which created the roar.[5]

This boiler-room imagery is absent from the arbitrage trading room at International Securities. Instead of a low ceiling, the observer finds high ceilings and a huge open space filled with rows of desks, computers, and traders. Instead of a roar, the observer hears a hushed buzz among the traders immersed in the flickering numbers on hundreds of flat-panel screens. Instead of an oppressive space, the observer finds generous corridors, elegant watercolors on the walls, and a dramatic view of Manhattan. Instead of agitated employees, the observer finds relaxed traders in business-casual wear leisurely circulating about the trading room, coffee in hand. Instead of writhing arms and torsos, we see equations and formulas scribbled hurriedly on a large whiteboard located prominently near the center of the trading room. And instead of a fake fireplace, the room is populated by nonhuman "intelligent agents," the computer programs executing automated trades, referred to by the traders as "robots."

The difference between the boisterous Wall Street trading room of the 1980s, accurately described by Tom Wolfe, and the almost academic atmosphere that we found in the arbitrage trading room at International Securities is a clue that something has happened to trading in the intervening decades. That difference can be understood as a product of the "quantitative revolution" that swept through the world of finance during this period. We characterize *quantitative finance* as a distinctive combination of connectivity, knowledge, and computing. Along each of these dimensions, finance was a leader; and it was the combination of these elements that

---

[5] Tom Wolfe, *The Bonfire of the Vanities*, 1987, p. 58.

yielded the quantitative revolution. With the creation of the NASDAQ in 1971, Wall Street had an electronic market long before any other industry. With the development of Bloomberg data terminals in 1980, traders in investment banks were connected to each other in an all-inclusive computer network well before other professionals. With the development of formulas for pricing derivatives such as the Black-Scholes formula in 1973, traders gained powerful mathematical tools. And, with the dramatic growth in computing power, traders were able to combine these equations with powerful computational engines. This mix of formulas, data to plug into them, computers to calculate them, and electronic networks to connect them was explosive, leading to a decisive shift to quantitative finance.[6] As a result, finance today is mathematical, networked, computational, and knowledge intensive. We focus on arbitrage because it is the trading strategy that best represents this powerful combination.

To date, the leading analytic strategy used by sociologists studying modern finance has been to focus on one or another of the key components of the quantitative revolution. Exemplary, in this light, is the study by Knorr Cetina and Bruegger,[7] which analyzes one of the key trends of the quantitative revolution—the rise of electronic markets—arguing that electronic trading has altered the relationship between market participants and physical space. Their work is pathbreaking for the insight that the numbers on the screens of the electronic traders do not *represent* a market that is elsewhere; instead, the market is "*appresented.*" Like the conversations of instant messaging (but unlike, say, a movie or TV show), electronic markets constitute an on-screen reality that lacks an off-screen counterpart. This has important implications for the practice of quantitative finance. Just as the eyes of traders in a commodities pit are glued to the gestures of other traders, so Knorr Cetina and Bruegger found that the eyes of their currency traders were glued to the screen—because in both cases that is where the market is. Electronic markets, they assert, have brought the marketplace to the traders' screens, prompting the traders to shift from a "face-to-face world" to a "face-to-screen world" and bringing about the "diminishing relevance of the physical setting" (p. 23).

While Knorr Cetina and Bruegger focus on the rise of connectivity in finance, MacKenzie and Millo focus on another leg of the quantitative

---

[6] Nicholas Dunbar, *Inventing Money: The Story of Long-term Capital Management and the Legends Behind It,* 2000.

[7] Karin Knorr Cetina and Urs Bruegger, "Global Microstructures: The Virtual Societies of Financial Markets," 2002.

revolution, the rise of mathematical formulas and their consequences for trading.[8] The mathematical formulas of modern finance, they argue, do not *represent markets* so much as constitute part of a network (also made up of people, computers, ideas, etc.) that *intervenes in markets* in the sense developed by Michel Callon.[9] A model is *performative* if its use increases its predicitive ability. As an example of such a "performative" that does not just mirror a reality but is constitutive of it, they point to the role of the Black-Scholes formula in predicting and later setting option prices on the Chicago Board Options Exchange.

The two studies are nicely complementary: Knorr Cetina and Bruegger examine the network connectivity of electronic trading but ignore formulas entirely; MacKenzie and Millo address the role of formulas but ignore the connectivity of electronic trading. But if we are to understand the organization of trading in the era of modern finance, we must examine all three pillars of the quantitative revolution: network connectivity, mathematical formulas, and computing. It is precisely this combination that gives the study of modern arbitrage—as the trading strategy that most powerfully (and, to date, most profitably) exploits the mathematics and the machines of modern market instruments—such analytic leverage.

In taking the limitations of these studies as our point of departure, the opportunity we seize, however, is not just to examine as an ensemble the pieces they had begun to analyze separately. Amidst the circulating information of Knorr Cetina and the diffusing equations of MacKenzie, we find little about the core problem facing any trader—how does one recognize an opportunity? We will argue that traders do so by making of their trading room a laboratory, by conducting experiments, by deploying an array of instruments to test the market. In the practices through which value is calculated, equivalencies are constructed, and opportunities realized; tools count. Calculation is distributed across the human and nonhuman agents and instruments enacting the trade. But, if calculation involves both the mathematics and the machines of quantitative finance, the process, even when it is automated, is (as we shall see) far from mechanical: at this level of performance, calculation involves judgment. Moreover, calculation is not detached: whereas the trader is emotionally distant from any

---

[8] Donald MacKenzie and Yuval Millo, "Negotiating a Market, Performing Theory: The Historical Sociology of a Financial Derivatives Exchange," 2003; and see also Donald MacKenzie, *An Engine Not a Camera: How Financial Models Shape Markets*, 2006.

[9] Michel Callon, "Introduction: Embeddedness of Economic Markets in Economics," 1998. On performativity, see especially the essays in Donald MacKenzie, Fabian Muniesa, and Lucia Siu, eds., *Do Economists Make Markets? On the Performativity of Economics*, 2007.

particular trade, to be able to take a position, the trader must be strongly attached to an evaluative principle and its affiliated instruments. In the field of arbitrage, to be opportunistic you must be principled; that is, you must commit to an evaluative metric.

Second, our focus on the problem of identifying value leads us to take into account the dynamics identified by Knorr Cetina, MacKenzie, and their coauthors but to draw radically different analytic conclusions. For Knorr Cetina and Bruegger, the displacement of physical locale in favor of the "global microstructures" on the screen is explained by the ever-increasing rapidity of the circulation of information. We, too, initially approached our research setting as a world of globally instantaneous information. By studying sophisticated derivative traders, able to produce formulas that quantify unknown magnitudes, we hoped to demarcate a world of pure information that could stand as a benchmark against which we could differentiate other calculative settings. And, yes, we encountered a world abundant in information, delivered with dazzling, dizzying speed. But after months of fieldwork, we realized that, as increasingly more information is almost instantaneously available to nearly every market actor, the more strategic advantage shifts from economies of information to the sociocognitive process of interpretation.[10] Precisely because all its competitors have access to the same information, the trading room we studied makes profits (considerably higher than industry-average profits) not by access to better or timelier information but by fostering interpretive communities in the trading room.

Similarly, learning from MacKenzie and Millo about how the diffusion of formulas shapes markets, we go on to ask the next question. If everyone is using the same formulas, how can anyone profit? The more that formulas diffuse to perform the market, the more one's profits depend on an original performance. That is, the premium shifts to innovation. As with information (which you must have, but which in itself will not give advantage) so with formulas: the more widely diffused, the more you must innovate.

What then facilitates interpretation and fosters innovation? The answer came only when we stopped regarding the trading room simply as a "setting" and began to regard the spatial configurations of this particular locale as an additional dimension alongside the combination of

---

[10] Karl Weick, *The Social Psychology of Organizing*, 1979; John Seely Brown and Paul Duguid. *The Social Life of Information*, 2000; and Gernot Grabher, "The Project Ecology of Advertising: Tasks, Talents and Teams," 2002.

equations, connectivity, and computing. In analyzing the *modus operandi* of modern finance, we came to see that its *locus operandi* could not be ignored. That is, whereas Knorr Cetina and Bruegger dismiss physical locale in favor of interactions *in cyberspace*, we found that trading practices are intimately tied to the deployment of traders and instruments *in the room*.

Arbitrage trading can be seen as an economy of information and speed. So is flying a fighter aircraft in warfare. Without the requisite information and the requisite speed, neither trader nor pilot could do the job. But maneuvering in the uncertain environment of markets, like maneuvering in the fog of battle, requires situated awareness.[11] As we shall see, the configuration of the trading room, as a specific locale, provides the sociospatial resources for this sense making. A trading room is an engine for generating equivalencies. Such associations are made *in situ*; that is, they entail the use of financial formulas that result from associations among people working in the same physical place.

The cognitive challenge facing our arbitrage traders—a challenge central to the process of innovation—is the problem of recognition. On one hand, they must, of course, be adept at *pattern recognition* (e.g., matching data to models, etc). But if they recognize only patterns that are already familiar within their existing categories, they will not be innovative.[12] Innovation requires another cognitive process that we can think of as *re-cognition* (making unanticipated associations, conceptualizing the situation anew, breaking out of lock-in).

The organization of the trading room, as we shall see, is equipped (quite literally) to meet this twin challenge of exploiting knowledge (pattern recognition) while simultaneously exploring for new knowledge (practices of re-cognition).[13] Each desk (e.g., merger arbitrage, index arbitrage, etc.) is organized around a distinctive evaluative principle and its corresponding cognitive frames, metrics, "optics," and other specialized instrumentation for pattern recognition. That is, the trading room is the site of diverse, indeed rivalrous, principles of valuation. And it is the interaction across this heterogeneity that generates innovation.

---

[11] For an application of interpretive theories of organization to the military, see Karl Weick and Karlene H. Roberts, "Collective Mind in Organizations: Heedful Interrelating on Flight Decks," 1993.

[12] John H. Clippinger, "Tags: The Power of Labels in Shaping Markets and Organizations," 1999.

[13] We are reinterpreting March's exploitation/exploration problem of organizational learning through the lens of the problem of recognition. See James G. March, "Exploration and Exploitation in Organizational Learning," 1991.

Arbitrage, or Quantitative Finance in the Search for Qualities

Arbitrage is defined in finance textbooks as "locking in a profit by simultaneously entering into transactions in two or more markets."[14] If, for instance, the prices of gold in New York and London differ by more than the transportation costs between those cities, an arbitrageur can realize an easy profit by buying in the market where gold is cheap and selling it in the market where it is expensive. As such, classical arbitrage lacks sociological as well as economic interest: it relates markets that are the same in every dimension except for an obvious one such as, in this case, the geographical. Reducing arbitrage to an unproblematic operation that links the obvious (gold in London, gold in New York), as textbook treatments do, is doubly misleading, for modern arbitrage is neither obvious nor unproblematic. It provides profit opportunities by associating the unexpected, and it entails real exposure to substantial losses.

Arbitrage is a distinct form of entrepreneurial activity that exploits not only gaps across markets but also the overlaps among multiple evaluative principles. Arbitrageurs profit not by having developed a superior way of deriving value but by exploiting opportunities exposed when different evaluative devices yield discrepant pricings at myriad points throughout the economy.

As a first step to understanding modern arbitrage, consider the two traditional trading strategies, *value* and *momentum* investing, that arbitrage has come to challenge. Value investing is the traditional "buy low, sell high" approach in which investors look for opportunities by identifying companies whose "intrinsic" value differs from their current market value. They do so by studying a company's annual reports, financial results, products, and executives; they then compare the intrinsic value that emerges from this analysis with the market price of the company.[15] Value investors are essentialists: they believe that property has a true, intrinsic, essential value independent from other investors' assessments, and that they can attain a superior grasp of that value through careful perusal of the information about a company. Value investors map the many aspects of a company by translating them into abstract variables—e.g., return, growth, risk—and collapsing them into a single number ("value") with the use of formulas such as discounted cash flow. They proceed with the belief that mispricing will eventually be corrected—that is, that enough investors will eventually

---

[14] John C. Hull, *Options, Futures, and Other Derivative Securities*, 1996.
[15] Benjamin Graham and David L. Dodd, *Security Analysis: Principles and Techniques*, 1934.

"catch up" with the intrinsic value and drive the price toward it, producing a profit for those who saw the mispricing first.

In contrast to value investors, momentum traders (also known as "chartists") turn away from scrutinizing companies toward monitoring the activities of other actors on the market.[16] Like value investors, their goal is to find a profit opportunity. However, momentum traders are not interested in discovering the intrinsic value of a stock. Instead of focusing on features of the asset itself, they turn their attention to whether other market actors are bidding the value of a security up or down. Alert to trends, they believe in the existence of "momentum," a self-sustaining social process amenable to discovery by studying patterns in the time series of the stock—its chart. In contrast with value investing, a momentum strategy can involve buying when the price is extremely high, as long as the patterns in the chart suggest that it is getting higher. Preoccupied with vectors and directionality, momentum traders plot trajectories. Like the fashion-conscious or like nightlife socialites scouting the trendiest clubs, they derive their strength from obsessively asking, "where is everyone going?" in hopes of anticipating the hot spots and leaving just when things get too crowded.

Like value and momentum investors, arbitrageurs also need to find an opportunity, an instance of disagreement with the market's pricing of a security. They find it by making associations. Instead of claiming to have a superior ability to aggregate and process information about intrinsic assets (as value investors do) or to have better information on what other investors are doing (as momentum traders do), the arbitrage trader tests ideas about the correspondence between two securities. Confronted by a stock with a market price, the arbitrageur seeks some other security— or bond, or synthetic security such as an index composed of a group of stocks, etc.—that can be related to it, and prices one in terms of the other. The two securities have to be similar enough so that their prices change in related ways, but different enough so that other traders have not perceived the correspondence before. As we shall see, the posited relationship can be highly abstract. The tenuous or uncertain strength of the posited similarity or covariation reduces the number of traders that can play a trade, hence increasing its potential profitability.

Arbitrage, then, is a distinct trading strategy. Whereas value investment is essentialist and momentum trading is extrinsic, arbitrage is associational. Whereas the value investor pegs value on intrinsic worth,

---

[16] Charles Smith, *Success and Survival on Wall Street: Understanding the Mind of the Market*, 2001.

and the momentum trader tracks the value assessments assigned by other investors, arbitrage traders locate value by making associations between particular properties or qualities of one security and those of other previously unrelated or tenuously related securities.

Arbitrage hinges on the possibility of interpreting securities in multiple ways. Like a writer seeking to coin a striking literary metaphor, an arbitrage trader reaches out to associate the value of a stock to that of some other, previously unidentified security. By associating one security to another, the trader highlights different properties (qualities) of the property he is dealing with.[17]

In contrast to value investors, who distill the bundled attributes of a company to a single number, arbitrageurs reject exposure to a whole company. In contrast to corporate raiders, who buy companies for the purpose of breaking them up to sell as separate properties, the work of arbitrage traders is yet more radically deconstructionist. The unbundling they attempt is to isolate, in the first instance, categorical attributes. For example, they do not see Boeing Co. as a monolithic asset or property but as having several properties (traits, qualities) such as being a technology stock, an aviation stock, a consumer-travel stock, an American stock, a stock that is included in a given index, and so on. Even more abstractionist, they attempt to isolate such qualities as the volatility of a security, or its liquidity, its convertibility, its indexability, and so on.

Thus, whereas corporate raiders break up tangible assets of a company, modern arbitrageurs carve up abstract qualities of a security. In our field research, we find our arbitrageurs actively shaping trades. Dealing with the multiple qualities of securities, as narrow specialists they position themselves with respect to one or two of these qualities, but never all. Their strategy is to use the tools of financial engineering to shape a trade so that exposure[18] is limited only to those equivalency principles in which

---

[17] At the outset of our investigation, quantitative finance seemed an improbable setting to find actors preoccupied with qualities. On the qualification of goods in other settings and for theoretical discussions of economies of qualities, see François Eymard-Duvernay, "Coordination des Echanges par l'entreprise et Qualité des biens," 1994; Olivier Favereau and Emmanuel Lazega, eds., *Conventions and Structures in Economic Organization: Markets, Networks and Hierarchies*, 2002; Michel Callon, Cecile Meadel, and Vololona Rabeharisoa, "The Economy of Qualities," 2002; and Harrison White, *Markets from Networks*, 2002.

[18] The exposure created by a trade is given by the impact that a change in some variable (such as the price of an asset) can have on the wealth of the trader. Following the quantitative revolution in finance, traders think about their own work in terms of *exposure*, not in terms of *transactions*. Hence, for example, they do not use the expression "buy IBM" but say "to be long on IBM," which means that a trader stands to profit when the price of IBM rises. Similarly, they do not say "sell" but "be short on." The reason for this change in terminology is that, through the use of derivatives, traders can attain a given exposure in different ways.

the trader has confidence. Derivatives[19] such as swaps, options,[20] and other financial instruments play an important role in the process of separating the desired qualities from the purchased security. Traders use them to slice and dice their exposure, wielding them in effect like a surgeon's tools—scalpels, scissors, proteases—to give the patient (the trader's exposure) the desired contours.

Paradoxically, much of the associative work of arbitrage is therefore for the purpose of "disentangling"[21]—selecting out of the trade those qualities to which the arbitrageur is not committed. The strategy is just as much not betting on what you do not know as betting on what you do know. In merger arbitrage, for example, this strategy of highly specialized risk exposure requires that traders associate the markets for stocks of the two merging companies and dissociate from the stocks everything that does not involve the merger. Consider a situation in which two firms have announced their intention to merge. One of the firms, say the acquirer, is a biotech firm and belongs to an index, such as the Dow Jones (DJ) biotech index. If a merger arbitrage specialist wanted to shape a trade such that the "biotechness" of the acquirer would not be an aspect of his/her positioned exposure, the arbitrageur would long the index. That is, to dissociate this quality from the trader's exposure, the arbitrageur associates the trade with a synthetic security ("the index") that stands for the "biotechness." Less categorical, more complex qualities require more complex instruments.

When, as in some forms of merger arbitrage, the process of dissociating is taken to the extreme, we could say that merger arbitrageurs trade in securities in order to bet on events. By hedging against all qualities of

---

[19] Derivatives are financial instruments whose value is derived from the value of something else. They make it possible, for example, to trade in the risk of an asset without holding the underlying asset itself. Derivatives can be based on very different types of assets or indexes. Some types of derivatives markets are not based on the underlying value of an asset such as a commodity, stock, bond, or interest rate. An index of the weather, for example, can be the basis for weather derivatives, which can be used by farmers to hedge against drought or harsh conditions, by ski resort owners to hedge against warm winters, or by the manufacturers of umbrellas or throat lozenges to hedge against a lack of rain or cold. Carbon emission derivatives markets could become some of the largest markets of any kind. They are an acute version of the more general process of creating an asset out of a risk. For a basic introduction to derivatives for nonspecialists, see Jakob Arnoldi, "Derivatives: Virtual Values and Real Risks," 2004. For a more elaborated but still highly accessible discussion, see Dick Bryan and Michael Rafferty, *Capitalism with Derivatives: A Political Economy of Financial Derivatives, Capital and Class,* 2006; and especially Dick Bryan and Michael Rafferty, "Financial Derivatives and the Theory of Money," 2007.

[20] A *swap* is an agreement to exchange rights or obligations. A stock *option* is a derivative security that gives its holder the right to buy or sell a stock at a certain price within a given time in the future.

[21] For a related usage, see Michel Callon, "An Essay on Reframing and Overflowing: Economic Externalities Revisited by Sociology," 1998.

the stock other than the merger itself, the merger arbitrageur, in effect, is betting about the likelihood of a discrete event. You cannot go to a betting window to wager that two companies will merge (or not) on January 3. But with enough sophisticated instruments, you can shape your exposure to something very close to such a position.

Arbitrageurs do not narrow their exposure for lack of courage. Despite all the trimmings, hedging, and cutting, this is not a trading strategy for the fainthearted. Arbitrage is about tailoring the trader's exposure to the market, biting what one can chew, betting on what one knows best, and avoiding risking money on what one does not know. Traders expose themselves profusely—precisely because their exposure is custom-tailored to the relevant deal. Their sharp focus and specialized instruments give them a clearer view of the deals they examine than the broader views of the rest of the market. Thus, the more the traders hedge, the more boldly they can position themselves.

Arbitrageurs can reduce or eliminate exposure along many dimensions, but they cannot make a profit on a trade unless they are exposed on at least one. In fact, they cut entanglements along some dimensions precisely to focus exposure where they are most confidently attached. As Michel Callon and colleagues argue, calculation and attachment are not mutually exclusive.[22] To be sure, the trader's attachment is distanced and disciplined; but however emotionally detached, and however fleeting, to hold a position is to hold a conviction.[23]

How do unexpected and tenuous associations become recognized as opportunities? In the following sections we examine the trading room to see how cognition is distributed and diversity is organized. Before examining the instruments that mediate the markets, we look first at the deployment of the traders themselves within the room. After examining the spatialized sociability of the trading room, we examine the *equipment*— the teams and the tools—of arbitrage.

The Trading Room as a Space for Associations

The trading room at International Securities offers a sharp contrast to the conventional environment of corporate America. In the traditional corpo-

---

[22] Callon, Meadel, and Rabeharisoa, "The Economy of Qualities"; and Callon and Muniesa, "Markets as Calculative Devices."

[23] Zaloom correctly emphasizes that, to speculate, a trader must be disciplined (Caitlin Zaloom, "The Discipline of the Speculator," 2004). In addition to this psychological, almost bodily, disciplining, however, we shall see that the arbitrage trader's ability to take a risky position depends as well on yet another discipline—grounding in a body of knowledge.

rate office, space is used to emphasize status differences as the hierarchy of concentric rings effectively isolates the highest-ranking employees. At International Securities, by contrast, space is used to create an atmosphere conducive to association. Instead of having its senior managers scattered at window offices along the exterior of the building, the bank puts managers in the same desks as their teams, accessible to them with just a movement of the head or hand. Unlike a standard corporate office with cubicles and partitions, the trading room layout, like that of a newsroom or a new-media design studio, is an open-plan arrangement where information roams freely.

At 160 people, the trading room is small by current Wall Street standards. But this small number and the open-plan layout were deliberately chosen to allow the type of low-key interaction that encourages experimentation and intellectual risk-taking. Bob, the manager of the trading room, says of some other managers, "they'll tell you, 'communication, communication,' but you wonder." To illustrate the contrast, he refers to the trading room of another international bank located in Connecticut:

> It's the size of three aircraft carriers. And the reason for it is that it is a source of pride to the manager. It is difficult to see how traders can communicate shouting at each other across two aircraft carriers. At [name of bank], what you'll find is chaos that looks grand.

Instead, at the trading room of International Securities,

> The key is [to avoid] social awkwardness. Two traders are talking to each other. A third needs a piece of information. He has to interrupt. 'Can I interrupt? Can I interrupt?' The key there is the social cost of the interruption. Part of my job is to keep those costs down.

Whereas the traders of the 1980s, acutely described by Tom Wolfe as "Masters of the Universe," were characterized by their riches, bravado, and little regard for small investors, the quantitative traders at International Securities have MBA degrees in finance, PhDs in physics or applied math, and are more appropriately thought of as engineers. None of them wear suspenders. Yet promoting sociability among these engineers/traders is not an easy task. Whereas Tom Wolfe's traders were gregarious to the point of bullying, arbitrageurs in the era of mathematical finance are intellectually overconfident but socially inept:

> A trader is like an engineer type. Difficult when they think they're right. Abrasive. And not very social. Not socially adept. I can easily

find you ten traders in the room who would be miserable at a cocktail party.

If such individualism is not addressed, it can result in fragmented territoriality in the trading room.[24] International Securities avoids such territoriality by moving traders around. "I rotate people as much as I can," Bob says, "because sitting near each other is the best rule of thumb to predict that they will talk to each other." However, Bob is careful not to displace them too disruptively. He describes his approach as "not really shifting, more like drifting," and he continues:

> Once two traders have been sitting together, even if they don't like each other, they'll cooperate, like roommates. So, everyone gets moved every six months on average. But not everyone at a time. It's like those puzzles with one empty space in which you move only one piece at a time.

This emphasis on cooperative interaction underscores that the cognitive tasks of the arbitrage trader are not those of some isolated contemplative, pondering mathematical equations and connected only to an on-screen world. Cognition at International Securities is a distributed cognition. The formulas of new trading patterns are developed in association with other traders. Truly innovative ideas, as one senior trader observed, are slowly developed through successions of discreet one-on-one conversations:

> First you talk to others. You tell someone else, 'I've got this great idea,' and if he tells you 'I read it yesterday in *Barron's*,' you drop it. If you get a positive take, then you work it around.

An idea is given form by trying it out, testing it on others, talking about it with the "math guys," who, significantly, are not kept apart (as in some other trading rooms), and discussing its technical intricacies with the programmers (also immediately present).[25] Because they have been mixed and stirred by the subtle, continual reshuffling of seating arrangements in

---

[24] Underscoring the importance of sociability, the bank not only deliberately restricts the number of people to 160 but also has a strict "low-monitor" policy enforced by Bob that prevents traders from stacking their Bloomberg monitors two or three high. "We try," he says, "to keep the PCs at a low level so that they can see the rest of the room."

[25] Unlike the practice at many other arbitrage hedge funds, the trading room at International Securities accommodates not only traders and their assistants but also a diversity of employees, including salesmen, analysts, operation officers, and computer programmers. Flouting an industrywide trend of relegating these latter employees to a back office, International Securities has kept programmers and operations officers in its money-making core. They not only stay in the trading room but are given desks as large as the traders', and their area of the room has the same privileged feel as the rest. The objective, Bob states, is to prevent differences in professional status

the room, traders can test the ideas on those with whom they were once "like roommates" but who might now be sitting in different parts of the room. Appropriately, the end of this process of formulation (and the beginning of the next stage of material instrumentation, see below) is known as a "victory lap"—a movement around the room in and through which the idea was generated. Place facilitates sociability to make associations.

And where is Bob, the trading room manager? He sits in the middle of the room despite the fact that he has a very well-appointed office in one corner, complete with designer furniture, a small conference table, and, to watch the markets, a home-cinema-size Bloomberg screen that can be controlled from a wireless mouse and keyboard. But he prefers to sit in a regular trader's desk in the middle of the room.

> I have that office over there—you just saw it. But I like this place better [referring to his desk]. Here, I am more connected. No one would come to tell me stories if they had to come into my office. Also, here I get a feel for how the market is doing. I have to know this, because the atmosphere definitely influences the way these guys trade.

In this way, the trading room at International Securities overturns the traditional concentric circles of status. Rather than enjoying less accessibility, the trading room manager is the most accessible. He is most easily reached; and he is best positioned to observe, indeed to sense, what is happening in the room.

What is happening is more than exchange of information. To be sure, traders must have access to the most timely and complete array of information; but this is not enough. In addition to being a nexus of data flows, the trading room is a room of bodies. Taking its collective "pulse" is a means to take the pulse of the markets. Whereas Knorr Cetina and Bruegger find their foreign currency traders "viscerally plugged into the screen reality of the global sphere,"[26] our arbitrage traders are reflective about how they are acutely attuned to the social reality of the local sphere:

> The phone and online communication are inefficient. It takes longer for people to tell each other what they want. You miss body language. Body language and facial expressions are really important. You're not conscious of body language and so it's another channel of communication, and it's one that's not deliberate. So it's a good

---

from undermining interaction among these groups. If placed in a different building, says Bob, "they might as well be in a different planet."

[26] Knorr Cetina and Bruegger, "Global Microstructures," p. 15.

source for what's happening. I don't try to get too conscious of how I'm reading body language and facial expressions. I just let it work its way to where it's useful.

Bob's observations (and those of many other traders with whom we spoke) highlight that cognition in the trading room is not simply distributed. It is also a specifically situated cognition. A trader needs tools—the financial instruments of derivatives and the material instruments to execute a trade. But in addition to these calculative instruments, the trader also needs a "sense of the market." Knowing how to use the tools combines with knowing how to read the situation. This situated awareness is achieved by drawing on the multiple sensors (both human and instrumental) present within the room.

The trading room thus illustrates a particular instance of Castells's paradox: as more information flows through networked connectivity, the kinds of interactions grounded in a physical locale become more important.[27] New information technologies, Castells argues, create the possibility for social interaction without physical contiguity. The downside is that such interactions can become repetitive and programmed in advance. Given this change, Castells argues that as distanced, purposeful, machine-like interactions multiply, the value of less-directed, spontaneous, and unexpected interactions that take place with physical contiguity will become greater.[28] Thus, for example, as surgical techniques develop together with telecommunications technology, the surgeons who are intervening remotely on patients in distant locations are disproportionately clustering in two or three neighborhoods of Manhattan where they can socialize with each other, learn about new techniques, float new ideas, and so on.[29]

From the perspective of arbitrage as association, trading rooms can be seen as the "space of place" where novel associations emerge. The associations established by the arbitrageurs are shaped by the patterns of association in the room. One exemplary passage from our field notes finds a senior trader formulating an arbitrageur's version of Castells's paradox:

It's hard to say what percentage of time people spend on the phone vs. talking to others in the room. But I can tell you the more elec-

[27] Manuel Castells, *The Rise of the Network Society*, 1996.

[28] Nigel Thrift, "On the Social and Cultural Determinants of International Financial Centres: The Case of the City of London," 1994; and Saskia Sassen, "The Spatial Organization of Information Industries," 1997.

[29] Castells's observations are consistent with findings in much of the literature on automated control rooms. See, for example, Christian Heath, Marina Jirotka, Paul Luff, and Jon Hindmarsh, "Unpacking Collaboration: The Interactional Organization of Trading in a City Dealing Room," 1995.

tronic the market goes, the more time people spend communicating with others inside the room.

The Trading Room as an Ecology

Pattern Recognition at the Desk

From looking at the trading room as a simple society of individuals, we now turn to examine the teams that compose the trading room as a more complex organization of diversity. This organization of diversity begins by demarcating specialized functions. The basic organizational unit, "team," has a specific equipment, "desk." The term *desk* denotes not only the actual piece of furniture where traders sit but also the team of traders—as in "Tim from the equity loan desk." Such identification of the animate with the inanimate is due to the fact that a team is never scattered across different desks. In this localization, the different traders in the room are divided into teams according to the financial instrument they use to create equivalencies in arbitrage: the merger arbitrage team trades stocks in companies in the process of consolidating, the options arbitrage team trades in "puts" and "calls"[30] (the derivatives that lend the desk its name), and so on. The desk is an intensely social place. The extreme proximity of the workstations enables traders to talk to each other without lifting their eyes from the screen or interrupting their work. Lunch is at the desk, even if the sandwich comes from a high-end specialty deli. Jokes are at the desk, a never-ending undercurrent of camaraderie that resurfaces as soon as the market gives a respite.

Each desk has developed its own way of looking at the market, based on the principle of equivalence that it uses to calculate value and the financial instrument that enacts its particular style of arbitrage trade. For example, traders at the merger arbitrage desk value companies that are being acquired in terms of the price of the acquiring firm and specialize in asking, "how solid is company X's commitment to merge?" For merger arbitrage traders, the companies in the Standard & Poor's 500 Index are little more than a set of potential acquirers and acquisition targets. In contrast, traders at the index arbitrage desk exploit discrepancies between the price of index securities (e.g., futures on the S&P 500) and the actual average price of the companies that constitute such indexes. Given the minuscule and rapidly vanishing nature of these discrepencies, they need to

---

[30] A *put* is a financial option that gives its holder the right to sell. A *call* gives the right to buy.

trade in high volume and at a high speed. Traders at the convertible bond arbitrage desk look at stocks as bonds, and specialize in information about stocks that would typically interest bondholders such as their liquidity and likelihood of default. The traders at the customer sales desk, meanwhile, take orders from and propose orders to customers outside the confines of the room. Although not specialized in a distinct financial instrument, this most sociable team in the room provides a window on the anxiety level of customers and thus of the market at large by the sound of its traders' voices on the phone and the banging of headsets against their desks in frustration.

A desk generates its own form of pattern recognition. For example, merger arbitrage traders, keen on finding out the degree of commitment of two merging companies, look for patterns of companies' progressive approximation in stock prices. They probe commitment to a merger by plotting the "spread" (difference in price) between acquiring and target companies over time. As with marriages between persons, mergers between companies are scattered with regular rituals of engagement intended to persuade others of the seriousness of their intent. As time passes, arbitrage traders look for a pattern of gradual decay in the spread as corporate bride and groom come together. A similar correspondence of tools and concepts can be found at other desks.

Such joint focus on sensory and economic patterns creates, at each desk, a distinctive community of practice around an evaluative principle, with its own tacit knowledge. Traders at a desk develop a common sense of purpose, a real need to know what each other knows, a highly specialized language, and idiosyncratic ways of signaling to each other. This sense of joint membership translates into friendly rivalry toward other desks. A customer sales trader, for example, took us aside to denounce statistical arbitrage as "like playing video games. If you figure out what the other guy's program is, you can destroy him. That's why we don't do program trades," he explained, referring to his own desk. Conversely, one of the statistical arbitrage traders told us, in veiled dismissal of manual trading, that the more he looks at his data (as opposed to letting his robot trade) the more biased he becomes.

Within each desk, there is a marked consistency between the trading strategy, mathematical formulas, and tools for pattern recognition that traders use. Merger arbitrage traders, for example, plot spreads on their screens but do not use convertible bond valuation models; neither do they employ Black-Scholes equations nor draw on principles of mean-reversion. Convertible arbitrage traders, by contrast, use bond valuation models but do not obsess about whether the spread between two merging companies is widening or narrowing. Customer sales traders are more keen on executing their clients' orders on the day they receive them than on following for months the evolution of the spread between two merging stocks.

The complex trades that are characteristic of our trading room, however, seldom involve a single desk/team in isolation from others. It is to these collaborations that we now turn.

Distributed Cognition across Desks

The desk, in our view, is a unit organized around a dominant evaluative principle and its arrayed financial instruments (devices for measuring, testing, probing, cutting). This principle is its coin—if you like, its specie. But the trading room is composed of multiple species. It is an ecology of evaluative principles. Complex trades take advantage of the interaction among these species. To be able to commit to what counts, to be true to its own principle of evaluation, each desk must take into account the principles and tools of other desks. Recall that shaping a trade involves dissociating some qualities in order to give salience to the ones to which your desk is attached. To identify the relevant categories along which exposure will be limited, shaping a trade involves active association among desks. Co-location, the proximity of desks, facilitates the connections needed to do the cutting.

Whereas in most textbook examples of arbitrage the equivalence-creating property is easy to isolate, in practice it is difficult to fully dissociate. Because of these difficulties, even after deliberate slicing and dicing, traders can still end up dangerously exposed along dimensions of the company that differ from the principles of the desired focused exposure. We found that traders take into account unintended exposure in their calculations in the same way that they achieve association: through co-location. Physical proximity in the room allows traders to survey the financial instruments around them and assess which additional variables they should take into account in their calculations.

For example, the stock loan desk can help the merger arbitrageurs on matters of liquidity. Merger arbitrage traders lend and borrow stock as if they could reverse the operation at any moment of time. However, if the company is small and not often traded, its stock may be difficult to borrow, and traders may find themselves unable to hedge. In this case, according to Max, senior trader at the merger arbitrage desk, "The stock loan desk helps us by telling us how difficult it is to borrow a certain stock." Similarly, index arbitrageurs can help merger arbitrageurs trade companies with several classes of shares. Listed companies often have two types of shares, so-called A- and K-class stock. The two carry different voting rights, but only one of the two types allows traders to hedge their exposure. The existence of these two types facilitates the work of merger arbitrageurs, who can execute trades with the more liquid of the two classes and then transform the stock into the class necessary for the hedge. But such transformation can be prohibitively expensive if one of the two classes is illiquid. To find out, merger arbitrageurs turn to the index arbitrage team, which exploits price differences between the two types.

In other cases, one of the parties to the merger may have a convert provision to protect the bondholder (that is, its bonds can be converted into stocks if there is a merger), leaving merger arbitrage with questions about how this might affect the deal. In this case, it is the convertible bond arbitrage desk that helps merger arbitrage traders clarify the ways in which a convertibility provision should be taken into account. "The market in converts is not organized," says Max, in the sense that there is no single screen representation of the prices of convertible bonds. For this reason,

> We don't know how the prices are fluctuating, but it would be useful to know it because the price movements in converts impacts mergers. Being near the converts desk gives us useful information.

In any case, according to Max, "even when you don't learn anything, you learn there's nothing major to worry about." This is invaluable because, as he says, "what matters is having a degree of confidence."

By putting in close proximity teams that trade in the different financial instruments involved in a deal, the bank is thereby able to associate different markets into a single trade. As a senior trader observed,

> While the routine work is done within teams, most of the value we add comes from the exchange of information between teams. This is necessary in events that are unique and nonroutine, transactions that cross markets, and when information is time sensitive.

Thus, whereas a given desk is organized around a relatively homogeneous principle of evaluation, a given trade is not. Because it involves hedging exposure across different properties along different principles of evaluation, any given trade can involve heterogeneous principles and heterogeneous actors across desks. If a desk involves simple teamwork, a (complex) trade involves collaboration. This collaboration can be as formalized as a meeting (extraordinarily rare at International Securities) that brings together actors from the different desks. Or it might be as primitive as an undirected expletive from the stock loan desk that, overheard, is read as a signal by the merger arbitrage desk that there might be problems with a given deal.

Practices of Re-cognition

How do the creativity, vitality, and serendipity stemming from the trading room yield new interpretations? By interpretation we refer to processes of categorization, as when traders answer the question "what is this *a case of*?" but also processes of recategorization such as making *a case for*. Both work by association—of people to people, but also of people to things, things to things, things to ideas, and so forth.

We saw such processes of re-cognition at work in the following case of an announced merger between two financial firms. The trade was created by the "special situations desk," its name denoting its stated aim of cutting through the existing categories of financial instruments and derivatives. Through close contact with the merger arbitrage desk and the equity loan desk, the special situations desk was able to construct a new arbitrage trade, an "election trade," that recombined in an innovative way two previously existing strategies, merger arbitrage and equity loan.

The facts of the merger were as follows: on January 25, 2001, Investors Group announced its intention to acquire MacKenzie Financial. The announcement immediately set off a rush of trades from merger arbitrage desks in trading rooms all over Wall Street. Following established practice, the acquiring company, Investors Group, made an offer to the stockholders of the target company to buy their shares. It offered them a choice of cash or stock in Investors Group as means of payment. The offer favored the cash option. Despite this, Josh, head of the special situations desk, and his traders reasoned that a few investors would never be able to take the cash. For example, board members and upper management of the target company were paid stocks in order to have an incentive to maximize profit. As a consequence, "it would look wrong if they sold them," John said. In other words, their reasoning included "symbolic" value, as opposed to a purely financial profit-maximizing calculus.

The presence of symbolic investors created, in effect, two different payoffs—cash and stock. The symbolic investors had access only to the smaller payoff. As with any other situation of markets with diverging local valuations, this could open up an opportunity for arbitrage. But how to connect the two payoffs?

In developing an idea for arbitraging between the two options on "election day" (when shareholders of the target company would have to "elect" one of their options, cash or stock), the special situations desk benefited crucially from social interaction across the desks. The special situations traders sit in between the stock loan and merger arbitrage desks. Their closeness to the stock loan desk, which specializes in lending and borrowing stocks to other banks, suggested to the special situations traders the possibility of lending and borrowing stocks on election day. They also benefited from being near the merger arbitrage desk, as it helped them understand how to construct an equivalency between cash and stock. According to Josh,

> [The idea was generated by] looking at the existing business out there and looking at it in a new way. Are there different ways of looking at merger arb? . . . We imagined ourselves sitting in the stock loan desk, and then in the merger arbitrage desk. We asked, is there a way to arbitrage the two choices, to put one choice in terms of another?

The traders found one. Symbolic investors did not want to be seen exchanging their stock for cash, but nothing prevented another actor such as International Securities from doing so directly. What if the special situation traders were to borrow the shares of the symbolic investors at the market price, exchange them for cash on election day (i.e., get the more favorable terms option), buy back stock with that cash and return it to symbolic investors? That way, the latter would be able to bridge the divide that separated them from the cash option.

Once the special situation traders had constructed the bridge that separated the two choices in the election trade, they still faced a problem. The possibilities for a new equivalency imagined by Josh and his traders were still tenuous and untried. But it was this very uncertainty—and the fact that no one had acted on those possibilities before—that made them potentially so profitable. The uncertainty resided in the small print of the offer made by the acquiring company, Investors Group: How many total investors would elect cash over stock on election day?

The answer to that question would determine the profitability of the trade: the loan and buyback strategy developed by the special situations traders would not work if few investors chose cash over stocks. IG, the acquiring company, intended to devote a limited amount of cash to the election offer. If most investors elected cash, IG would prorate its available cash (i.e., distribute it equally) and complete the payment to stockholders with shares, even to those stockholders who elected the "cash" option. This was the preferred scenario for the special situation traders, for then they would receive some shares back and be able to use them to return the shares they had previously borrowed from the "symbolic" investors.

But if, in an alternative scenario, most investors elected stock, the special situations desk would find itself with losses. In that scenario, IG would not run out of cash on election day, investors who had elected cash such as the special situations traders would obtain cash (not stocks), and the traders would find themselves without stock in IG to return to the original investors who had lent it to them. Josh and his traders would then be forced to buy the stock of IG on the market at a prohibitively high price.

The profitability of the trade, then, hinged on a simple question: Would most investors elect cash over stock? Uncertainty about what investors would do on election day posed a problem for the traders. Answering the question "what will others do?" entailed a highly complex search problem, as stock ownership is typically fragmented over diverse actors in various locations applying different logics. Given the impossibility of monitoring all the actors in the market, what could the special situation traders do?

As a first step, Josh used his Bloomberg terminal to list the names of the twenty major shareholders in the target company, MacKenzie Financial. Then he discussed the list with his team to determine their likely action. As he recalls,

> What we did is, we [would] meet together and try to determine what they're going to do. Are they rational, in the sense that they maximize the money they get?

For some shareholders, the answer was straightforward: they were large and well-known companies with predictable strategies. For example, Josh would note:

> See . . . the major owner is Fidelity, with 13 percent. They will take cash, since they have a fiduciary obligation to maximize the returns to their shareholders.

But this approach ran into difficulties in trying to anticipate the moves of the more sophisticated companies. The strategies of the hedge funds engaged in merger arbitrage were particularly complex. Would they take cash or stock? Leaning over, without even leaving his seat or standing up, Josh posed the question to the local merger arbitrage traders:

> "Cash or stock?" I shouted the question to the merger arbitrage team here who were working [a different angle] on the same deal right across from me. "Cash! We're taking cash," they answered.

From their answer, the special situations traders concluded that hedge funds across the market would tend to elect cash. They turned out to be right.

The election trade illustrates the ways in which co-location helps traders innovate and take advantage of the existence of multiple rationalities among market actors. The election trade involved a recombination of the strategies developed by the desks around the special situations traders. Proximity to the stock loan desk allowed them to see an election day as a stock loan operation, and proximity to risk arbitrage allowed them to read institutional shareholders as profit maximizers, likely to take cash over stock. But proximity mattered because it created opportunities for interaction across the distinctive views on markets offered by the evaluative principles of merger, stock loan, and risk arbitrage. Electronically connected to markets of global reach, the traders at International Securities reach out to colleagues only a few paces away to calibrate the tools of their trade. The trading room is an ecology of knowledge in which heterarchical collaboration is the means to solve the puzzle of value.

The Trading Room as a Laboratory

In the previous section we showed how calculation is not individual and asocial but instead is distributed across desks in the trading room. In this section we argue that calculation is also distributed across sociotechnical networks of tangible tools that include computer programs, screens, dials, robots, telephones, mirrors, cable connections, and so on.

Although financial instruments (derivatives such as futures, options, swaps, etc.) are deemed worthy of study in the *Journal of Finance*, these material instruments supposedly belong to the province of handymen, contractors, and electricians. But traders know they are important, if only because they spend so much time acquiring skills to use, construct, and maintain these instruments. Without instruments for visualizing properties of the market, they could not see opportunities; and without instruments for executing their trades, they could not intervene in markets. No tools, no trade.

To see opportunities, traders put on the financial equivalent of infrared goggles, which provide them with the trader's equivalent of night vision. They also delegate calculation to robots that single-mindedly execute their programmed theories, and they scan the room for clues that alert them to the limits in the applicability of these theories.

One cannot appreciate the degree to which quantitative finance is knowledge intensive without considering the complexity of the traders' tools. According to Knorr Cetina and Bruegger, traders do not quite match up to scientists: when compared to high-energy physicists and their twenty-year-long experiments, traders appear as having flat production functions that do not transform data but merely transpose it onto the screen.[31] By contrast, we found our traders' tools remarkably close to Latour's definition of scientific instruments as inscription devices that shape a view.[32] Scientific instruments, whether a radio telescope, a Geiger counter, or a petri dish, display phenomena that are often not visible to the naked eye. They reveal objects in space, radiation waves, or minuscule bacteria that could otherwise not be discerned. Similarly, the traders' tools reveal opportunities that are not immediately apparent. Both scientists and traders derive their strengths—persuasiveness in the former, profits in the latter—from original instrumentation.[33]

Perhaps the most salient instruments at International Securities are the traders' Bloomberg workstations and their individually customized screens.[34] These dramatic, extrawide, high-contrast Bloomberg flat panel monitors serve as their workbench. Bloomberg terminals include a specialized monitor, color-coded keyboard, and a direct intranet cable connection to Bloomberg L. P. Even more expensive than the physical terminals is the software that comes with them, structured around five areas that include data (prices, volume, etc.), analytics for parsing and visualizing the data, news (from a thousand journals around the world), trading support, and information on trade execution.[35] Just as traders are on the lookout

[31] Knorr Cetina and Bruegger, "Global Microstructures."

[32] Bruno Latour, *Science in Action: How to Follow Scientists and Engineers through Society*, 1987.

[33] For insightful treatments of the interaction between valuation and technology in the field of finance, see Preda's historical study of the ticker and its effects on investor behavior, and Muniesa's study of the use of telephones in trading rooms. (Alex Preda, "Socio-technical Agency in Financial Markets: The Case of the Stock Ticker," 2006; and Fabian Muniesa, "Reserved Anonymity: On the Use of Telephones in the Trading Room," 2002.)

[34] Screens in trading rooms are but one example of the ubiquity of screens in the digital era. Think of cinema screens, television screens, and screens for overhead projectors. Then add screens for personal computers, mobile phones (estimated by Nokia at around two billion worldwide in 2006), video games, ATMs, PDAs, cash registers, airport monitors, surveillance monitors, medical equipment, and so on. We have likely reached the moment when there are more screens than human beings on the planet. For diverse accounts of screens populating the social, see Sherry Turkle, *Life on the Screen*, 1998; Lucas D. Introna and Frenando M. Ilharco, "On the Meaning of Screens: Towards a Phenomenological Account of Screeness," 2006; and Mimi Sheller, "Mobile Publics: Beyond the Network Perspective," 2004.

[35] The demands for instrumentation to assist quick pattern recognition in data on crisscrossed markets makes trading rooms a critical field for the development of visualization tools. Because hedge funds are flush with cash, software developers are rushing in to fill the need. "What you see is what you risk," writes a strategist in Microsoft's Visualization and Financial Engineering unit. (See Michael Pryke, "Money's Eyes: The Visual Preparation of Financial Markets," 2008.) With enormous resources entering this field, I expect that trading rooms will figure prominently in the next move from visual to haptic (touch and grasp) approaches to computer interfaces. That is, look for new recombinant innovations at the overlap of research for computing for the blind and

for specialized software, they individually tailor their digital workbenches in ways as elaborate as they are diverse: at International Securities, no two screens are the same. Screen instruments are not mere transporters of data but select, modify, and present data in ways that shape what the trader sees. As screens they reveal information, but they also filter and conceal.

Take, for example, the case of Stanley H., junior trader at the customer trading desk. Like others at his desk, Stan executes arbitrage trades for clients. He does not need to come up with new trades himself; he needs only to find out the points in time at which he can execute the client's orders. For this purpose, he needs to know the general direction of the market, current developments regarding the companies he is trading, and whether he can trade or not. His is a world of the here and now. To grapple with it, Stan has arranged on his screens instruments such as a "magnifying glass," trading "baskets," and "active links."

Stan's point of departure is the baseline information that everyone has: a Bloomberg window that graphs the Dow Industrials and the NASDAQ market indexes to give him information on the market's general direction, bullish or bearish. Next to it, another instrument provides a more personalized perspective. A window that he calls his "magnifying glass" displays sixty crucial stocks that he considers representative of different sectors such as integrated circuits, oil, or broadband. Visually, the numbers in this window momentarily increase in size when an order is received, resembling a pulsating meter of live market activity. Stan complements the magnifying glass with the "footprints" of his competitors in tables that display rival banks' orders in the stocks that he trades.

Stan's screens include a clipboard for his operations, an arrangement that simplifies and automates part of the cognitive work involved in making the trades. This is composed of several "trading baskets," windows that show the trades that he has already done. An additional instrument shows pending work. This is contained in an Excel spreadsheet in which Stan introduces entries with "active links" to stock prices, that is, cells that are automatically updated in real time. In the cells next to the links Stan has programmed the conditions that the clients give to him (e.g., "set the spread at 80"). As a result, another cell changes color depending on whether the conditions are met or not (cyan means they are; dark green means they are not). The computer, then, does part of the calculation work for Stan. Instead of having to verify whether the conditions hold to execute each of

---

that for financial engineering. On tangible computing, see Paul Dourish, *Where the Action Is: The Foundations of Embodied Interaction*, 2004.

the trades, he follows a much simpler rule: trade if the cell is cyan, do not trade if it is dark green.

Stan is a toolmaker as much as a "trade maker," a craftsman of tools as much as a processor of information. He devotes considerable deliberation to the conscious inscription of his screens. Every day, one hour before the markets open, he arrives at the trading room to prepare his setup; part of that preparation is readying the screens. One by one, Stan opens each of his windows and places them in their customary place, ensures they have their own color and size, creates new active links as customers order new trades, and discusses possible technical issues with the computer programmers.

Two desks away, Richard C. at the convertible bond arbitrage desk looks at stocks from a very different perspective—as if they were bonds. As noted above, traders in convertible bond arbitrage such as Richard seek to exploit the value of the so-called convertibility option that is sometimes included in bonds. This allows the bondholder to convert the bond into a stock, in effect morphing one type of security into another. To assess the value of the option to convert, Richard uses Bloomberg's proprietary "Convertible Bond Valuation" model, which returns an estimated value of the bond given basic parameters such as volatility of the stock, its delta, gamma, and so forth. Richard's models can be seen as a pair of goggles that highlight the hidden value of convertibility options.

Close to the bond arbitrage desk, Max Sharper at the merger arbitrage desk exploits profit opportunities when companies merge. As noted, merger arbitrage traders long the company that is the acquisition target and short the acquirer. In doing so, their trades end up as a bet on the probability that the merger will take place. To decide whether or not to bet on a merger, Max plots the "spread" or price difference between the companies in merger talks. If two companies merge they will be worth the same, and their spread will be zero. As the merger unfolds, a small spread denotes market confidence in the merger, and a large spread denotes skepticism. Max plots the spread in time to read from it the "implied probability" that the market assigns to the merger. As with the other traders, Max's spread plots serve as an optical device that brings into focus actors' confidence about a given merger.

The visualization techniques of on-screen instruments, then, are as varied as the principles of arbitrage that guide each desk. Stan's desk executes trades, and the magnifying glasses, trading baskets, rivals' footprints, and active links on his screens display momentary instances of open windows of opportunity in a geometric array of white, green, blue, and cyan squares with numbers dancing in them, lending his screens the appearance of an animated painting by Piet Mondrian. Richard's desk buys and sells convertible bonds, and the bond valuation models on his screens display a more conventional text interface, a boxy black-on-white combination suggestive of 1980s-style minicomputer screens. The spread plots for betting on mergers on Max's screens show charts, narrow white lines that zigzag in a snakelike manner from left to right over the soothing blue background of his monitor.

The traders' reliance on such goggles, however, entails a serious risk. In bringing some information into sharp attention, the software and the graphic representations on their screens also obscure. In order to be devices that magnify and focus, they are also blinders. According to one, "Bloomberg shows the prices of normal stocks; but sometimes, normal stocks morph into new ones," such as in situations of mergers or bond conversions. If a stock in Stan's magnifying glass—say, an airline that he finds representative of the airline sector—were to go through a merger or bond conversion, it would no longer stand for the sector.

An even more serious risk for the traders is that distributing calculation across their instruments amounts to inscribing their sensors with their own beliefs. As we have seen, in order to recognize opportunities, the trader needs special tools that allow him to see what others cannot. But the fact that the tool has been shaped by his theories means that his sharpened perceptions can sometimes be highly magnified misperceptions, perhaps disastrously so. For an academic economist who presents his models as accurate representations of the world, a faulty model might prove an embarrassment at a conference or seminar. For the trader, however, a faulty model can lead to massive losses. But for the trader, there is no option not to model: no tools, no trade. What the layout of the trading room—with its interactions of different kinds of traders and its juxtaposition of different principles of trading—accomplishes is the continual, almost minute-by-minute, reminder that the trader should never confuse representation for reality.[36]

Instead of reducing the importance of social interaction in the room, the highly specialized instruments actually provide a rationale for it. "We

---

[36] Recalling René Magritte's 1929 painting *The Treachery of Images* ("Ceci n'est pas une pipe"), biochemist Mike Hann produced an image showing the model of a protein molecule with the inscription "Ceci n'est pas une molecule" to remind his colleagues "that all of the graphic images presented here are not molecules, not even pictures of molecules, but pictures of icons which we believe represent some aspects of the molecule's properties" (http://mgl.scripps.edu/people/goodsell/mgs_art/hann.html). Traders do the same, populating their monitors with cartoons and other reminders that speak, in so many words, "This model is not a market." Arbitrage trader Emanuel Derman writes, "All models are wrong, some are just more useful than others" (Derman, "Modeling and Its Discontents," 2007).

all have different kinds of information," Stan says, referring to other traders, "so I sometimes check with them." How often? "All the time."

Hence, just as Latour defined a laboratory as "a place that gathers one or several instruments together,"[37] trading rooms can be understood as places that gather diverse market instruments together. Seen in this light, the move from traditional to modern finance can be considered as an enlargement in the number of instruments in the room, from one to several. The best scientific laboratories maximize cross-fertilization among disciplines and instruments. For example, the Radar Lab at MIT in the 1940s made breakthroughs by bringing together the competing principles of physicists and engineers.[38] Similarly, the best trading rooms bring together heterogeneous value frameworks for creative recombinations.

Monitoring the Price Mechanism

Another example of distributed calculation can be found in "robots," computer programs used by statistical arbitrage traders that automate the process of buying and selling stocks. As with the other market instruments of the trading room, robots bring benefits but also pose new challenges that are solved by intermingling the social, the cognitive, and the artifactual.

Robots are representations as well as tools for automation. Inscribed with the trader's beliefs, they execute only the trading strategy they were programmed to perform. For example, in deciding whether to buy or sell stocks, a mean-reversion robot takes into account only whether the prices are close to or distant from their historic average price, while an earnings robot, on the other hand, considers only the companies' earnings. Robots enact a complex set of assumptions about the market, and they process an active selection of the available data that are consistent with it.

Sociability in the room is crucial from the moment of the robot's inception, a process of codifying tacit knowledge into algorithms and computer code. This takes place at the whiteboard, in meetings of heterogeneous perspectives that might include, for example, an index arbitrage trader, a computer programmer, and a merger arbitrage trader. Starting at the whiteboard, an idea for a trade mutates in form, from a trader's utterances, to graphs on the board, to abstract models, to mathematical equations, and, finally, into computer code. The robot is quite literally codified knowledge.

[37] Latour, *Science in Action*.

[38] Peter L. Galison, *Image and Logic: A Material Culture of Microphysics*, 1997. On the architecture of science see also Peter L. Galison and Emily Thompson, eds., *The Architecture of Science*, 1999.

Once codified into a program, the robot goes to work with traders specialized in implementing computer programs, such as the statistical arbitrage desk. But the story does not end here. Piloting a robot requires inputs from a kind of emergent traffic control—cues and signals from other parts of the room. More accurately, the case is an illustration of Wanda Orlikowski's challenge to the codified/noncodified distinction and related taxonomic dichotomies. As she argues, successful knowledge performance, "knowledge in practice," requires combinations of explicit and tacit knowledge.[39]

Consider the case of Tom, a trader at the statistical arbitrage desk. Instead of trading manually, Tom uses and maintains a robot. Automated trading poses the same challenge as driving a car at a high speed: any mistake can lead to disaster very quickly. "I have," Tom says, "a coin that comes up heads 55 percent of the time." With margins as low as 0.05, the only route to high returns is trading a very high volume or, as Tom says of the coin, "the point is to flip it a lot." As with Formula 1 car racing or high-speed boating, traders need excellent instrumentation. Indeed, they have navigation instruments as complex as those of an airplane cockpit. Yet, as it turns out, these are not enough. The price mechanism has to be monitored, and calibrated; and for that purpose Tom obtains crucial cues from the social interactions at the desks around him.

To illustrate the sensitivity of results to timely data (in which the units of measurement are frequently seconds rather than minutes), Tom recounts an instance in which a slight time delay lost millions of dollars for a competing bank—and earned as much for International Securities. On that specific day, some banks had been receiving price information with a delay because of problems with the Reuters server. Price movements had been large all through the day, and the market index had risen very quickly. In a rising market, a delay makes the index appear consistently below its real level. In contrast to spot prices, prices for futures contracts were arriving to all banks with no delay. As a result, index arbitrage traders at one bank (traders who exploit differences between spot and S&P 500 futures) perceived as inexpensive securities that were in fact very expensive, and bought extensively. Tom and others at International Securities, in contrast, were getting timely information on both spot and futures prices. Tom recounts:

> While they were buying, we were selling . . . the traders here were writing tickets until their fingers were bleeding. We made $2 million in an hour, until they realized what was happening.

[39] Wanda J. Orlikowski, "Knowing in Practice: Enacting a Collective Capability in Distributed Organizing," 2002.

The episode illustrates the challenges of working with robots. When trading at Formula 1 speed, "the future" is only seconds away. When the speed of trading amplifies second-by-second delays, the statistical arbitrage trader must be attuned to a new kind of problem: by how many seconds are the data delayed? That is, traders have to remind themselves of the time lag that elapses between what they see—the numbers on their screens—and actual prices. The prices that matter are those that reside in the computer servers of the market exchange, be it the NASDAQ or the New York Stock Exchange, for that is where the trades are ultimately executed. What traders see on-screen are bits and bytes that have been transported from the exchange to the trading room in a long and sometimes difficult path of possible delays. If traders mistakenly take delayed data for real-time data, losses will pile up quickly. In that situation, delegating the trading decisions to the robot could lead to disaster. How do the statistical arbitrage traders prevent these disasters from taking place?

The first line of defense against the risks of high-volume, high-speed, automated trading is more technology. Tom's robot provides him with as many dials as a cockpit in an airplane. He trades with three screens in front of him. Two of them correspond to powerful Unix workstations, and the third one is a Bloomberg terminal. One Unix terminal has real-time information about his trades. Across the top of one, a slash sign rotates and moves from side to side. It is a "pulse meter" to gauge the "price feed," that is, the speed with which information on prices is arriving. The character stops moving when prices stop arriving. It is very important to be aware when this happens, because the price robot can get confused. According to Tom, "it thinks that prices aren't changing and it imagines false opportunities, while in reality prices are moving but not arriving to it."

Tom benefits from numerous additional dials. On the right-hand corner of his second Unix station Tom has five squares; each of them is a speedometer that indicates how quickly the orders are getting through the servers of the specialists or the electronic communication networks. If they are green, everything is fine. If they are yellow, the network is congested and deals are delayed. If they are red, servers are clogged. The clocks in the Unix workstations are synchronized every day to the National Institute of Standards atomic clock. In addition to a large display of an analog clock in his computer, Tom has two "CPU meters," which measure congestion in the bank's order flow. When International Securities' computers are engaged for long periods of time, orders take longer to execute. Thus, to monitor prices in the market, traders must monitor the price mechanism—literally, they must monitor the machines that bring and make prices.

Technology, however, is not the only answer to the problem of execution, for the dials that measure the accuracy of the technology are a representation themselves. Technology, in other words, answers one question, "is the robot getting the data?" but raises another one, "is the robot right in what it says?" We call this infinite-regress problem the "calibration" problem.

The nuclear accident at Chernobyl showed an acute case of calibration problems. Radiation was so high that the dials of the Geiger counters in the control room of the Soviet nuclear power station did not register any abnormal level of radiation even at the peak of the radioactive materials' escape. The dials, calibrated to register nuances, failed to detect the sharp increase in radiation levels. Technology permits the execution of automated tasks, but it requires appropriate calibration.

How to solve the calibration problem? Tom solves it by drawing on the social and spatial resources of the trading room. He sits in between the merger arbitrage desk and the systems desk. According to Tom:

> When you hear screams of agony around you, it indicates that perhaps it is not a good time to trade. If I hear more screams, maybe I should not use the system even if it's green.

Similarly, price feeds in stocks and futures have to arrive at the same speed. By sitting near the futures arbitrage desk, the statistical arbitrage trader can remain alert to any anomaly in the data feed. In addition to getting a sense of when to turn off their robots, stat arb traders interpret cues from nearby desks to gauge when to take a particular security out of automated trading. The instruments of representation that make up the technology of finance retain their value only so long as they remain entangled in the social relations that spawned them. A trader's tools are sociotechnical.

This sociotechnical character, finally, governs the placement of the robots in the trading room. While promoting association through proximity, the trading room also uses distance to preserve the requisite measure of variety among the robots. Instead of minimizing differences to produce a "one right way" to calculate, the trading room actively organizes diversity. Of the four statistical arbitrage robots, a senior trader observed:

> We don't encourage the four traders in statistical arb to talk to each other. They sit apart in the room. The reason is we have to keep diversity. We could really get hammered if the different robots would have the same P and L [profit and loss] patterns and the same risk profiles.

Seemingly at odds with the policy of putting all the traders of the same function at the same desk, the statistical arbitrage traders and their robots are scattered around the room. Why? Because the robots, as the traders say, are partly "alive"—they evolve. That is, they mutate as they are maintained, retooled, and refitted to changes in the market. They are kept separated to reduce the possibility that their evolution will converge (thereby resulting in a loss of diversity in the room). But they are, of course, not pushed out of the room entirely, because a given stat arb unit must not be too far from the other types of arbitrage desks—proximity to which provides the cues about when to turn off the robots.

The Pursuit of New Properties

In the preface to *Novum Organum*, one of the founding documents of modern science, published in 1620, Francis Bacon wrote that "in every great work to be done by the hand of man it is manifestly impossible, without instrumentation and machinery, either for the strength of each to be exerted or the strength of all to be united."[40] These observations about the importance of instrumentation were a key part of Bacon's broader goal to outline a new course of discovery. Writing in an age when the exploration, conquest, and settlement of territory was enriching European sovereigns, Bacon proposed an alternative strategy of exploration. In place of the quest for property, for territory, Bacon urged a search for properties, the properties of nature, arguing that this knowledge, produced at the workbench of science, would prove a yet vaster and nearly inexhaustible source of wealth.[41]

Like Bacon's experimentalists, arbitrage traders have moved from exploring for *property* to exploring for the underlying *properties* of securities. Just as Bacon's experimentalists at the beginnings of modern science were in search of new properties of nature, so our quantitative traders have, in their quest for profits, gone beyond traditional properties of companies such as growth, solvency, or profitability. Their pursuit of new properties has taken them to abstract financial qualities such as volatility, convertibility, or liquidity—as different from accounting-based measures of property as Bacon's search for new properties was from the conquest of territory. And just as Bacon was advocating a program of inductive, experimentalist science in contrast to logical deduction, so our arbitrage

---

[40] Francis Bacon, *Novum Organum (The new organ)*, [1620] 1960, p. 35.

[41] We owe this insightful reading of Bacon's writings, including *Novum Organum* and his (often unsolicited) "advices" to his sovereigns, Elizabeth I and James I, to Monique Girard.

traders, in contrast to the deductive stance of neoclassical economists, are actively experimenting to uncover properties of the economy.

Whereas Bacon's New Instrument[42] was part of a program for "The Interpretation of Nature," the new instruments of quantitative finance—connectivity, equations, and computing—visualize, cut, probe, and dissect ephemeral properties in the project of the interpretation of markets. In the practice of their trading room laboratories, our arbitrage traders are acutely aware that the reality "out there" is a social construct consisting of other traders and other interconnected instruments continuously reshaping, in feverish innovation, the properties of that recursive world. In this coproduction, in which the products of their interventions become a part of the phenomenon they are monitoring, such reflexivity is an invaluable component of their tools of the trade.

Our arbitrageurs' search for new properties is thus an expression of the self-referential character of advanced capitalism. Having brought more and more domains of social life within market frameworks, the capitalist search for value turns upon itself. Where it once found markets for physical goods, markets for money, markets for symbolic goods, and markets for futures, it now finds markets for markets, markets for risk, and markets for abstracted properties such as indexability and volatility. Value is found in increasingly immaterial forms.[43] But the very possibility of such increasingly virtual value rests on specifically material forms. Markets in derivatives, markets in weather, markets in risk, markets in volatility, and markets seemingly in time itself are not possible "without instrumentation and machinery" (recalling Bacon's terms). They require enormous computing capacity, powerful algorithms, and network connectedness of global scope. As risk becomes tradable and markets for markets increasingly entangled, this networked hypercoupling creates new forms of uncertainty with the possibilities of crises cascading throughout the system.

For these reasons, sociologists and other social scientists need to make the study of technology a part of the tools of our trade. When economists or sociologists study technology, it is most frequently as a specialized subfield—the social studies of science, for instance, or the economics of technological innovation. Such research is invaluable. But we should also incorporate the study of technology in the core subfields of our disciplines. In our epoch, for example, organizational design is inseparable from design of the digital interface. Similarly, to understand not only the

---

[42] *Novum Organum* translates as "New Instrument." Bacon contrasts the deductive method of "Anticipation of the Mind" to his own method of "Interpretation of Nature" (p. 37).

[43] Arnoldi, "Derivatives"; Daniel Miller, "Materiality: An Introduction," 2005; and Nigel Thrift, *Knowing Capitalism*, 2005.

mathematics but also the machines that make up the sophisticated market instruments of quantitative finance, we need to analyze the entanglements of actors and instruments in the sociotechnology of the laboratories of finance.

Epilogue

On September 11, 2001, the work of the arbitrageurs at International Securities was interrupted by a sudden explosion in the building adjacent to theirs, one of the Twin Towers in the World Trade Center. As they rushed to the windows of their trading room in the World Financial Center, the traders saw Tower 1 go up in flames. From that vantage point, some saw the frightful approach of the second plane. That crash brought terror to the trading room, and a tumultuous escape to the Hudson River. By the time the towers fell, many of the International Securities traders were on boats to New Jersey. Fortunately, no one in the firm was harmed.

The building, however, was badly damaged, making the trading room dangerous and inaccessible. The World Trade Center had collapsed at its doorstep. The windows of the trading room were pierced and shattered by debris from the fallen towers. Dust and ash, possibly containing asbestos and toxic chemicals, had entered the room and penetrated the computers, clogging their fans, overheating them, and rendering them unusable and unsafe for repair. The building was deemed structurally unsafe, and access to it was prohibited for months. As a result, the lively trading room that had once supported the innovative work of interpretation became a dark hole with no electricity, no connectivity, and no assurance of safety from toxic chemicals.

In an emergency meeting on the night of 9/11, the team in charge of equity trading at International Securities concluded that recovery from the attack would be long and hard, and that it would take from three weeks to three months for them to be trading again. The bank had only one equities trading room in the United States; there was no backup site to which they could go. The bank did have another available facility, a back office in a New Jersey suburb, but the only resource that the traders could count on there was spare space in a basement where the firm stored corporate-style minicomputers for processing payroll data. The basement had no workstations, no desks, and no high-speed connectivity.

Yet, barely six days after 9/11, by the time the New York Stock Exchange reopened on September 17 the traders at International Securities were trading again. We were privileged to witness how this was accomplished.

Several days after the attack, we sent an e-mail of concern to ask if everyone had escaped unharmed. To our relief, we learned that no one was injured. To our surprise, the return e-mail included an invitation, indeed, an insistence, that we come over to New Jersey to witness the recovery process. "It is chaotic," wrote the manager of the trading room, "but also very inspiring." Our presence would be "a reminder of normal times." As ethnographers, we felt enormously honored to be welcomed to document these extraordinary efforts.

Thus, on September 19 we were back among traders in our role as observers, this time in an improvised trading room in a converted basement warehouse in New Jersey. The temporary trading room was barely an hour's drive away from Manhattan, but it felt a universe away from the excitement and activity of Wall Street. Located in a suburban corporate park, the building was surrounded by similar low-rise corporate offices, used by manufacturing companies such as Colgate or AT&T. Just around the corner, a farm announced "Hay For Sale." The surroundings offered an endless succession of down-market shopping malls, Wal-Marts and Dunkin Donuts; one could drive around for an hour and never find espresso coffee. What had been the back office of International Securities had now, in effect, become its front office. The basement room had a makeshift feel to it: no windows, a low ceiling, and walls painted in industrial yellow, more fitting for a storage room than a trading room. Indeed, one week before our visit the place was still being used to store the mainframes used by the bank's data center. Correspondingly, the dress code had shifted from business casual to jeans and boots.

Our traders were in New Jersey, unquestionably in a basement storage room in New Jersey. But a sign taped prominently on the wall gave different bearings: "20th Floor, Equities." In other parts of the same enormous room one could read other signs: "21st Floor, Fixed Income," and "19th Floor, Risk Management." Our traders were still between the nineteenth and the twenty-first floors, but now horizontally rather than vertically. Moreover, within the constraints of those temporary quarters, they had arranged their desks to reproduce the layout of the Financial Center trading room. For example, every trader in the "agency trading" desk remained together, sitting on the same desk. In the Financial Center trading room they had sat on a spacious desk between the stock loan and the special situations desk. In New Jersey, they camped on a table partly occupied by two photocopiers and three fax machines, in what used to be the fax station of the data center. They camped, but they stayed together. The desks also preserved their relative locations, reconstructing the cognitive order of the trading room at the Financial Center. When the managers of the agency and special situations desks found themselves sitting again alongside each other, they reverted to their old routine of checking perceptions against each other, probing each other's beliefs, and designing together new arbitrage trades. At some point, one of them exclaimed in exhaustion, "Everybody seems to be thinking with my brain today!" a reflection that the distributed cognition afforded by the desk pattern was again taking place.

The traders could replicate the floor plan of the Financial Center trading room, but not the technology. Direct data from the New York Stock Exchange were not available. "Trade Manager v1.4a," the platform of hardware and software that registered and processed trades (also called the "trading engine"), was not working. The customary phone turrets with twenty lines each were also not available, and the traders had to make do with off-the-rack single-line phones (which they slammed with the usual energy). Instead of Sun workstations, they were working on Pentium IIs and laptops, some brought from the traders' homes, some rescued from the data center, some hurriedly purchased in the days following the attack. Instead of having virtually unlimited bandwidth, they now had to adapt to limited network connections that did not allow all desks in the room to trade simultaneously.

The Breakdown of Technology Is Society Made Visible

The traders' response to September 11 contains important insights for a sociotechnical view of organizations. We have argued that arbitrageurs associate stocks by associating people, artifacts, and ideas in the same place. Conceptually, it is tempting to split this sociotechnical network into humans and machines—people who think and talk versus machines that obey preprogrammed commands. But such separation is misconceived. "Technology," writes Bruno Latour, "is society made durable."[44] Yet, what happens when technology breaks down, when traders who are accustomed to twenty dedicated phone lines apiece must share phones, when traders whose style of trading is based on speed and volume must suddenly operate with minimal bandwidth? The breakdown of the trading technology at International Securities opened up for us a window on its sociotechnical network—a network that operated seamlessly and invisibly in the Financial Center trading room. The breakdown of technology is society made visible.[45]

---

[44] Bruno Latour, "Technology Is Society Made Durable," 1991.

[45] To take a trivial example, consider the photocopy machine in your department. It is likely that you think about the photocopier as a piece of technology—that is, until it breaks down and

To those of us working in New York City, September 11 brought home
the visibility of sociotechnical networks. Six of the members of my research
team at the Center on Organizational Innovation (COI) were conducting
ongoing ethnographic research downtown. In addition to Daniel and myself at the WFC, four others were involved in field research in Silicon Alley,[46] and several others, including John Kelly, quickly became involved in
studying response and recovery. I was very proud of my graduate students
who put their dissertations on hold to study how a city was responding
to crisis. We focused on the interface of technology and organization in
firms in or near Ground Zero, talking with people individually and in
groups, from large companies as well as small and medium-size firms.

On December 5, 2001, the COI organized a roundtable discussion with
senior executives and contingency planning specialists from key WTC
firms.[47] The passages quoted below and in the accompanying sidebars are
excerpted from the transcript of that meeting. Although these executives
were responsible for recovering the infrastructure—the communications
systems that are the nervous system of global finance—their observations
did not focus on technology nor, for that matter, on contingency planning.
No one said, "Our technology saved us," or "our preparedness plan really
worked." Despite being technology officers, they all pointed to social relationships as a key feature of organizational response.

The most memorable account, appropriately, was a story about stories
from an executive at a major bond-trading firm in the Trade Center that
suffered terrible casualties. On the evening of 9/11, the survivors of the
leadership group met, knowing that they had to be trading when the bond
markets reopened in the same week. Because bond markets had already
opened on the morning of September 11 before the terrorist attack, the

---

you recognize that it is part of a sociotechnical network including the department secretary who
needs to call the service company, the dispatchers, and the repair person who comes out to fix the
machine. On the breakdown of technology as society made visible after 9/11, see John Kelly and
David Stark, "Crisis, Recovery, Innovation: Learning from 9/11," 2002; Daniel Beunza and David
Stark, "The Organization of Responsiveness: Innovation and Recovery in the Trading Rooms of
Wall Street," 2003.

[46] Monique Girard, Amanda Damarin, Paul-Brian McInnerney, and Gina Neff. Paul-Brian
was actually on site carrying out research in a nonprofit technology assistance program on September 11. His field notes from that day are an extraordinary piece of ethnography.

[47] The companies included Merrill Lynch, Cantor Fitzgerald, Deutsche Bank, Sun Microsys-
tems, SunGard, Fred Alger Associates, and other medium- and small-size firms. All quotations
are anonymous as per the agreement with our participants. That anyone in the center of the
maelstrom could possibly find time to talk to us in the days and months after 9/11 was remarkable. The fact that many really wanted to speak, and did so in a spirit of openness, candor, and
contribution to the general good, made a great impression on us. We cannot overstate our admi-
ration for them.

> **"Without the Human Element, Preparedness Wouldn't Have Done Anything"**
>
> We're never going to have this happen to us again when another bomb goes off in the basement or garage of the World Trade Center, but you know there are so many different levels of what happened in this tragedy that how do you prepare yourself for something that is truly the unseen?
>
> Without that human element of commitment to task, commitment to each other, preparedness wouldn't have done anything. The best plan never would have been opened up.
>
> I'm sure preparedness contributed . . . but even where preparedness was not there, people just innovated around it.
>
> [We were] already highly communicative and worked together very well as a team, which became the essence of how we were able to recover.
>
> If you're talking about measuring preparedness, the key question is how effectively can people work together and collaborate.
>
> By ensuring people had the right focus, we were able to achieve some sort of miracle. We weren't able to do this in our traditional modes of thinking, and the last thing I really want to stress is that if you empower people, if you give them the authority to solve a problem, they will solve it. I can't stress that enough.

firm faced huge exposure; and without access to the traders' positions, it could face financial ruin when the markets reopened. The firm had followed all the guidelines for contingency planning. Its system had backed up the traders' data—at not just one but, in fact, two off-site locations, one across the Hudson River, another across the Atlantic. But the survivors could not access the system without the missing traders' IDs and passwords. As the executive recounts:

> We had forty-seven hours to get [ready for] September 14, when the bond markets reopened and there was one situation that our Technology Department had that they spent more time on than anything else. . . . It was getting into the systems, [figuring out] the IDs of the systems because so many people had died and the people that knew how to get into those systems and who knew the backup . . . and the second emergency guy were all gone. The way that they got into those systems? They sat around the group, they talked about where they went on vacation, what their kids' names were, what their wives' names were, what their dogs' names were,

> ### "What Made the Difference Was a Kind of High-Touch, Low-Tech Solution"
>
> Simple human contact is something we shouldn't design out of the solutions at all. What made the difference . . . for every company that came back successfully [was] that kind of touch, high-touch, low-tech solution.
>
> An overwhelming message is how resilient, creative, innovative people are in a crisis, and that's the hardest thing to measure.
>
> The organizations that had a culture of dispersed employees . . . functioned a lot better during the emergency than those that were traditionally organized.
>
> Vendors and suppliers in our information technology areas, in communications, and across the board really were absolutely outstanding. It's very easy to criticize these people routinely. They're the brunt of bad jokes. It's sort of corporate yucks to go around and make fun of the infrastructure and who supplies it. But in this case it was exceedingly generous. I can't begin to tell how much we could count on the relationships we had with vendors, consultants, and clients. People were willing to do whatever they had to do to reconnect to us and whether that meant working around the clock so that we could be open on the fourteenth, they were there. You know, those relationships can never be replaced with anything.

you know, every imaginable thing about their personal life. And the fact that we knew things about their personal life to break into those IDs and into the systems to be able to get the technology up and running before the bond market opened, I think [that] is probably the number one connection between technology, communication, and sociology.

The problem this team of coworkers solved was not strictly a technical problem—their computing infrastructure was technically functional. Nor was it strictly a human problem—there were plenty of these to be sure, for the firm's human loss was staggering. This problem was about the interface between people and their technology. There was a breakdown at a key point of this interface, the use of passwords to regulate human command and control of the technical systems.

Interface is not a boundary, separating us from our technology, but a border that is usually traversed transparently in our practices of using technology to mediate our social behavior. Normally, an interface is working best when we are not aware of it. Once basic skills and tasks are sedimented in muscle memory and cognitive models, we are mainly aware of our social objectives rather than all the button pressing we have to do to manage them. When interfaces break down, we notice them and see how they are working. For these bond market traders, the interface—the passwords that were lost with the colleagues they now mourned—was sociotechnical. And what saved the day, and perhaps the firm, was how well they knew each other. To get access to the system codes, the team relied on noncodified personal knowledge.[48]

The account of the bond market trading firm also highlights the role of redundancy in preparing for crisis. Like the speed and volume of information in the trading room, redundancy—typically understood as system backups—is necessary but not sufficient. This type of *replicative redundancy*, in which critical systems are backed up or replicated, conforms to the dominant style of risk management, in which future states of the world can be calculated and assigned some probabilistic value. Having adopted a strategy of concurrent computing after the 1993 bombing of the World Trade Center's underground garage, the bond-trading firm had replicated its critical systems. But replicative redundancy in planning for situations of calculable risk, as we saw for this firm, is not sufficient to deal with situations of uncertainty that even the best plans cannot anticipate. One contingency planner at our December 2001 meeting eloquently captured the distinctive character of extraordinary crisis:

> You know that line from Tolstoy that goes something like "All
> happy families are the same, but unhappy families are uniquely
> miserable." It's the same for us. Every normal day is like every
> other, but every really big crisis is unique. That's why you can't just
> plan for crises.

In a unique crisis, one cannot know in advance what resources one will need, or even know in advance what might be a resource. Thus, in addition to replicative redundancy, our research also suggests the importance of *generative redundancy* in response to crisis. This redundancy differs from slack, which is merely more of the same resource. Generative redundancy is a "redundancy" of difference. And it is for this reason that it can be generative. In situations of radical uncertainty, diversity of ties and diversity of means increase the likelihood that interaction will yield creative solutions. Lateral ties that cut across official vertical structures—such as knowing your coworkers' home phone numbers or addresses—are redundant but not simply replicative. Organizations that tolerate more than one

---

[48] This knowledge, moreover, had not been acquired by the firm by prying into the personal lives of the employees and entering it into some central database.

way of doing things are similarly willing to sacrifice some allocative efficiency in the short run in the interest of dynamic adaptability. These redundancies contributed to emergent self-organization when corporate hierarchy was catastrophically disrupted, and they allowed for the flexible redefinition of roles and resources in a time of crisis.

In the conventional view, there exists a trade-off between preparedness and competitiveness. Replicative redundancy is a necessary business practice, but it is a pure cost that does not in normal times contribute to organizational competitiveness. This view of preparedness typically gives advantage to companies that are larger and more bureaucratic. Generative redundancy, on the other hand, might contribute to preparedness *and* daily competitiveness. Heterarchical structures that help at times of crisis can facilitate innovativeness at all times.

Resourceful Recognition

A sociotechnical network is far more complex than the simple sum of social and technical ties. The severance of technical ties, for example, cannot automatically be fixed by new social ones. This became clear in the sign "20th Floor, Equities" placed on the wall, and its insistence in reproducing the old trading floor structure of International Securities embodied in that designation. The sign not only reminded traders that the equities trading room was located between risk management and fixed income; it also familiarized the unfamiliar. According to Callon, a sociotechnical network "is not connecting identities which are already there, but a network that configures ontologies. The agents, their dimensions and what they are and do, all depend on the morphology of the relations in which they are involved."[49]

After the attack, the International Securities traders were left wondering whether their firm would continue to exist, whether the trading room would operate again, what they should do, and even who they were. The basement turned those survivors back into traders. To the question of *who am I?* the computers, desks, and open-plan space answered *a trader.* To the question of *what should I do?* the "20th Floor" sign answered, *begin to trade with whatever resources you can scramble together.*

Faced with broken and missing technologies, the traders recombined old and new tools to start trading again. At the agency trading desk, for example, junior traders manually performed operations—such as booking, registering, and breaking up trades—that would have been automated

---

[49] Callon, "Embeddedness of Economic Markets."

just days earlier in the World Financial Center. With these manual operations effectively taking them back to the trading technologies of five years earlier, most of the younger traders (some with PhDs in physics) quickly had to learn from older hands familiar with manually writing up tickets.

At first, the traders were using the most primitive modem connections. Within a week they got access to Bloomberg data. But the statistical arbitrage traders, for whom "the future" is just seconds away, were still stymied. "I can't trade with historical data," complained one stat arb trader, referring to the fact that Bloomberg data were fifteen minutes behind the New York Stock Exchange. Nonetheless, some statistical arbitrage traders made up for the lack of direct data from the NYSE by adjusting their work practices. Instead of monitoring their trading robots, they became active participants in the price mechanism. "Welcome to cut and paste land," one stat arb said to us by way of greeting as we approached his makeshift desk in New Jersey. By "cut and paste" he referred dismissively to his nonstop activity, transporting orders from the e-mail system to the trading engine by force of pointing and clicking his mouse. He labored in this fashion because the lack of price feed in the Unix system forced him to manually connect one interface to the other. As a result, he said, "I have very little time left to do anything else" such as monitoring the market and the speed of the price feeds, his typical job.

Eventually the makeshift trading room got a T1 line with high-speed connection to the NYSE. But insufficient connectivity gave rise to a situation in which not all traders had enough bandwidth to trade simultaneously. When, for example, the index arbitrage desk was active, other desks could not trade. Even though this pitted the bonuses of index arbitrageurs against those of other desks, the rest of the traders in the room did not let the bottleneck escalate into conflict among desks. The episode is an example of another, equally important trait of bricolage: tolerance with a less than ideal situation.

What is the lesson from the makeshift trading room for the organization of responsiveness? Responsiveness, the experience of these traders suggests, is a combination of anticipation and improvisation. The bank had a space, but it was far from perfect. Yet the traders managed to be trading in it from day one. How? By engaging in bricolage. The bank had a warehouse, with square feet and little else. In that square footage the traders saw a resource—and used it to arrange the desks in almost the same configuration as in their former trading room and to improvise technically with remarkable success to talk to other banks, enter orders, and connect to the market.

Like good bricoleurs, the traders did not let imperfection stand in the way of action. In addition to recombining old and new tools, some traders became clerks, others manual operators, and others became roommates of bandwidth, sharing cable to the NYSE. These changes in role status did not detract from their status as traders; in fact, this was how they reaffirmed their status as traders.[50] Sometimes things have to change to remain the same. Their identity as trader was inscribed on their business cards. But what do traders do? They trade. By repositioning themselves in the damaged sociotechnical networks, the traders found ways to trade. Innovation is not having new resources to accomplish new tasks but recognizing configurations that others would not see as resources. Responsiveness is grounded in this resourceful recognition.

[50] For a more elaborated account of the crises of identity facing the traders at International Securities, see Daniel Beunza and David Stark, "Resolving Identities: Successive Crises in a Trading Room after 9/11," 2005. The trading room faced not one crisis—the immediate aftermath of September 11—but many, including a crisis that threatened the integrity of the firm when the merger arbitrage unit left the New Jersey facility and moved to midtown Manhattan. We demonstrate that a given crisis was resolved by restoring identities but that identities, once restored, redefined the situation and led to new crisis. That is, the successive waves of crisis were produced by each success in managing crisis.

5

From Field Research to the Field of Research

In the three ethnographic chapters that comprise the empirical core of this book, I observed the building of tools in mechanical engineering, software engineering, and financial engineering. I now turn attention to the analytic tools for understanding the social processes that underlie economic activity in organizations. From my field research I return to my field of research, offering several lines of inquiry for economic sociology as it faces new challenges in the turbulent twenty-first century.

Economic sociology is arguably the newest and the oldest field in sociology. Only recently recognized by the discipline as a subfield,[1] economic sociology can claim to be as old as the discipline itself. Each of the founding figures of sociology (e.g., Marx, Weber, Durkheim, Simmel) made important contributions to the study of economic life. Thus, when the field reemerged in the mid-1980s, it did so with a wealth of concepts, great legitimacy resting on reference to the founding figures, and, nearly immediately, a throng of adherents.[2]

Together with its rapid institutionalization, the "new economic sociology" also emerged with the lines of its major theoretical approaches already clearly drawn. Institutional analysis, network analysis, and organizational ecology are the three major contending perspectives,[3] each with its own methodologies and canonical texts. This combination of new and old allows for conservation of past successes but also poses a problem of its own: how to avoid being trapped in already well-established formulations of problems in the context of already sharply delineated approaches. Posed as caricature, is the "new economic sociology" already prematurely aged? Less polemically, how can economic sociology avoid becoming locked into its early successes?

[1] Economic sociology was formally recognized as a section of the American Sociological Association in 2001.

[2] Reflecting this enormous legitimacy, economic sociology, unlike many other new subfields, did not need to launch niche journals, establish a footing, and then attempt to break into the mainstream. From inception, the established journals of the discipline were open to its contributors. Many of its formative papers, for example, were published in the *American Journal of Sociology* and the *American Sociological Review*.

[3] Rational choice might once have seemed a contender. But that perspective, which is at odds with a discipline whose irreducible unit is not the rational individual but a relation, has waned over the past decade.

While recognizing the possibilities for lock-in, I also recognize the possibilities for renewed vibrancy, especially where new lines of research are being created through friction at the overlap of contending approaches. In building on the institutionalists, organizational ecologists, and network analysts, the next steps in the development of the field are likely to occur through recombinations of aspects of each of these perspectives. Such recombinant sociology might be startling to some, so well entrenched are the three camps in economic sociology. But the field's potential lies as much in exploiting the friction at the overlap among these perspectives as in accumulating further work along well-grooved lines within each of the traditions.

By so doing, we can build on the advances of network analytic, organizational ecology, and institutionalist concepts, retaining their analytic insights while amplifying or modifying them to explore new problems. We can, for example, build on network analytic insights that the structure of social relations shapes behavior—but modify them by noting that the "social" comprises not only human agents but also instruments, artifacts, and concepts. Sociology, as the science of association, then, would not only study the associations of humans to humans; and network analysis would be enriched by exploring the associations among the persons, artifacts, and concepts that populate the social.[4] Viewed in such network terms, calculation is seen as socially distributed across a network of humans and their nonhuman artifacts in distinctive calculative spaces.

We can build on the organizational ecologists' insights about the importance of organizational diversity—but modify them by suggesting that, if diversity enhances adaptability at the level of a social system, diversity also matters for adaptability at the organizational level. That is, we shift from the ecologists' diversity of organizations to the organization of diversity. In so doing, the role of diversity also shifts from the ecologists' emphasis on diversity as important in selection to an emphasis on diversity as important in mutation. The generative role of diversity is thereby highlighted. The organization of diverse, even rivaling, performance criteria and evaluative principles contributes to adaptability by preserving a more diverse organizational "gene pool," increasing the likelihood of possibly fruitful recombinations in times of unpredictable change.

We can build on the institutionalists' insights about the importance of cognition and their refusal to reduce action to "choice" or "decision." By focusing on cultural categories as resources for action, the institutionalists shatter the old binaries of means versus ends and of constraint versus

[4] Bruno Latour, *Reassembling the Social*, 2005.

choice, replacing this dichotomy with the notion of practical action. The challenge is to retain the insight that embodied practical action should not be reduced to choice or decision without reducing cognition to unreflective activity. As the organizational environment is changing from the relatively stabilized institutional environment of the mid to latter part of the twentieth century to a much more turbulent environment sparked by accelerating technological change, actors in organizations are aware that what is taken for granted today can be out-of-date tomorrow. Cognizant that they cannot take their knowledge for granted, they look for practices to break the grip of habit. In so doing, they challenge us to explore the organizational groundings for a reflexive cognition. Whereas organizations relying on institutionalized routines were preoccupied with the elaboration of classificatory codes to cope with the problem of legitimation, today's organizations are preoccupied with the social technologies of search to cope with the problem of recognizing opportunities. Whereas unreflective activity was the property of institutions, we can turn to study reflexive cognition in the troubling situations that generate it.

In the following sections, I explore several lines of inquiry. My task is emphatically not to create a new map of the field, demarcate new boundaries, and name new hybrids. Such an exercise would be antithetical to the spirit of loosening up the field. If we need new maps, they should be ones with *terrae incognitae,* nether zones of an entirely different kind of risk and of opportunity for exploring problems not yet known and not already categorized. That is the challenge for the next generation of economic sociologists.

In the meantime, because, like the field, I am already too ensconced in its debates, I adopt a narrative of retrospection and projection,[5] examining where the field has been and pointing to developments that promise fresh approaches attuned to the analytical challenges of a changing world. If I maintain that, for organizations, possibilities for innovative recombinations arise from reflexivity produced by the friction of contending

[5] This narrative of retrospection and projection echoes the rhetorical strategy of "from … to …" used by DiMaggio and Powell in their formative statement for the new institutionalism: "Placed in the context of the transformation in the sociological theory of action we have described, the differences between the old and new institutionalisms in organizational analysis become understandable. The shifts in theoretical focus from object-relations to cognitive theory, from cathexis to ontological anxiety, from discursive to practical reason, from internalization to imitation, from commitment to ethnomethodological trust, from sanctioning to ad hocing, from norms to scripts and schemas, from values to accounts, from consistency and integration to loose coupling, and from roles and routines have quite naturally altered the questions that students of organization have asked and the kinds of answers they have offered." Paul J. DiMaggio and Walter W. Powell, "Introduction," in *The New Institutionalism in Organizational Analysis,* 1991, pp. 26–27.

principles, the same holds for my views on developments in my own field. Drawing on lessons of my own research, I argue that we should seek new insights and analytical leverage at the points of contestation between established schools of thought. It was by maintaining a position of insider/outsider[6] that I was free to simultaneously engage institutionalism, network analysis, and organizational ecology, finding fertile ground for new concepts where the competing schools overlapped. Therefore, in pointing out new directions for economic sociology and organizational analysis, I highlight areas promising cross-fertilization.

From Classification to Search

The "new institutionalism" in economic and organizational sociology has been preoccupied with classifications from the time of its founding statement, in which John Meyer and Brian Rowan observed that "institutionalized rules are classifications built into society as reciprocated typification and interpretation."[7] For Meyer and Rowan, rationalized formal structures are more defining of modern society than markets or technology. "Postindustrial society," they write, is "the society dominated by rational organization even more than by the forces of production" (p. 345). The classificatory codes of institutionalized rules, they argue, particularly come into play in activities where output cannot be easily evaluated (such as schools, R & D units, or the service departments of corporations). In these cases, institutionalized classificatory rules increasingly serve as the operative performance criteria. The legitimacy of rationalized formal structures is the alternative to the efficiency criteria of the market. The coexistence of multiple performance criteria within organizations is an uneasy one: "Categorical rules conflict with the logic of efficiency" (p. 355).

To resolve conflicts between rules and efficiency, Meyer and Rowan observe that organizations buffer, or in their words "decouple," actual prac-

---

[6] My work draws on institutionalism, network analysis, and organizational ecology, borrowing from each while belonging to none. From a position of insider/outsider, my work exists in and is the product of multiple crosscutting networks: an ethnographer who coauthors studies using network analysis; a network analyst who coauthored a paper advocating institutional analysis; and an institutionalist who coedited a collection drawing on organizational ecology for evolutionary models of systemic transformation. See, respectively, David Stark and Balazs Vedres, "Social Times of Network Spaces: Network Sequences and Foreign Investment in Hungary," 2006; David Stark and Victor Nee, "Toward an Institutional Analysis of State Socialism," 1989; and Gernot Grabher and David Stark, "Organizing Diversity: Evolutionary Theory, Network Analysis, and the Postsocialist Transformations," 1997.

[7] John W. Meyer and Brian Rowan, "Institutionalized Organization: Formal Structure as Myth and Ceremony," 1977, p. 341.

tices from formalized governance. Where conformity to institutionalized rules is ritualized or "ceremonial," technical interdependencies can be worked out under the radar. But, however buffered or decoupled, ceremonial rules cannot be ignored. The legitimation of ceremonial conformity to formalized codes matters for the success and survival of organizations: "Thus, organizational success depends on factors other than efficient coordination and control of productive activities . . . the survival of some organization depends more on the ceremonial demands of highly institutionalized environments" (pp. 352–353).

Two elements in this founding statement of institutional analysis are most telling. First, in observing the entanglement of multiple performance criteria, Meyer and Rowan explicitly recognize that organizations are the sites of competing and coexisting principles of value. Alongside market assessments of worth, they identify "ceremonial criteria of worth" (p. 351). Second, the principle guiding the alternative ordering of value operates according to a classificatory logic. Institutionalized formal structures are rational because they are "classificatory," "categorical," and "codified": "New and extant domains of activity are codified in institutionalized programs, professions, or techniques, and organizations incorporate the packaged codes" (p. 344).

This founding statement was enormously generative, providing inspiration to Paul DiMaggio and Walter Powell's article on organizational isomorphism,[8] in which they demonstrated how adoption of institutionalized rules tends to reduce variety as it operates across organizations to override diversity in local environments.[9] If Meyer and Rowan provided the fuel, DiMaggio and Powell's article was the booster rocket that launched the new institutionalism in sociology. Whether in work on how institutions shape organizations (through, for example, coercive or mimetic isomorphism) or in research inspired by Neil Fligstein's work on how institutions

---

[8] Paul J. DiMaggio and Walter W. Powell, "The Iron Cage Revisited: Institutional Isomorphism and Collective Rationality in Organizational Fields," 1983.

[9] DiMaggio and Powell's "Iron Cage" article also stimulated organizational ecologists, who developed the notion that selection mechanisms could operate with more than one performance criterion. The idea that success could depend, in part, on legitimacy challenged conventional ways of thinking about efficiency: "Because organizations compete among themselves for scarce resources, membership, and legitimacy, efficiency in mobilizing each of these affects survival chances. In this sense, organizations face efficiency tests. However, the efficiency testing assumed in current ecological theory is much more complicated than simple testing for technical efficiency in producing some product or service. Efficiency in mobilizing resources or in currying political favor may often be more decisive in affecting survival chances than narrow technical efficiency." Michael T. Hannan, "Uncertainty, Diversity, and Organizational Change," 1986, pp. 90–91.

shape markets,[10] the emphasis everywhere was on rules, codes, and classifications. While economists have prices and production functions, sociologists have categories and systems of classification.

In this approach, institutionalization is, above all, institutionalization of bureaucratic rationality. Organizations, for example, are embedded in rationalized systems of rules classifying job categories. Markets are embedded in regulatory frameworks, accounting codes, and technical standards—each formally elaborated, bureaucratically rationalized, and hence governed by a classificatory logic delineating the categories of persons, objects, and practices and demarcating boundaries of eligibility and liability. By characterizing practical action as the unreflective enactment of classificatory scripts, sociological institutionalism reduced strategic action to rule making: "Strategic action is the attempt by social actors to create and maintain stable social worlds (i.e., organizational fields). This involves the creation of rules to which disparate groups can adhere."[11]

Whereas the old institutionalism was based on "values, norms, attitudes," the new institutionalism was about "classifications, routines, scripts, schema," noted DiMaggio and Powell in the introduction to their important collection titled *The New Institutionalism in Organizational Analysis*.[12] Influential because of the high quality of the contributions, the collection deserved its prominence also because it marked the high-water point of what we can now see as the second wave of bureaucratization. Whereas the first, as DiMaggio and Powell note in the opening paragraphs of "The Iron Cage Revisited," involved the creation of large corporate and state bureaucracies, the second involved the rationalization[13] of the organizational environment and an attending refinement of the classificatory regulation of its internal processes.[14]

Classification is the key social process of bureaucracy. Within the field of business organizations, think of the early scientific managers' classifications of tasks and the analysis of their component motions. At the level of national administration, consider the importance of census categories

---

[10] Neil Fligstein, *The Architecture of Markets: An Economic Sociology of Capitalist Societies*, 2001.

[11] Neil Fligstein, "Social Skill and Institutional Theory," 1997, p. 398.

[12] DiMaggio and Powell, "Introduction," p. 13.

[13] Bureaucratized conventions are rationalized in a dual sense of the word. Their codification is standardized, and their rationale (however much misrecognizing actual intentions and effects) is made explicit. On codification and formalization see especially Pierre Bourdieu, "Habitus, Code, et Codification," 1986.

[14] The century's turn, however, marked a new set of processes that are not expressed as bureaucratic rationalization. For a discussion of these changes, see essays in Paul DiMaggio, ed., *The Twenty-First-Century Firm: Changing Economic Organization in International Perspective*, 2001.

for the bureaucratic classification of populations as well as the creation of systems of accounts to represent national economies.[15] At the supranational level, observe the proliferation of taxonomies of products within the European Union;[16] and at the global level, think of the international classifications of disease and their consequences for the organization of medicine.[17]

Processes of classification are and will remain an important feature of modern society and contemporary organizations. But there are indications that such a classificatory logic is giving way to—certainly being augmented by—an alternative logic. Whereas the rationality of hierarchy is organized around processes of classification, emerging heterarchical forms are organized around processes of search. Like classification, search is a fundamental human activity. And just as institutionalism identified the spread of rationalized classificatory codes as an important development in the interorganizational environment of the latter part of the twentieth century, so transformations in the organizing logic of search are an important feature of the broad social field in the twenty-first. In arguing that the study of search is a necessary counterpart to the study of classifications, I begin with search technologies, briefly explore the role of search in organizations, and then reexamine the logic of search.

If classification is the key social process of rational bureaucracy, the file and the filing cabinet are its paradigmatic technologies.[18] How to be organized? Organize your files—classify, categorize, sort, file. Whereas the filing cabinet is the principle technology of bureaucratic rationalization, the search engine is the paradigmatic technology of our era. Among the many new information technologies that are reshaping work and daily life, perhaps none is more transformative than the new technologies of search. A filing cabinet, of course, is also a technology that facilitates a kind of search, a search based on knowledge of its system of classification; and, in the early years of the digital age, the first search engines were essentially based on a similar logic of filing, one familiar to those of us who are old enough to remember when accessing a document on one's PC required remembering in which directory it was stored. Yahoo and its early

[15] Alain Desrosières, "Official Statistics and Business," 1994; and Alain Desrosières, *The Politics of Large Numbers: A History of Statistical Reasoning*, 1998.

[16] On Europeanization as a kind of normalization—a process of meeting norms and standards numbering in the tens of thousands—see László Bruszt and David Stark, "Who Counts? Supranational Norms and Societal Needs," 2003.

[17] Geoffrey Bowker and Susan Leigh Star, "Knowledge and Infrastructure in International Information Management: Problems of Classification and Coding," 1994.

[18] JoAnne Yates, *Control Through Communication: The Rise of System in American Management*, 1989.

competitors, for example, hired human editors who categorized websites to build and maintain directories.

Things changed when the founders of Google reorganized search from a classificatory to a network logic. The key step was a shift to a new measure of authority. By what criterion, they wondered, can we direct the user to an authoritative site? Why not use the nonhierarchical, network structure of the Web, connections through hyperlinks, as the generator of authority? Instead of relying on hired staff to make authoritative judgments, build on the decisions of literally millions of creators of websites who point to other websites. Dispense with an elaborate system of classification. Instead, give every website a "Google rank score" based on the weighted number of websites that link to it (with the pointing sites being more highly weighted to the extent that they have more sites linking to them). In place of a hierarchical structure based on classificatory principles, build a heterarchical structure based on horizontal authority and network principles.

Search engines organized around *collaborative filtering* similarly use network principles. If you have used a recommender system—"people who bought (or highly rated) this book also bought . . ."—you are familiar with collaborative filtering even if you have never heard the term.[19] Here, too, the key idea is that the search engine, in this case a recommender system, does not need to classify your tastes (e.g., country and western vs. classical in music, thrillers vs. comedies in film). It just needs to match your past choices (purchases, rankings) to those of other users who have made similar, though not identical, choices. Emphatically, collaborative filtering does not build profiles of users based on preexisting, or even emergent, categories. Instead it builds user profiles from network ties. But whereas most social network analysts in sociology conceive of networks as ties between persons, here the network analysis builds on ties between persons and things.

These new social technologies exploit, radically in recombination, the three basic activities of life on the Web: *search, link, interact*. With a telephone and a phone directory, of course, I can search (find the number), link (place the call), and interact (order a backpack for my son). But I cannot search based on the structure of links; neither can I interact based on the structure of searches nor link based on the structure of interactions.

[19] Malcolm Gladwell presents a good introduction to collaborative filtering in "The Science of the Sleeper," 1999. For useful technical descriptions, see Upendra Shardanand and Pattie Maes, "Social Information Filtering: Algorithms for Automating Word of Mouth," 1995; and Jonathan L. Herlocker, "Algorithmic Framework for Performing Collaborative Filtering," 1999.

The new information technologies, however, work precisely through these recombinatorics.

These new applications, moreover, move well beyond frivolous cases such as looking for a movie. Informatics researchers in the digital library at the Los Alamos Laboratory, for example, have constructed an adaptive recommendation system that mines enormous scientific databases (containing over three million records). Luis Rocha's *TalkMine* is a hybrid Collective/Structural/Content system that fully exploits the recombinatorics of search, link, and interact.[20] Like other innovative researchers in informatics, Rocha is attempting to correct the key deficiency of programs that model search as *information retrieval*, that is, the assumption that the existing, often static, structure of an information resource contains all the relevant knowledge to be discovered. But knowledge, especially in fast-breaking fields, is evolving and, as such, new categories and new associations are emerging. Once the vast databases are seen as an associative knowledge structure, the goal is to make them accessible as evolving knowledge repositories. The means is to build on the ways in which users interact with information resources to infer emerging linguistic categories.

Rocha's program is explicitly hybrid. In network terms, it examines the semantic properties of information resources (networks, for example, of the relationship between keywords and other linguistic categories in and across documents). But it uses a set structure called "evidence sets," an extension of fuzzy logic, to model linguistic categories.[21] In network terms, it also finds patterns of association among documents by following ties among information resources created by users. But, unlike collaborative filtering, this system of "collective recommendation" tracks the paths users follow in the structure of information as they retrieve documents. The more some sets of documents tend to be retrieved together in paths followed by different users, the closer they become in the structure of the information resource. With this hybridity, the system counteracts some of the shortcomings of each of its component elements.[22]

TalkMine works by conceptualizing the interactions between users and information resources (and indirectly to other users) as an extended

[20] Luis M. Rocha, "Adaptive Webs for Heterarchies with Diverse Communities of Users," 2001.

[21] For details see Luis M. Rocha, "Evidence Sets and Contextual Genetic Algorithms: Exploring Uncertainty, Context and Embodiment in Cognitive and Biological Systems," 1999.

[22] It corrects, notably, the shortcoming of purely collective approaches in which positive feedback can lead to an excessive adaptation to the interests of the majority of users, thus reducing the diversity of knowledge by recommending only the most retrieved documents in a given area as, for example, in the "best of" lists found at websites such as Amazon.

conversation. New categories emerge by treating users themselves as information resources with their own specific contexts defined by their own information proximity. That is, users make new associations as they search for, link to, and interact with knowledge forms. Simplifying here: a user can enter a search term that is not stored as a keyword category in any location in the system. Let's assume, for example, that the keyword *heterarchy* does not initially exist in the Philosophy of Social Science library. After I conduct this search a number of times, the keyword *heterarchy* is created in the library, even though it does not contain any document about this topic. As I modify my search by including other keywords and retrieving documents that are appropriate for my local context, the keyword *heterarchy* becomes associated with *distributed intelligence, diversity, recombination, adaptability,* and so on. As other users make similar associations, the new category is tagged to documents whose authors did not include it as a keyword. From that point on, a user who enters *distributed intelligence* might find some documents also tagged with *heterarchy*; and a user who enters *heterarchy* might be directed to papers at the Santa Fe Institute and to research by scholars in widely disparate fields.

Note that in the shift to search we have not abandoned the concept of "category" but have highlighted a different aspect. The notion of category here refers to temporary constructs rather than to already-stabilized taken-for-granteds. A category is temporarily constructed by integrating knowledge from several information resources and the interests of users expressed in the interactive process.[23] As a temporary container of knowledge, it resembles transient, context-dependent knowledge arrangements characterized by Andy Clark as "on the hoof" category constructions.[24] Such "short-term categories bridge together a number of possibly highly unrelated contexts, which in turn creates new associations in the individual information resources that would never occur with their own limited context."[25]

Why should the study of search play a significant role in economic and organizational sociology? I present four reasons, in ascending order of importance. First, search has become big business. Although Amazon.com,

[23] "In this sense, in human cognition, categories are seen as linguistic constructs used to store temporary associations built up from the integration of knowledge from several neural subnetworks. The categorization process, driven by language and conversation, serves to bridge together several distributed neural networks, associating tokens of knowledge that would not otherwise be associated in the individual networks." (Rocha, "Adaptive Webs," p. 18).

[24] Andy Clark, *Associative Engines: Connectionism, Concepts, and Representational Change,* 1993; and Andy Clark, "Leadership and Influence: The Manager as Coach, Nanny, and Artificial DNA," 1999.

[25] Rocha, "Adaptive Webs," p. 25.

as the breakthrough in online retail, was the iconic firm in the first wave of the Internet boom, Google is the paradigmatic firm in our era, transforming how we work, shop, and even how we locate ourselves in social and physical space. We should not chase the fashionable, but search is not a fad. As a major business model, it demands our attention.

Second, collaborative filtering and its successor programs are changing the strategy of marketing from demographic categories to network properties. Important contributions to the former strategy were made by variable-based methods in sociology, through their preoccupation with demographic categories (age, sex, race, education, income, census tracts, etc.) and social classifications of taste cross-categorized with these. Marketing will never dispense with categories. A product so novel that it could not be recognized as belonging to, or at least overlapping with, some category of products and persons could never be sold. But the new social networking sites already suggest a new strategy of emergent classification. They mark a shift to a new economy in which value is not embedded in social relations but in which social relations are a primary source of value. In place of defining a product and designing a brand, foster a network and let the users tag the products. Knowledge of network properties is a valuable investment, in short, a kind of property. When social relations are the valuable property, the network, as much or perhaps even more so than the products, defines the (evolving) brand. To the extent that economic sociology has an applied arm, social network analysis is providing the methods for this growing strategy.

Third, if firms are shifting from classificatory to network marketing, they are also shifting from classification to search in their internal processes. As more work is organized in the temporary project form, job categories become less salient in allocating and rewarding work.[26] Because job categories do not disappear overnight, we see a proliferation of new, frequently hybrid, titles. My favorite, which we encountered among the new-media workers in chapter 3, is "technology evangelist." More importantly, when organizations were bureaucratically organized along lines of hierarchical reporting, access to knowledge could, indeed, be represented as "information retrieval." But this changes when the ability of the firm to be competitive (or for the nonprofit, effective) in adapting to and shaping its environment rests in a sustained capacity to generate a recombination of knowledge across units. Products and parts can be categorized, jobs can be classified, but knowledge, especially that at the forefront of a field,

---

[26] Thomas Lemieux, W. Bentley MacLeod, and Daniel Parent, "Performance Pay and Wage Inequality," 2007.

resists classification. Or, perhaps more accurately, we should say that organizations that want to stay ahead in their field need to resist the tendency to rely on codified (and hence, easily replicated) knowledge.[27]

As a symptom of this change, when the firm or the nonprofit is conceived of as a "knowledge organization," we find an increasingly fearsome preoccupation with knowledge management. Much of this knowledge management is about search—and many organizations have adopted systems similar to that developed by Luis Rocha for the Los Alamos Laboratory. Critical to these systems is the notion of emergent categorization.[28] Some of these schemes are faddish, as for example in the major international consulting firms where there is a premium on new *terms*, behind which there might or might not be actual new *concepts*. And many practitioners complain that the work of metatagging is an additional burden on their time. Nonetheless, at the base of these efforts at knowledge management is the very serious problem of the increasing complexity of knowledge in organizations. As Noshir Contractor argues, the more knowledge is decentralized and distributed across persons, practices, documents, and information infrastructure, the question is not simply "who knows whom?" or "who knows what?" but "who knows who knows what?"[29] Better search engines can contribute, but they cannot themselves solve the problem: How does the organization know what it knows?[30]

Fourth, and most important, search is central to the recasting of economic sociology because it is the process that best exemplifies the challenges of contemporary organization. "Organizational structure," writes complexity theorist Michael Cohen, "is a search heuristic." Cohen further argues that search is particularly central when an organization confronts a difficult environment: "Combinatorial complexity makes the design of search processes a crucially important activity."[31]

As I argued in the opening pages and throughout this book, the most critical searches for organizations are the kinds that cannot be powered by search engines. In genuine explorations of the unknown, the innovative organization, like Elmore Leonard's detective in *Mr. Paradise*, does not know exactly what it is looking for until it finds it. In fact, as John Dewey

---

[27] Bruce Kogut and Udo Zander, "Knowledge of the Firm, Combinative Capabilities, and the Replication of Technology," 1992.

[28] John H. Clippinger, "Tags: The Power of Labels in Shaping Markets and Organizations," 1999; and Brook Manville, "Complex Adaptive Knowledge Management: A Case from McKinsey & Company," 1999.

[29] Noshir S. Contractor and Peter R. Monge, "Managing Knowledge Networks," 2002.

[30] Pablo Boczkowski, *Digitizing the News: Innovation in Online Newspapers*, 2004.

[31] Michael D. Cohen, "The Power of Parallel Thinking," 1981.

acutely grasped in his work on inquiry, we come to know what we are look-ing for only in the process of transforming the world. In these most inno-vative of inquiries, there is not something out there in the world waiting to be found. David Lane and Robert Maxfield, studying situations in which the structure of the firm's world undergoes cascades of rapid change, state the problem clearly: "The world in which you must act does not sit pas-sively out there waiting to yield up its secrets. Instead, your world is under active construction, you are part of the construction crew—and there is not any blueprint."[32]

Conventionally, we might think that organizations know what they are looking for: profit, value, opportunities. But no organization can find profit, value, or opportunity in the abstract. As we saw in the trading room examined in chapter 4, no trader ever made a profit on an abstract op-portunity. In fact, tales of abstract opportunities are typically stories about *missed* opportunities. Traders might make associations that are highly ab-stract, but the actual deals must be maddeningly, literally split-secondly, concrete. To be opportunistic, in the positive as opposed to pejorative sense of the term, is to be able to find moments for action that others, who knew what they were looking for, were unable to recognize. The trading room, a setting that at first glance is all about the rapid analysis of infor-mation, is in fact organized to facilitate the kind of interpretive search that makes startling new associations. The new-media start-up in chapter 3 similarly searches for previously unrecognized associations among clients, software programs, users, and business models in a highly uncertain field. In chapter 2 the toolmakers in socialist Hungary would seem to operate in a field that is rigidly fixed, certain, and stultifying. And, at first, they know exactly what they are looking for—recognition of the worth of their craft skills. But, in recognizing an opportunity, they come to recognize new, unexpected, identities.

How can actors and organizations search for unexpected opportunities and recognize them when they find them? The first step is to learn how to unlearn the lessons of early success. It is to this challenge that we turn.

From Diversity of Organizations to the Organization of Diversity

Each evening during their hunting season, the Naskapi Indians of the Lab-rador peninsula determined where they would look for game on the next

---

[32] David Lane and Robert Maxfield, "Strategy under Complexity: Fostering Generative Rela-tionships," 1996, p. 216.

day's hunt by holding a caribou shoulder bone over the fire.[33] Examining the smoke deposits on the caribou bone, a shaman would read out, for the hunting party, the points of orientation of the next day's search. In this way, the Naskapi introduced a randomizing element to confound a short-term rationality that would have concluded that the one best way to find game would be to look again tomorrow where they had found game today. By following the divergent daily maps of smoke on the caribou bone, they avoided locking in to early successes that, while taking them to game in the short run, would have depleted in the long run the caribou stock in that quadrant and reduced the likelihood of successful hunting. By breaking the link between future courses and past successes, the tradition of shoulder-bone reading was an antidote to path dependence in the hunt.

I am not arguing that we should organize search with a roll of the dice. Nonetheless, the lesson from Labrador does nicely express one group's attempt to deal with the counterpart, in that region's ecology, to the nonergonomic QWERTY keyboard.[34] Indeed, studies in evolutionary economics and organizational analysis do suggest that organizations that learn too quickly sacrifice efficiency. Allen and McGlade, for example, use the behavior of Nova Scotia fishermen to illustrate the possible trade-offs of exploiting old certainties and exploring new possibilities.[35] Their model of these fishing fleets divides the fishermen into two classes: the rationalist "Cartesians," who drop their nets only where the fish are known to be biting, and the risk-taking "Stochasts," who seek new schools of fish. In simulations where all the skippers are Stochasts, the fleet is relatively unproductive, because knowledge of where the fish are biting is unutilized; but a purely Cartesian fleet locks onto the "most likely" spot and quickly fishes it out. More efficient are the models that, like the actual behavior of the Nova Scotia fishing fleets, mix Cartesian exploiters and Stochastic explorers.

James March's simulation in "Exploitation and Exploration in Organizational Learning" yields similar results. He finds that groups composed of uniformly quick learners frequently underperform groups with a mix of quick and slow learners. Organizations that learn too quickly veer toward *exploitation* at the expense of *exploration*, thereby locking in to sub-

---

[33] This account is drawn from Karl E. Weick, "Organization Design: Organizations as Self-designing Systems," 1977, p. 45. The notion of a conceptual shift from adaptation to adaptability was initially formulated with Gernot Grabher (see Grabher and Stark, "Organizing Diversity").

[34] W. Brian Arthur, "Competing Technologies, Increasing Returns, and Lock-In by Historical Events," 1989.

[35] Peter M. Allen and J. M. McGlade, "Modeling Complex Human Systems: A Fisheries Example," 1987.

optimal routines and strategies.[36] Scott Page runs similar simulations but modifies some of the parameters. He demonstrates that a pool of problem solvers with less ability but with more diverse perspectives outperforms a pool of more uniformly able problem solvers because the latter quickly find merely local optima. From these simulations and other game theoretic research, Page concludes: "Diversity trumps ability."[37] The purely Cartesian fleet in Allen and McGlade's study, like the organizations of homogeneously smart learners in March's and Page's simulations, illustrate the potential dangers of positive feedback and the pitfalls of tight coupling.[38]

Like infantry officers who instructed drummers to disrupt the cadence of marching soldiers while they were crossing bridges, lest the resonance of uniformly marching feet bring calamity, I draw the lesson that dissonance contributes to organizational learning and economic evolution.

Unlike firms in the stabilized organizational environments assumed by the new institutionalists, organizations in radically destabilized environments cannot limit their search to the institutionally familiar. In fields with unpredictable markets sparked by accelerating technological change, you cannot hunt tomorrow where you found game today. Restated in the language of the new economics of complex adaptive systems,[39] the problem for firms in uncertain environments is that the very mechanisms that foster allocative efficiency might eventually lock development into a path that is inefficient, viewed dynamically. Within this framework, our attention turns from a preoccupation with *adaptation* to a concern with *adaptability*, shifting from the problem of how to improve the immediate "fit" with the environment to the problem of how to reshape organizational

---

[36] James G. March, "Exploration and Exploitation in Organizational Learning," 1991; see also Daniel A. Levinthal and James G. March, "The Myopia of Learning," 1993.

[37] Scott E. Page, *The Difference: How the Power of Diversity Creates Better Groups, Firms, Schools, and Societies*, 2007. Michael Cohen was the first researcher to run simulations demonstrating that, with the proper structure of interaction, organizations are able to get powerful search performance out of weak parts. Cohen, "The Power of Parallel Thinking"; and Michael D. Cohen, "Conflict and Complexity: Goal Diversity and Organizational Search Effectiveness," 1983.

[38] Edwin Hutchins found that more communication is not always better. If all networks are allowed to communicate with others from the outset, dense communication patterns yield confirmation bias as the social group rushes "to the interpretation that is closest to the center of gravity of their predispositions, regardless of the evidence." Restricting the level of early communication across subgroups, then enabling it subsequently, reduces overall confirmation bias as the buffered networks can balance predispositions against the evidence. (Edwin Hutchins, *Cognition in the Wild*, 1995, pp. 292–295.) Clark notes the implications for communication among jurors—too-early communication can dissipate the collective advantage of a jury over an individual decision. (Andy Clark, *Being There: Putting Brain, Body, and World Together Again*, 1997.)

[39] John Holland, "Complex Adaptive Systems," 1992; and W. Brian Arthur, *Increasing Returns and Path Dependence in the Economy*, 1994.

structure to enhance its ability to respond to unpredictable future changes in the environment.[40] The radical lesson that heterarchical organizations put into practice can be posed even more provocatively: strictly speaking, in terms that I elaborate later, they are willing to sacrifice allocative efficiency (adaptation) in the short run for dynamic efficiency (adaptability) over the long haul.

Although the trade-off is not formulated in terms of adaptation *versus* adaptability, sociologists working within the organizational ecology approach are alert to the loss of organizational diversity produced by institutional isomorphism. As Michael Hannan observes, economic systems with a greater variety of organizational forms are more responsive to environmental change:

> Organizational diversity . . . constitutes a repository of solutions to the problem of producing certain sets of collective outcomes. These solutions are embedded in organizational structures and strategies. If so, reductions in organizational diversity imply losses of organized information about how to adapt (produce) to changing environments. Having a range of alternative ways to produce certain goods and services is valuable whenever the future is uncertain. A society that retains only a few organizational forms may thrive for a time. But once the environment changes, such a society faces serious problems until existing organizations can be reshaped or new ones created. A system with greater organizational diversity has a higher probability of having in hand some solution that is satisfactory under changed environmental conditions.[41]

In short, at the societal level, adaptability is promoted by the *diversity of organizations*.

Hannan's insights are useful for understanding an organizational failure of historic proportion—the failure of socialism as an economic system. The structural weakness of the command economy was not only that it famously lacked market selection mechanisms (firms were not allowed to go bankrupt or fail) but also that it placed all its economic resources in one organizational form, the large, state-owned enterprise. In its early stages, this form was remarkably successful in transforming a predominantly agrarian society into an industrial power capable of mass-producing the materiel for industrial-age warfare. But the communist system, imposed on the occupied countries of Eastern Europe precisely at the time of its

---

[40] Gernot Grabher, "Adaptation at the Cost of Adaptability? Restructuring the Eastern German Regional Economy," 1997.

[41] Hannan, "Uncertainty," p. 85.

greatest success, locked in to the state enterprise form as the only legitimate organizational vehicle.[42] While one-party monopoly rule eliminated competition, repressed dissident opinion, and suppressed organizational diversity in the political and public realms,[43] communism not only eliminated market competition but also suppressed the coexistence and competition of organizational forms in the economy. In the subsequent transformation from an industrial to a postindustrial age, the system lacked requisite variety and so was unable to adapt economically, politically, or militarily.

As my example indicates, I agree with the population ecologists that organizational diversity matters at the level of economic systems. Precisely because I agree that this insight is a powerful one, I want to extend it from the societal to the organizational level. As a preliminary exercise, I propose that we reexamine the excerpted passage quoting Hannan above, substituting *firm/organization* where terms or context indicate society/system. The insight remains. Firms, or organizations more generally, with greater diversity in ways of doing things are more likely to have the capacity to adapt when the environment changes.

In moving from the societal to the organizational level, then, we shift from the ecologists' *diversity of organization* to the heterarchical *organization of diversity*.[44] Organizational diversity is most likely to yield its fullest evolutionary potential when different organizational principles coexist in an active rivalry within the firm.

Why does diversity matter at the organizational level? My answer requires that we make one further modification to the ecological frame-

---

[42] The "second economy" of private producers, as we saw in chapter 2, was legitimated only in the waning years of communism. In Hungary, it was illegal in the early 1950s, enjoyed an alegal or "not illegal" status in the 1970s, and was only partially legitimated in 1982. See István R. Gábor, "The Second (Secondary) Economy," 1979.

[43] In institutionalist terms, the Soviet system was coercive isomorphism of unprecedented scale and scope, encompassing nearly every domain of life, business, politics, science, education, sports, media, even community organizations such as garden clubs, associations of stamp collectors, and societies for architectural preservation.

[44] "[T]he sphere of complexity is that of organized diversity, of the organization of diversity" (Edgar Morin, "Complexity," 1974, p. 558). The shift that I am proposing—from considering variation within a population of organizations (characteristic of organizational ecology) to attention to the organization of diversity inside firms—is broadly comparable to the difference between population biology and new work in computational biology on the origins of organization. "In contrast to the traditional approach, a constructive dynamical system specifies the interactions among objects not externally, but rather internally to the objects as a function of their structure.... A self-maintaining system is one which continuously regenerates itself by transformations internal to the system." (Walter Fontana and Leo Buss, "'The Arrival of the Fittest': Toward a Theory of Biological Organization," 1994, p. 3.) For a cogent discussion of the evolution of *variability* and genetic control of genotype-phenotype mapping, see Gunter P. Wagner and Lee Altenberg, "Complex Adaptations and the Evolution of Evolvability," 1996.

work. Recall Hannan's statement that "having a range of alternative ways to produce certain goods and services is valuable" because it increases the "probability of having in hand some solution that is satisfactory." My argument is somewhat different. Diversity matters not because it preserves already-known solutions at hand. Instead, it contributes to adaptability by preserving a more diverse organizational "gene pool," increasing the likelihood of possibly fruitful *recombinations* in times of unpredictable change. Note that this modification considers more radically unexpected environmental change for which there might not be preexisting solutions.

Note, moreover, that this modification, which shifts emphasis from the elements to their recombination, is entirely consistent with evolutionary thinking. It is, however, curiously absent in the population ecology of organizations literature, where we find, despite the (appropriately cautious and always distanced) adoption of biological metaphors, little mention of cross-fertilization, mixing, or recombinations of organizational materials.

Organizational diversity in itself does not make for adaptability. There must be interaction across forms, principles, and cultures to generate new solutions. It is mating that matters. Not entirely in jest, organizational analysis needs more sex. In organizational ecology there are births and deaths but no cross-fertilization. In network analysis we find linking but no real coupling. Institutions reproduce, but there is no mating.

Billie Holiday sang it: "Birds do it / Bees do it / Even educated fleas do it. . . ." Biologists say it: "Novelties come from previously unseen association of old material. To create is to recombine," wrote the great French biologist Francois Jacob. Or, in the words of Santa Fe Institute researcher John Holland, "Recombination plays a key role in the discovery process, generating plausible new rules from parts of tested rules."[45] Mathematicians say it;[46] musicians say it;[47] even educated sociologists say it: "Values mate to change."[48]

Up in Boston . . . (as Billie Holiday would sing), even Harvard economists say it. Working on the "new growth theory" to open up the black

---

[45] Francois Jacob, "Evolution and Tinkering," 1977; Holland, "Complex Adaptive Systems."

[46] Henri Poincaré: "To create consists precisely in not making useless combinations and in making those which are useful and which are only a small minority. Invention is discernment, choice. Among chosen combinations the most fertile will often be those formed of elements drawn from domains which are far apart." (Henri Poincaré, *Foundations of science* [1908] 1982, p. 386.)

[47] Glenn Gould, "Forgery and Imitation in the Creative Process," 1994.

[48] Harrison C. White, "Values Come in Styles, Which Mate to Change," 1993. White similarly observes: "All organizing is the attempted weaving together of bits and hunks of preexisting organization, preexisting not only to disappear into a merged form" (Harrison C. White, *Identity and Control*, 1992, p. 105).

box of technological change in order to model the pace of technological change endogenously, Martin Weitzman introduces

> a production function for new knowledge that depends on new recombinations of old knowledge. The core of the analytical structure is a theory of innovation based on analogy with the development of new cultivated varieties by an agricultural research station. "Recombinant innovation" refers to the way that old ideas can be reconfigured in new ways to make new ideas.[49]

Drawing on Schumpeter's definition of entrepreneurship as "the carrying out of new combinations,"[50] Weitzman argues for "the combinatoric power of a recombinant growth process" (p. 355).

The research of economists Lester and Piore, to which I referred in the opening pages of the introduction, similarly examines how different domains of knowledge are brought together to form something new and original. In this process, they argue that "ambiguity is the critical resource out of which new ideas emerge. . . . The cell phone emerged in the space created by the ambiguity about whether the product was a radio or a telephone; by playing with that ambiguity, the device became something that was different from either of them."[51]

Lester and Piore further observe that radio and telephone technologies each claim a distinct commercial and engineering tradition, with the segment of the radio industry from which cellular technology was derived being particularly distinctive, based on two-way radios mounted in police cars and fire engines. "The cultural differences between radio and telephone engineering were deep rooted."[52] In chapter 3 we saw similar disciplinary differences in the new-media field, as the diverse communities of software programmers, designers, business strategists, information architects, and merchandising specialists each invoked distinctive traditions to validate their particular skills and value orientations.

When I invoke "combinations," I do not mean to evoke the simple mixtures of cookbook recipes (combine the flour, salt, and baking powder). The more they are innovative, the more recombinant processes are likely to be, at least initially, discordant rather than harmonious. If one chooses river metaphors, the terms of merging or confluence are too easy; instead,

---

[49] Martin L. Weitzman, "Recombinant Growth," 1998, p. 332.

[50] "As a rule, the new combinations must draw the necessary means of production from some old combinations . . . development consists primarily in employing existing resources in a different way, in doing new things with them." Joseph A. Schumpeter, *The Theory of Economic Development*, 1934, p. 68.

[51] Richard K. Lester and Michael J. Piore, *Innovation: The Missing Dimension*, 2004, p. 54.

[52] Lester and Piore, *Innovation*, p. 17.

think turbulence and eddies. Even more apt, think collision, certainly friction.

With this latter term, friction, we confront a very different tradition in economics. With the notion of "transaction cost" Oliver Williamson brought the notion of friction into economics. Whereas today, economists—such as Brian Arthur, Martin Weitzman, and others—are conversant with models from biology and biophysics, back in the 1970s Williamson was linking economics back to physics, the discipline on which economics had modeled itself prior to the fascination with cybernetics in the post–World War II era.[53] But whereas friction was a central concept in physics, it held no place in economics. In this, Williamson recognized an opportunity. But if friction, through the concept of transaction costs, became a new concept in economics, it was with reference to a negative phenomenon that actors sought everywhere to reduce.

Economic sociology is reversing the negative valence. Neil Fligstein's work within the institutionalist approach, for example, can be read as introducing a positive value. Fligstein shows that the notion of a market without friction is a fiction—no friction, no markets. Similarly, in the debate on the "transition" from socialism, I questioned the notion of a "smooth" transition, wondering if marching in lockstep to the blueprints of "designer capitalism" was instead an example of too-quick convergence toward confirmation bias, with later political repercussions challenging the institutions of property and markets that were the intended goal of reform.[54] Hagel and Brown also challenge the idea of a "frictionless economy." At the organizational level, they make a positive case for "productive friction" between organizations and among the units within them.[55] The rivalry of evaluative principles that we saw in each of our case studies is an example of such creative friction.

If, with Schumpeter, I consider entrepreneurship as recombination, and I further regard recombinant processes as friction, it is a small step to conceive of entrepreneurship as the organization of friction. Friction cannot occur across a gap. Thus, in contrast to Ronald Burt, who finds entrepreneurial roles in "structural holes" in between otherwise cohesively interacting actors, I find entrepreneurship at the organizational overlap where performance criteria conflict and collide. To overlap, diverse orders of value must coexist on the same domain space. As principles, they are

[53] Philip Mirowski, *Machine Dreams: Economics Becomes a Cyborg Science*, 2001.

[54] David Stark, "Recombinant Property in East European Capitalism," 1996; and David Stark, "Ambiguous Assets for Uncertain Environments: Heterarchy in Postsocialist Firms," 2001.

[55] John Hagel III and John Seely Brown, "Productive Friction: How Difficult Business Partnerships Can Accelerate Innovation," 2005.

relatively independent and coherent, but they cannot be organizationally buffered. To "mate" they must mix it up.

By tolerating, even promoting, ambiguity among multiple performance criteria, entrepreneurship in heterarchical organizations sacrifices allocative efficiency. At any given time, perhaps a case can be made that there is one best way to do things. If so, in strict terms of allocative efficiency, all resources should then be organized within that frame. Allocatively efficient, such an organization would be perfectly adapted to its environment. Unwilling to sacrifice adaptability, the heterarchical organization sacrifices near-term efficiency in the interest of superior ability to redefine resources. Logically, this strategy tolerates some waste—logically, but not irrationally, since it tolerates waste toward the goal of generating wealth. Organizations that must go out and get new resources are less efficient than those that can redefine resources that are at hand but still need to be recognized as such. The problem of such re-cognition is the subject of the next section.

From Unreflective Taken-for-Granteds to Reflexive Cognition

One of the strongest features of the new institutionalism in economic sociology is its grounding in a theory of practical action in which cognition plays a central role. In their definitive statement, DiMaggio and Powell argue that the new institutionalism

> departs from Parsons' preoccupation with the rational, calculative aspect of cognition to focus on preconscious processes and schema as they enter into routine, taken-for-granted behavior (practical activity); and to portray the affective and evaluative dimensions of action as intimately bound up with, and to some extent subordinate to, the cognitive.[56]

Whereas the old institutionalism examined "unanticipated consequences," the new focuses on "unreflective activity" (p. 13).

This stress on a framework that "emphasizes the practical, semiautomatic, non-calculative nature of practical reason" and "re-establishes the centrality of cognition" (p. 24) should be understood as part of a strategy for defining a broad space for an institutionalist economic sociology during a time when "rational actor theory" (RAT) appeared to be making inroads within sociology. The move was a bold, preemptive strike, anticipating the

---

[56] DiMaggio and Powell, "Introduction," p. 22.

ambush at the very moment it was being mobilized: why let the RATs have all the "action"? Let them take *calculation*—so long as institutionalists define the more fundamental, underlying process, *cognition*.

The move was as brilliant as it was bold. DiMaggio, Powell, and their institutionalist colleagues shifted the ground from action as choice to scripts and routines as resources for action. Or, to put it another way, action is about habit as much as or more than about choice.[57] The old binaries of means versus ends and of constraint versus choice fall apart through a focus on resources for action.

But the emphasis on habituated action comes at a price. "Taken-for-granted scripts, rules, and classifications," DiMaggio and Powell argue, "are the stuff of which institutions are made" (p. 15). My problem is not to quarrel with this definition of institutions but to note that, in the process, there is a danger that *cognition* becomes reduced to the "taken-for-granted."[58] The challenge is to retain the insight that action should not be reduced to "choice" or "decision" without reducing cognition to "unreflective activity."

Economic sociology should find a place for reflexive cognition, first, because the economy has changed in the decades intervening since the period when the new institutionalists developed concepts acutely attuned to their times. Scripts, routines, and classifications of cultural taken-for-granteds worked as analytic tools because they worked as the operative recipes for behavior in the relatively stabilized institutional environments of the mid to latter part of the last century. They might still be operative in many sectors today. But I and other researchers find economic actors who are acutely aware that taken-for-granteds are likely to be out-of-date. When foresight horizons are shortened and the structure of their world is changing rapidly, actors cannot take knowledge of their world for granted.[59]

These actors, in a sense, take seriously the sociologists' insight that institutional scripts and organizational routines tend to lock in to unreflective activity. "You're right," they seem to be saying, "my organization is filled with routinized scripts." But, rather than accepting this as their sociological fate, they go on to look for practices to help unlock the grip of habit. Whether or not they learned from us, we can learn from them. In so

[57] In discussing the cognitive turn in social theory, DiMaggio and Powell (pp. 25–26) point especially to Bourdieu's analytic construct of *habitus*, embodied dispositions based on past experiences that provide a system of regulated improvisation. (Pierre Bourdieu, *Outline of a Theory of Practice*, 1977.)

[58] The phrase is striking in its ubiquity, occurring no fewer than nine times in DiMaggio and Powell's text.

[59] Lane and Maxfield, "Strategy under Complexity."

doing, we recognize practices in the economy (as well as in organizations in the public sphere) that we value in academia. As in all the studies that I am citing here, we value excellence because it critically reflects on and thus reshapes how we think about a field. A reflexive sociology recognizes capacities for reflexivity not only within our field but also among the actors we study.

How, then, can we retain a conception of action less as choice and decision and more as embodied, practical activity while opening a space for reflexive cognition? Whereas the new institutionalists took Bourdieu as their starting point, here, as elsewhere, I look to the American pragmatists. For John Dewey, the process of inquiry takes place in indeterminate situations:

> A variety of names serves to characterize indeterminate situations. They are disturbed, troubled, ambiguous, confused, full of conflicting tendencies, obscure, etc. It is the *situation* that has these traits. *We* are doubtful because the situation is inherently doubtful.[60]

Thus, whereas unreflective activity is a property of *institutions*, reflexive cognition must be studied in *situations*.[61] Following Dewey's insight, I adopted ethnography as the method that best allows the researcher access to situations. Moreover, as we moved from the shop floor to the new-media space to the trading room, we increasingly encountered sites that were generating "situations" by design.

The troubling situations of the Hungarian shop floor were the least intentional. They emerged from the fact that the toolmakers were simultaneously players in more than one game. They were employees of the socialist firm, playing with its assessments of value, formulas for overtime, and the compensations of special bonuses. But they were also members of a partnership, using the very same tools and equipment "on the off-hours" within their own system of accounting. Yet even this description parses the two games more sharply in time and space than was, in fact, the case because there were moments, not infrequent, when actors were making moves that were operating in more than one game at once. That the partnership exploited the ambiguity of this situation is the most obvious, but far from the only, example of perplexing situations examined in the ethnography.

Situations were generated in the new-media firm by the fact that the various communities of practice (designers, programmers, business strategists, and others) held divergent principles of evaluation. It was not simply

---

[60] John Dewey, "The Pattern of Inquiry," [1938] 1998, p. 171, emphasis in the original.

[61] Ann Mische and Harrison White, "Between Conversation and Situation: Public Switching Dynamics across Networks," 1998.

that a given community (designers, for example) had distinctive standards for evaluating their own work. Instead, each "discipline" used different performance criteria for assessing the value of the product the firm was constructing. Moreover, evaluative principles could not be neatly buffered into departments, because any given project combined adherents of each of the perspectives; nor could they be compartmentalized in time, because simultaneous (as opposed to sequential) engineering required close collaboration throughout the process. Note that the site generated situations. Emphatically, it was not the case that some manager announced, "we have a situation here," clarified the terms of the dilemma, and then everyone pulled together to come up with a solution. Instead of *responding to situations*, the divergent perspectives *produced situations* that provided opportunities for redefining the product in a fast-changing market. Instead of responding to the market, the new-media firm fostered rivalry of performance criteria to reconfigure new conceptions of the market.

Quick response to changes in their markets would seem to be the defining feature of the trading room. Indeed, speed was of the essence. With the dials on their instrument panels registering in fractions of seconds the delay between their trading engines and the New York Stock Exchange, many of the traders were like fighter pilots flying through the data streams at supersonic speed. Traders were organized in desks, each dedicated to a distinctive evaluative principle, to facilitate the process of quick pattern recognition. But if speed was necessary (and more so in some types of trading than others), it was not the only, nor even the primary, feature of this hedge fund trading.

To stay ahead of the competition, in addition to recognizing patterns that they had already identified, the traders needed to identify new types of associations among the abstracted qualities of the securities they were trading. To call this latter process "recognition" would fail to understand it because, in itself, the term could suggest that the traders recognized something that they had already encountered (as, for example, when you recognize a friend's voice on the telephone).[62] Instead, the process was much more active, in fact, constructivist. The traders were actively making a new type of association. Other than a simple recognition, this was re-cognition. In some situations, moreover, this re-cognition was not asking "what is this *a case of*?" and then relabeling it from one category to another, but was *making a case for* a new type of association. To generate such situations, the trading room was, as we saw, deliberately organized to

---

[62] For an engaging study of recognition, see Dan Sperber and Deirdre Wilson, *Relevance: Communication and Cognition*, 1996.

facilitate interaction across desks with different evaluative principles. The trading room was a cognitive ecology.

Reflexive cognition is this kind of re-cognition. And the cognitive ecologies of heterarchical forms are the generative mechanism. Institutionalization naturalizes the social world: in the unreflective activity of the taken-for-granted, the cognitive order is taken as the natural order of things. The cognitive ecologies of heterarchical forms, by contrast, disturb the cognitive order.

As my ethnographic studies also indicate, reflexive cognition, moreover, is distributed cognition.[63] The kind of cognition that I have in mind is not the isolated thinker who reflects on her situation. It is a collective, collaborative, and sometimes conflictual social process that occurs in a situation. Neither is it some extraordinary, almost heroic, process of getting distance, standing apart, or gazing further ahead. The situation provides the materials for reflexive cognition not because I rise above it but because we mix it up. Not a metanarrative or higher-order representation, reflexive cognition is a practical activity of collective construction.

My notions of the trading room as a cognitive ecology and of the Hungarian shop floor as an ecology of games recall John Padgett and Chris Ansell's masterful study of Renaissance Florence.[64] For Padgett and Ansell, the notion of an "ecology of games"[65] figures as part of their more encompassing concept of "multivocality":

> the fact a) that single actions can be interpreted coherently from multiple perspectives simultaneously, the fact b) that single actions are moves in many games at once, and the fact c) that public and private motivations cannot be parsed. Multivocal action leads to Rorschach blot identities, with all alters constructing their own distinctive attribution of the identity of ego.[66]

In Padgett and Ansell's account, multivocality characterizes one player alone, Cosimo de Medici, who because of his distinctive location in otherwise disconnected networks was able to benefit from the ambiguity of

---

[63] The terms "cognitive ecology" and "distributed cognition" are from Ed Hutchins's *Cognition in the Wild*, an extraordinary study of navigation on a U.S. Navy vessel. On mind as embodied intelligence distributed across a social scaffolding, see especially Andy Clark, *Being There*. For Hutchins and Clark, all cognition is distributed cognition.

[64] John F. Padgett and Christopher K. Ansell, "Robust Action and the Rise of the Medici," 1993.

[65] The term was coined by Norton Long, "The Local Community as an Ecology of Games," 1958.

[66] Padgett and Ansell, "Robust Action," p. 1263.

his position. As they emphasize, it was not that Cosimo behaved ambiguously but that the disconnected others made divergent attributions to the same utterance (hence, "Rorschach blot identities").

With Padgett and Ansell, I am similarly interested not only in practical action in more than one game but in attributions and identities as well. The differences rest, in part, in the differences in our cases. Whereas they examine a case in which an individual was the nearly *singular point of contact* among the cognitive orders, I examine situations in which *multiple orders are overlapping*. Whereas Cosimo benefited from multivocality, the organization benefits from the reflexive cognition produced by the polyphonic orders. Whereas in the Florentine case the singular point of contact made possible "distinctive attributions of the identity of ego" (Padgett and Ansell's expression), in my cases the overlap of cognitive orders makes it possible to arrive at new attributions of the identities of many other entities.

This last point is the key lesson of Lane and Maxfield's study of the ROLM telephone system.[67] Back in the old days (before 1968), companies arranged their phone lines with a local AT&T telephone company and likely purchased their telephone equipment from an AT&T subsidiary. Opportunities opened when the FCC broke the phone company's monopoly on private branch exchanges (PBX). A PBX is a telephone exchange that serves a particular business or office. In 1973 ROLM was a small Silicon Valley company with fewer than one hundred employees that was an early mover in the field of computer control and digital switching for PBXs. The new digital system could slash the costs of long-distance calls, manage internal company connections, and provide some (and later many) of the features such as voice mail that we now associate with the telephone.

Selling the new equipment, Lane and Maxfield argue, required changes of attribution in "agent-artifact space." As a first step, such changes of attributions involved reaching into the companies that were the potential customers for the new technology. The key purchasing agents of business PBXs were the telecommunications managers (TMs). In a field where there had been little choice and few opportunities for any kind of creativity, the TMs were right down at the bottom of the management status hierarchy. They also tended to be ex–telephone company employees. With their bosses in higher management of the various companies where they worked, they shared the attribution that a PBX was just a switchboard connected to telephone sets at one end and an outside line at the other. Executives at ROLM, of course, did not share these attributions assigned to

---

[67] Lane and Maxfield, "Strategy under Complexity."

their digital PBX; but although they were confident that they were building something conceptually different, they had yet to actually recognize the possible features of the new technology. Instead of a strategy of insisting that they knew what their product could do, they took the course of building generative relationships to find out what it could be.[68]

ROLM account representatives and engineers began to work with the TMs of some major companies. Unlike the homogeneous attributions in conversations among AT&T salesmen and the TMs who saw everything eye to eye, there was much greater discursive heterogeneity in these conversations. Over time, members of the ROLM staff haltingly and then aggressively changed their attributions about the TMs. Although everything in their world pointed to the TMs as lowly custodians of infrastructural fixed costs, ROLM's agents began to attribute to them the role of information technology executives. To enlist the TMs in this attribution, they organized training courses dealing not only with the technology side but also with the skills of creative management to assist them in making the case to their bosses. Interactions between TMs and ROLM's technologists, in turn, fostered re-cognition of new possibilities for the system (for example, automatic call distribution, like those used by airlines to handle reservations, to route a large number of incoming calls among many specially trained employees). These business voice applications were incorporated into the third release of ROLM software, and it became a smash hit.[69] Originally conceived in limited terms as a more intelligent interface between a company and outsiders, the new system could be adopted to solve a wide range of business problems, providing productivity improvements in many aspects of their customers' operations. New attributions of identities enrolled allies who helped the company change attributions about its product.[70]

For Lane and Maxfield, attributions in agent-artifact space are consequential under conditions of complex foresight horizons when actors cannot take knowledge of their worlds for granted.

[68] "ROLM failed utterly to predict the effects of their entry into the PBX business. . . . Fortunately for ROLM, their success in the PBX market did not depend on their ability to foresee far into the future. . . . ROLM managers did not allow strategic plans to channel these relationships; instead, they let the relationships channel their strategic plans." Lane and Maxfield, "Strategy under Complexity," p. 235.

[69] Within five years of its first PBX sale, ROLM came to challenge AT&T for leadership in the then $1 billion PBX market.

[70] For another fascinating account of new attributions in agent-artifact space, see especially Trevor Pinch and Frank Trocco, Analog Days: The Invention and Impact of the Moog Synthesizer, 2004. Like the ROLM phone system, the Moog synthesizer became the leader in its field because its developers worked more closely with distributors and users—from whom it learned how to recognize new affordances of the technology.

They need information, of course—hence the strategic need for exploration and experimentation. But information takes on meaning only through interpretation, and interpretation starts with an ontology: who and what are the people and things that constitute the agent's world, and how do they relate to one another? . . . Hence the strategic need for practices that help agents "populate" their world: i.e., to identify, criticize, and reconstruct their attributions about who and what are there.[71]

Cognitive clashes can help generate new attributions, fostering re-cognition of new identities and new actors in our worlds.

While making attributions about the identities of others, we also make attributions about ourselves. The problem of identity is most acute in the case of the Hungarian toolmakers. When we first encountered them, we sensed that we were meeting people with strong identities. They understood who they were. As their situation became more complex, it seemed that their identities were shifting and with this their understanding of themselves. But the more carefully we examined these developments, the more we saw that they had strong identities throughout—not despite but because of these shifts. Identity lies in the discrepancy between current position and other possibilities. New, confounding situations can shift the discrepancy. Did the toolmakers fully understand their situations? Of course not, nor do we. Understanding can be overrated. There are times when it is better to use the situation than to understand it. The situation is not the object to be understood; instead, it is the opportunity for action to shift the discrepancy. John Dewey's type of situation, troubled but pregnant with possibilities, makes us think again about those situations in which we *find ourselves*.

From Shared Understandings to Coordination through Misunderstanding

It would probably be difficult to find a leading sociologist today who subscribes to the old "consensus" view of society. Various "conflict" schools, whether Marxist or Weberian, successfully challenged the notion that social order at the societal level is maintained because actors consciously embrace a dominant, unitary set of values. Where *consent* is still a relevant term, it has been thoroughly reconstructed. For example, in his remarkable ethnography of a shop floor in Chicago, *Manufacturing Consent*,

---

[71] Lane and Maxfield, "Strategy under Complexity," p. 227.

Michael Burawoy, a leading Marxist sociologist, argues that consent is an unconscious process.[72] Work is coordinated, order is maintained, and (ultimately) the capitalist system is reproduced not because subordinates accept the ideology of their bosses but because the locally grounded, practical activity of playing the piecework game of "making out" aligns workers' actions with the interests of the owners of capital.[73]

Most economic and organizational sociologists are less preoccupied with the problem of the reproduction of the capitalist system. Their problem is the coordination of activities among actors who are frequently heterogeneous in their skills and motivations. In studying the structure of organizations, the dynamics of markets, and the intricacies of economic exchanges, they ask, how can people cooperate to carry out complex projects? The answer is not value consensus in the old sense of the phrase; instead, like Burawoy's notion of consent, it is unconscious. Actors can coordinate, or can be coordinated (the emphasis differs across schools), because of the values that they share implicitly. Consciously articulated differences might pose obstacles, but heterogeneous actors can get the job done if, beneath these differences, there are shared understandings.[74]

The cases we have seen suggest a different kind of argument. Posed most polemically: there are circumstances in which coordination takes place not despite but because of misunderstandings. I should clarify at the outset that I am not arguing that shared typifications, let's call them shared understandings (unvoiced conventions or protocols that are part of the taken-for-granted), do not play a prominent role in coordination. If there is no point of commonality—something even so basic as "we need to get the job done," as we saw in the case of the new-media projects—coordination would be extraordinarily difficult if not impossible.

The misunderstanding that I want to highlight is not some chaotic confusion or random noise. It is structured, we could even say "organized," so long as we see organization as something that could be an emergent process and not necessarily the result of deliberate design. Above all, this is not misunderstanding of the "simply false" variety. The fruitfulness of

[72] Michael Burawoy, *Manufacturing Consent: Changes in the Labor Process under Monopoly Capitalism*, 1979.

[73] The primary evidence for this conclusion is that Burawoy, who subscribes to an entirely other worldview, finds himself playing the game. Unconscious practical action trumps consciousness.

[74] As institutionalists, DiMaggio and Powell go even deeper to the bedrock, underneath understanding, so to speak. Phrases such as "shared cognitions," "shared world view," "shared system of rules," and most frequently, "shared typifications" are used with positive connotations at least ten times in their now classic statement on the new institutionalism. (DiMaggio and Powell, "Introduction.")

John Dewey's problematic situations does not lie in untangling misconceptions or solving problems that have a right answer. Misunderstandings are not incorrect understandings.

The misunderstandings that I have in mind lie most frequently in conflicting attributions that actors are making. These can be conflicting attributions about persons (as we saw in the Padgett and Ansell study of Cosimo de Medici), but just as frequently they can be discrepant attributions about objects, artifacts, concepts, or other entities that populate our social worlds.[75] Our economies and our organizations are replete with such multivalent entities, and my analysis of organizations such as the three discussed in this book suggests that the misunderstandings produced through such discordant attributions may in fact facilitate as opposed to thwart coordination among heterogeneous actors within and across organizations.

I am using the term *misunderstanding* in a deliberately provocative way. But some provocation is necessary because as sociologists, or readers of sociology, or even just as participants in a society that is suffused with pop sociology ("let's get together and iron out our differences"), our thinking is deeply engrained with the notion that whereas differences make for conflict, shared understandings make for cooperation and coordination. Given the extent to which such notions are taken for granted, we can expect resistance to the idea of coordination through misunderstanding. The stretch to stress is that it is through *unshared* typifications, through uncommon attributions, through divergent or misaligned understandings that problematic situations can give way to positive reconstructions.

The most persuasive case for the positive role of misunderstanding is Peter Galison's marvelous study *Image and Logic: A Material Culture of Microphysics.*[76] A historian of science engaged in debates in his own field, Galison never uses the polemical term "coordination through misunderstanding." But the sensibility underlying his approach is the same as the perspective I am adopting.

Although we typically think about the strength of science as derived from its underlying unity, Galison's history of twentieth-century microphysics demonstrates that the culture of physics, for many the exemplary scientific field, was not unified. Galison identifies three dis-

---

[75] If you are persuaded by Padgett and Ansell's study that there could be an entity (in that case, a person) who could exist in multiple networks while operating with entirely divergent attributions about him, then ponder the possibility that there could be other entities, objects, concepts, artifacts that circulate in multiple worlds in which divergent attributions are made about them. Why let Cosimo alone have all the power of multivocality?

[76] Peter L. Galison, *Image and Logic: A Material Culture of Microphysics*, 1997.

tinctive cultures—the cultures of instrumentation, experimentation, and theory—each with its own standards of demonstration, separate identities and traditions, and tempos and dynamics of change.

Over the course of more than eight hundred pages, Galison describes in great detail how the three communities interact, asynchronously, across their incommensurable cultures. This interaction occurs in a social-technical space that Galison refers to as a "trading zone." But he emphasizes repeatedly that the parties to the trade do not necessarily agree on the meaning of the objects exchanged. These discrepancies go to the core concepts of the discipline. Galison finds "different communities using terms like 'mass' and 'energy' in significantly different ways." In the trading zone, "Two groups can agree on rules of exchange even if they ascribe utterly different significance to the objects being exchanged; they may even disagree on the meaning of the exchange process itself. Nonetheless, the trading partners can hammer out a *local* coordination despite vast *global* differences" (p. 783).

For Galison, exchange in the trading zone does not yield convergence to a single culture based on shared understandings building up over the course of the transactions. Instead, because the interactions are based on "incompatible valuations and understandings of the objects exchanged" (p. 804), exchange can take place without reducing the diversity of scientific cultures within microphysics:

> I will call this polycultural history of the development of physics intercalated because the many traditions coordinate with one another without homogenization. Different traditions of theorizing, experimenting, instrument making, and engineering meet—even transform one another—but for all that, they do not lose their separate identities and practices. (p. 782)

As Galison demonstrates, the dynamics of microphysics as a whole is not sparked because theorists, experimenters, and instrumentation engineers reach some uneasy yet stabilized consensus. Developments in microphysics occur not despite but because of the divergent misunderstandings. In Galison's concept of intercalation, physics is not a pure structure. Less like a crystal, more like the disordered atoms of semiconductors, the diverse subcultures of physics are layered.[77] And the strength of this

[77] Galison concludes with an apt metaphor about microphysics drawn from intellectual developments in the field itself: "For years, physicists and engineers harbored a profound distrust of disorder. They searched for reliability in crystals rather than disordered materials, and strength in pure substances rather than laminated ones. . . . It was the amorphous semiconductors, with their disordered atoms, that gave the consistent responses needed for the modern era of electronics.

lamination rests in its misalignment: "It is the disorder of the scientific community—the disunification of science—the intercalation of different patterns of argument—that is responsible for its strength and coherence" (p. 844).

Leigh Star and James Griesemer make a similar case for a positive role for misunderstanding in the process of cooperation among heterogeneous participants.[78] They argue that standardization, in which there is stabilized consensus about meanings, is but one mode for objects to circulate in the work of coordination.[79] Within the alternative mode, they identify "boundary objects," which have considerably discrepant meanings attributed to them. Boundary objects are not objects at the boundary or objects that make boundaries. Instead, they circulate across the boundaries of different social worlds sharing the same territory. To contribute to the work of coordination, boundary objects must be stabilized enough to circulate across sites, yet plastic enough to adapt to the local constraints and needs of the disparate parties deploying them. Robust enough to be recognizable in different settings, boundary objects are recognized by the different communities in distinctive ways.

In their history of the Museum of Vertebrate Zoology at the University of California, Berkeley, Star and Griesemer document how boundary objects such as maps, specimens, and field notes are given different meanings by zoologists, museum officials, patrons, amateur collectors, trappers, and university administrators. In contrast to Latour's account of the Pasteurization of France—which privileges Louis Pasteur as the scientific entrepreneur who becomes the obligatory passage point enrolling allies by translating their concerns[80]—Star and Griesemer extend the process of *interressement*. Not presupposing a primacy for any one viewpoint, they see all actors as attempting to enlist allies. Each actor has a project. The university administrator has a project, the museum director another, the trappers and amateur collectors still others, and so on. These are not different lenses on the same project, because there is no global project. It is not a project that circulates, accumulating different attributions along the

---

Structural engineers were slow to learn the same lesson. The strongest materials were not pure—they were laminated; when they failed microscopically, they held together in bulk" (*Image and Logic*, p. 843).

[78] Susan Leigh Star and James Griesemer, "Institutional Ecology, Translations, and Boundary Objects: Amateurs and Professionals in Berkeley's Museum of Vertebrate Zoology, 1907–1939," 1989.

[79] On the importance of ambiguity in standardized systems, and the counterproductive consequences of attempting to eliminate uncertainty from them, see Bowker and Star's analysis of the international classification of diseases: Bowker and Star, "Knowledge and Infrastructure."

[80] Bruno Latour, *The Pasteurization of France*, 1988.

way. Instead, boundary objects like specimens, notes, and maps are co-constructed at the overlap of social worlds, and the disparate attributions made to them facilitate coordination.

As an example from the world of finance, Donald MacKenzie and Yuval Millo show that disparate attributions played an important role in the adoption of the Black Scholes formula for pricing options on the Chicago Board of Trade (CBOT).[81] In this case, a good number of the participants in all likelihood did not understand the mathematics behind the Black Scholes model. But more interesting than this lack of comprehension is that traders, clearinghouse managers, CBOT officials, and SEC regulators understood (we might say misunderstood) Black Scholes differently. The formula could operate to price options for traders on the floor, to determine margin fees at the clearinghouses, and to regulate net capital requirements because "Black Scholes" was coconstructed as a boundary object at the overlap of the trading floor, the clearinghouses, and regulatory offices. Moreover, it could do the work of coordination within and across these domains despite the objective failure of the formula to correspond with the actual patterns of option prices in the wake of the October 1987 market crash.[82]

In short—whether in business, science, or finance—circuits of misunderstanding can facilitate "circuits of commerce."[83] If the parties in a situation would be forced to come to an explicit agreement on the meaning of objects, or the "rules of the game," or even what game is being played, their understandings might be so disparate as to forestall an agreement, resulting in a breakdown of coordination. Although the communities do not agree on the meanings of the rules or the nature of the game itself, through the circulation of objects with disparately ascribed meanings, each community can arrive to its own understanding of the situation without jeopardizing cooperation from others. As we saw in the three ethnographic cases of this book, and as these other studies illustrate, misunderstanding can facilitate coordination.

From Single Ethnographies to the Broader Sites of Situations

To study situations, my research collaborators and I conducted ethnographic field research in three different settings. Despite considerable range

---

[81] Yuval Millo and Donald MacKenzie, "The Usefulness of Inaccurate Models: The Emergence of Financial Risk Management," in press.

[82] Practitioners refer to this discrepancy as the "volatility skew."

[83] Viviana Zelizer, "Circuits of Commerce," 2004.

in the types of settings, in each case we studied a business activity (building machine tools, constructing websites, arbitrage trading) in a single organization (a rubber factory, a new-media start-up, an investment bank). The decision to conduct ethnographies of particular organizations was guided by theoretical considerations. Focusing on a single trading room, for example, was a way to address one of our initial research questions: Why, in an era of high-speed network connectivity, does an investment bank bring its arbitrage traders together in a single room? In a period in which some announce the "death of distance," how does place matter? By making observations in a single trading room, we were able to be attentive to microspatial processes at work. More generally, in moving from the population ecologists' notion of diversity of organization to the organization of diversity, it was important to demonstrate, in each of the cases, that competing evaluative principles were operating in a single organization. The decision to focus on business activities shared a similar motivation: study situations in a context where organizations have an external market orientation but in which there are multiple evaluative principles for coordination inside the organization.

But these boundary conditions impose serious limitations. First, my shift of the entrepreneurial unit from the individual to the organization did not go far enough. Because individual firms are the unit of formal and legal accounting, it did make sense to explore the accounts of actors inside such organizations. But increasingly the unit of action, the unit of innovation, and hence the unit of entrepreneurship is not the legally bounded firm but networks that span organizational boundaries.[84] Second, by restricting my case studies to business firms I did not mean to suggest that nonprofit organizations are not adopting heterarchical forms. But expanding the analysis outside the business sector should not be done simply to increase the number or variety of cases. Instead (and here developing the above-mentioned point about the unit of innovation), economic sociology needs to expand beyond firms because some of the most innovative recombinations involve interactions across types of organizations.

Innovations in pharmaceuticals and medical technologies offer rich examples. These are lucrative fields, but firms that seek high profits in these fields cannot develop and test their products entirely on their own. The problem is not simply that they depend on scientists (with their own criteria of worth) for advances in basic knowledge, or that they must cooperate with medical practitioners in research hospitals for clinical trials,

---

[84] This theme runs across the various essays in *The Twenty-First-Century Firm*, edited by Paul DiMaggio.

or that they depend on government regulatory agencies for approval of new products. It also happens that they require the cooperation—and can benefit from the lay knowledge and organizing abilities—of the patients themselves.

Steven Epstein, for example, studied the clash of community values and commercial values in the treatment of HIV-AIDS, showing that these differences in values can sometimes produce negotiations toward a mutual goal. AIDS activists wanted wider access to health care, including experimental new drug treatments; the pharmaceutical companies wanted to design and market new for-profit drug treatments. Although the resulting negotiations did not make drug companies community-oriented, changes in the approval process did incorporate many of the users' demands.[85] Similarly, Michel Callon and Vololona Rabeharisoa studied interactions across organizational forms and value framings in the case of muscular dystrophy.[86] At the outset, research and development was the sole province of scientists and doctors who dismissed input from the patient community as unknowledgeable intrusion on their domain. Patients, in this case the parents of childhood victims of the disease, impatient at the slow development of medical cures, began documenting (with photographs and detailed, daily, firsthand observations) the progression of the disease. Interactions between medical practitioners and the patient community focused on fund-raising. Researchers depended on the cooperation of the parents for the use of their children in telethons and other fund-raising events, but the parents increasingly demanded a voice in the direction of research. As the clash escalated, some doctors recognized that the now sizable collection of parent documentation of patient case histories was of considerable medical value, leading to a rapprochement of expert and lay knowledge.

The study of tornadoes offers a similar example. Professional meteorologists initially dismissed Oklahoma "storm chasers" as high-testosterone thrill seekers. But many of the storm chasers were doing more than seeking a dangerous adrenaline rush. First, in order to get close to tornadoes, they were sharing knowledge about the "behavior" of funnels as they fell from the sky to touch land. CB radios increased immediate communication during storms and widened the spread of this lay knowledge among a

---

[85] Steven Epstein, "The Construction of Lay Expertise: AIDS Activism and the Forging of Credibility in the Reform of Clinical Trials," 1995; and Steven Epstein, "Activism, Drug Regulation, and the Politics of Therapeutic Evaluation in the AIDS Era," 1997.

[86] Michel Callon, "The Increasing Involvement of Concerned Groups in R & D Policies: What Lessons for Public Powers?" 2003; and Michel Callon and Vololona Rabeharisoa, "Research in the Wild and the Shaping of New Social Identities," 2003.

larger dispersed community. Second, in documenting their exploits with video cameras and audio recording devices, the storm chasers were, along the way, also documenting the tornadoes. Interactions between professional meteorologists and these lay "activists" produced new forms of research, leading to real advancements in the understanding of destructive tornadoes and more reliable, highly localized forecasts for extreme-storm alerts to the public.[87]

In addition to these cases, where we saw such diverse relevant actors as families, gay activists, commercial interests, patient communities, university scientists, informal organizations of thrill seekers, and government agencies, we can think of new developments in fields like genetic testing and organ donation, where the relevant actors are also likely to include nongovernmental organizations (NGOs) that span international borders. How can we study these types of situations, where the most interesting interactions are not within an organization but across organizational forms?

Network analysis is one possible tool. But, as I pointed out in chapter 1, with few exceptions network analysis typically focuses on the patterns of ties to the exclusion of the diverse accounts of worth that might be operating in these interactions.[88] Rich in the study of structure, network analysis remains impoverished in the study of situations.[89] Another promising approach is multisited ethnography, in which the investigator studies several, perhaps diverse, settings.[90] But gaining deep familiarity with even

[87] Where is the commercial value in this story? Next to the football coaches of the public universities in Texas and Oklahoma, perhaps the most widely recognized personages in these states are the meteorologists of the large-city television stations. Increasing your market share with a reputable extreme-weather forecaster translates to higher rates for commercial advertising.

[88] László Bruszt, Balazs Vedres, and I are combining network analysis and accounts of worth in a project on civic activism. In a survey of the one thousand largest civic associations in Hungary, we gather network data by asking a representative of each organization to name its three most important organizational partners for each of its three most recent projects. To tap accounts of worth, we ask an open-ended question: Why is your organization valuable? We also ask them to rank items on the following list: Our organization is valuable because we are creative, caring, professional, taking initiative, challenging the status quo, unique, solvent, efficient, creating ties, exciting, independent, participatory, informative, visible, faithful to tradition, offering alternatives, transparent. For findings from this research project, see Balazs Vedres, László Bruszt, and David Stark, "Organizing Technologies: Genre Forms of Online Civic Association in Eastern Europe," 2004; and David Stark, Balazs Vedres, and László Bruszt, "Rooted Transnational Publics: Integrating Foreign Ties and Civic Activism," 2006.

[89] For an interesting exception, see Ann Mische, *Partisan Publics: Communication and Contention across Brazilian Youth Activist Networks*, 2008.

[90] On multisited ethnography, see especially George E. Marcus, *Ethnography through Thick and Thin*, 1998. For a multisited study on democratic participation and the variety of forms of civic assembly concerning the rebuilding of Lower Manhattan after 9/11, see Monique Girard and David Stark, "Socio-technologies of Assembly: Sense-Making and Demonstration in Rebuilding Lower Manhattan," 2007.

one setting requires considerable time. The danger of short-term ethnography is either that the analyst simply confirms prior assumptions or that, if surprises confound preconceptions and lead to new questions, there is too little time to resolve the confusion. Advocates of multisited ethnography respond that the trade-off between depth and range should not be overstated: following an object as it moves across organizational domains, for example, provides a kind of depth that would not be possible through single-sited ethnography.

Hybrids of network analysis and ethnography, of which actor-network theory (ANT) can be seen as the most fully elaborated variant, are most promising. From the standpoint of social network analysis, most research in the actor-network framework is not sufficiently structural and to date has not adopted or developed sophisticated quantitative network methods. From the standpoint of conventional ethnography, in its injunction to "follow the actors" ANT spreads too thin. But perhaps we ask too much of hybrids if we expect them to combine in some additive way the most elaborated forms of research in two traditions. In any case, it is too early to say what will happen when the predominantly French actor-network theory interacts with the predominantly American quantitative network analysis. I expect interesting developments. In the meantime, hybrids such as ANT are already bringing new insights into economic sociology with the notion that social networks involve not only associations of persons but also of persons, ideas, and material objects. As a consequence, for example, the study of markets is enriched with the study of "market devices."[91]

In addition to limiting my research to single-sited ethnographies in business contexts, I presented in this book ethnographies that were all limited to settings with relatively few employees (about 100 in the Hungarian machine shop, 150 at the maximum in the new-media start-up, 160 traders in the arbitrage unit). Can large organizations adopt heterarchical forms? That is an empirical question that lies outside the scope of this book and will require further research. One possibility is that heterarchical forms will be nested within larger organizations, which, for reasons of accountability to outside stakeholders, will have hierarchical structures. Large corporations—accountable to shareholders, tax authorities, and other government regulators—offer one type of research setting. More interesting, because at first glance implausible, are military organizations.

Military organizations might seem the last place where we would find heterarchical forms. Say the word *military* and we think *hierarchy*—for example, of promotion structures reaching up finely calibrated ranks and

[91] Fabian Muniesa, Yuval Millo, and Michel Callon, eds., *Market Devices*, 2007.

of orders issuing down clear lines of command and control. Military organization is profoundly hierarchical. Yet there are good reasons to expect to find emergent heterarchical forms there. Career structures are indeed bureaucratic, and military operations in the broad sense could not be effective without vertical lines of authority. But battlefields and peacekeeping missions are sites that also (and, some argue, increasingly) entail complex structures of distributed intelligence in which lateral ties of coordination are as decisive as vertical channels of command. Certainly there is lively debate currently taking place—not only in the military academies and war colleges but also among active military practitioners—about organizational structure.[92]

That debate is wide-ranging. A useful point of access, because it quickly touches on other aspects, is to start with the role of new information technologies in combat or peacekeeping. One side in the debate sees the greatest potential in new information technologies (IT) as powerful tools for centralization. New technologies, they argue, increase the volume, speed, and quality of information available to distant commanders, making them even more knowledgeable about the big picture. Meanwhile, electronic sensors and wireless telephony linked by satellite transmission give decision makers on another side of the globe direct, immediate access to the engagement. Armed with these technologies, the long-distance commander can shift the focal lens from the largest scope to the smallest, at the extreme seeing, in real time, the same image as that seen through an individual infantry soldier's night goggles. New technologies, in this argument, allow for greater centralization of command and control: the hierarchical superior can supervise the battlefield because he has superior vision, metaphorically and literally.

The other side in the debate responds: yes, orbiting infrared cameras can detect parts of the nonvisible spectrum, and night goggles can pierce the darkness, but no technologies can pierce the "fog of war."[93] Not unlike

---

[92] I first encountered this debate when I was invited to a series of meetings in Washington, DC, on organizational issues in the U.S. military services. This was before the Iraq war, while I was writing with Daniel Beunza and John Kelly about issues of technology and organization in recovery efforts after 9/11. I was asked to present my work on heterarchy. Attending these meetings were researchers and officials from the Department of Defense (DOD), faculty from West Point and the Air Force and Naval academies, and numerous active-duty senior officers, including several generals in the U.S. Army and senior naval officers, among them Admiral Arthur Cebrowski, the outspoken director of the Office of Force Transformation and former president of the Naval War College. The lengthy conversations that I had suggested to me that this would be a compelling area for future research.

[93] "Network Centric Warfare" is a central and contentious term in the debate. (David S. Alberts, John J. Garstka, and Frederick P. Stein, *Network Centric Warfare: Developing and Leveraging Information Superiority,* 2000.) Whereas some, perhaps especially civilian officials in the DOD,

the arbitrage traders who know that timely, voluminous information is vital but not sufficient, those who argue on this side of the debate see combat as a problem of sense making. Information is needed, but the critical challenge is interpretive. They further argue that this interpretation must be knowledge based. Knowledge is in the network, distributed across the horizontal ties linking heterogeneous units in the field. "I see different aspects of the battlefield, but it's a myth that I know more," one general remarked. "The real knowledge base of my organization is in the junior officers. I always have to keep that in mind because rising in rank produces a forgetfulness. They are the knowledgeable. Sure, we need to get information to them and from them. But what we are striving to do is to improve collaboration among them. That's the important area where we need to work with changes in technology and in organization."

Such collaboration is complex because it increasingly involves interdependencies among different military services. Naval officers, air force pilots, and army captains are all trained as warriors, but within distinctively different subcultures. Meshing these must be resolved laterally in real time without recourse to further commands from hierarchical superiors. But the complexity of the contemporary military mission (whether combat or peacekeeping) goes beyond interservice collaboration. Whether German, French, Dutch, British, or American, a young infantry captain must frequently operate in a network with other actors who have diverse interests, values, and objectives that are not easily harmonizable with military goals. These can be representatives of national governments, of disputing political parties, and of highly localized community groups or tribal authorities. They also frequently include representatives of transnational NGOs whose definitions of the situation might depart not only from that of the military but from those of each other as well, as in cases of conflicts between humanitarian aid and human rights organizations.[94] It is not enough that the young captain "take these interests into account" when making decisions.

---

see "network" as a communication channel reaching from top to bottom, others see it as an aspect of decentralization, empowering field-level officers. This latter group explicitly adopts the language of "peer-to-peer" as the critical new opportunity in the use of new technologies. (David S. Alberts and Richard E. Hayes, *Power to the Edge*, 2003; see also Dan Baum, "Battle Lessons: What the Generals Don't Know," 2005.) "Transformation" was the watchword of Donald Rumsfeld's program of reorganization, inspired in part by the notion of a "Revolution in Military Affairs." But its meaning was also contentious, as reflected in the business card given to me by Major General Dean Cash following a very lively dinner conversation. On the back of General Cash's elaborately embossed business card one reads the following: "Everyone wants transformation. Nobody wants to change."

[94] For a thoughtful discussion of the complexities of multiple perspectives in the battlefield, see David Kennedy's *Of War and Law*, 2006, especially pp. 111–164.

Success in her own mission requires gaining information, building trust, sharing information, and producing knowledge through that heterarchical network.

For these reasons, military organizations pose sites for the study of situations where contentious orders of worth are in play. There are good reasons, however, why they pose a special-limit case. Although we can readily accept the statement of the interactive designer at the new-media start-up who said that, whereas he reports to his project leader, he is accountable to everyone who counts on him, we would be uncomfortable to think that accountability in military affairs operates on a predominantly lateral dimension. We might concede that, in the heat of battle, effective command and control is actually about horizontally coordinated initiative. And we might even acknowledge that authority in tactical operations is distributed laterally among relatively junior officers. But such thinking confronts real limits because we correctly sense that there is a line across which distributed authority turns into "passing the buck." And so we, the public, demand the vertical accountability of hierarchy. When we send our young people into danger and violence, instructing them to be obedient and responsive to their superiors, we do so in the belief that this justifies our holding their superiors responsible. The chain of command reaches down because it is also a chain of accountability extending upward and, ultimately, outward as the means to hold superiors accountable to us.

But we should not be too quick to assume that hierarchy resolves problems of accountability. Sadly, the principle of hierarchical accountability too often stops at the bottom, all too rarely extending even one rank above. The inhumane and illegal treatment of detainees in American prisons such as Abu Ghraib was shameful because it happened. But it is a national disgrace because no military superiors or their civilian superiors in the Department of Defense have been held accountable.

Heterarchical forms pose distinctive problems of accountability. One who is accountable to many in different registers can be one who is accountable to none. Yet this formulation of the problem inadequately states the dilemmas. Beginning with the term *one*, it has been scripted by a taken-for-granted, implicitly assuming that the unit of accountability is the individual. For some time, network analysts in economic sociology have been arguing that the actual unit of action is not the individual or the isolated firm but a network. It is time that we consider how this account of economic action has implications for theories of accountability in general and for legal theory in particular. In legal theory the unit of accountability is the person—an individual person or a legal person (an incorporated entity). Legal theory is now grappling with new complexities that arise in cases such as sweatshop labor, in which the multinational sporting goods companies seldom own production facilities but in which tight coordination through subcontracting ties makes the network the effective unit of action.[95] Developments in legal theory are but a particular example of a more general problem: how, then, to make heterarchical networks accountable. That problem is yet another challenge for pioneering research in economic sociology. It is to related problems of heterarchy in the broader social arena that I turn in my concluding remarks.

[95] On the conceptual problems for legal theory of recognizing networks as new moral actors, see the insightful work of Günther Teubner, "Beyond Contract and Organization? The External Liability of Franchising Systems in German Law," 1991; also Richard M. Buxbaum, "Is 'Network' a Legal Concept?" 1993; and Karl-Heinz Ladeur, "Towards a Legal Theory of Supranationality: The Viability of the Network Concept,"1997.

Reprise

Search, inquiry, discovery. This was the theme with which I began this book. In the introductory chapter, I presented a line of argument that moved through inquiry, uncertainty, diversity, ambiguity, and reflexivity to develop the concept of heterarchy. My own search took me, in subsequent chapters, to heterogeneous actors in disparate settings—toolmakers in an antiquated Hungarian factory, new-media workers in the ultracool setting of Silicon Alley, and arbitrage traders in the sleek glass hothouse of the World Financial Center. My ethnographic case studies, then, were an inquiry about inquiry as I followed these disparate actors in their search for worth. In the previous chapter, I used insights from my field research to inquire about my own field of research, reflecting on where it has been and suggesting some lines of further inquiry. In this reprise, I inquire about the social costs of heterarchy and reflect on the problems these pose as we move out from particular organizations to the broader society.

In recent work in network analytic approaches to economic sociology, one can observe a typical pattern that operates according to a recognizably standardized formula: identify a problem or set of problems created by markets, specify a problem or set of problems created by hierarchies, and then explicate how these problems endemic to markets and hierarchies are resolved by networks. Full stop. That strategy has been enormously successful. But the next step, which few have taken,[1] would be to examine the problems generated by network forms of organization. Thus, taking the next step, in the terms of this book, what are the problems created by heterarchies?

First, as we saw most acutely in the case of the new-media workers, there are the personal costs. At the individual level, being accountable to many, in different registers, can be emotionally exhausting. Burnout, as Gideon Kunda powerfully demonstrates in an ethnographic study of a high-tech firm,[2] is curiously both a badge of extreme dedication (giving your all for the company) and a mark of shame (failure in the management

---

[1] For an important departure from this pattern, see Joel M. Podolny and Karen L. Page, "Network Forms of Organization," 1998. I examine the problems of accountability created by heterarchical forms in "Ambiguous Assets for Uncertain Environments," 2001.

[2] Gideon Kunda, *Engineering Culture: Control and Commitment in a High Tech Corporation*, 1993.

of the self). The most valued employee is the one who pushes right to the psychological edge without falling over the emotional precipice.

Here the study of heterarchies has much to gain from the concepts of the new institutionalists, for it is not the case that heterarchies do not have their own forms of organizational scripts and taken-for-granteds. A habitus of tolerance would be one example of a cultural script that is taken for granted in a heterarchical setting where diverse evaluative principles are in play.[3] But mutual tolerance is likely one of the few unequivocally benign personality traits. Others reflect more complex and perplexing dilemmas. As I suggested in the epilogue of chapter 3, when held to account in many registers, we can be accountable to none, or ultimately only to ourselves, for only one's self can be the true judge of one's contribution—exactly the situation with the potential for performance anxiety and burnout.

Yet many of us would not want to work for organizations in which we were expected to withhold our creativity. We join them precisely because they challenge us to the fullest so we can come to recognize our worth on our own terms. We value the autonomy that comes from working in settings of nonhierarchical self-management. But this ethic of personal responsibility requires identities that turn the work of management (emphatically not by others) onto the management of the self.[4] We need more studies of the new organizational habitus that is emerging when the quest for innovation becomes relentless.

Second, the performance anxiety that we find at the individual level manifests itself at a societal level. Here I turn from the specific features of heterarchical organizational forms to the more general features of the hyperentrepreneurial capitalism in which it is set. Such hyperentrepreneurial capitalism can be thought of in exactly the terms with which I opened this book: at the societal level, a search when we do not know what we are looking for—now a search so extreme that, as a society, we are in danger of not even recognizing whatever it is when we find it. Such a search is inexhaustible. It has brought great wealth, advances in science and medicine, and new applications of technology that can increase enjoyment, health, and longevity not just for a few but for many. Yet, surely, it is also a malady.

---

[3] Luc Boltanski and Ève Chiapello, *The New Spirit of Capitalism*, 2005.

[4] Whereas Taylorism was about the management of the working class, and human relations was about the management of middle managers, the latest developments are about managing the personalities of senior management. If consultancies were formerly directed toward improving performance at the bottom line, the new consultancies advise senior personnel about their personal performance. See especially Nigel Thrift, *Knowing Capitalism*, 2005.

In hyperentrepreneurial capitalism, any domain can be an object of profit-maximizing activity. Although we want the manufacturers of our children's medicines to be entrepreneurial in a relentless pursuit of improved, effective, and safe pharmaceuticals, and although we would like our car manufacturers and energy providers to rely less on government protection and be truly entrepreneurial in the pursuit of green transportation and sustainable energy, do we really want our spiritual leaders to be entrepreneurs? Such are the MBA ministers of megachurches such as VictoryChurch.tv and LifeChurch.tv in my hometown of Oklahoma City, where we find the conflation of economic value and spiritual values in disturbing forms.[5]

Hyperentrepreneurial capitalism is a relentless search not only for new domains of activity but also for new sources of creativity.[6] It finds a new source in the employees of heterarchical organizations, where it learns that creativity knows fewer bounds when it can be unbound from hierarchical control. In this, it continues developments anticipated by the movement of Communities of Practice, through which organizations came to recognize that activities that were not formally organized, and which were frequently crosscutting of formal organizational boundaries, could be richly generative of creative performance.[7] But it also finds creativity in energies that exist far outside the boundaries of any kind of professional communities, as when consumers are brought into the production process. Like the notion of "self-management," with its positive connotations combined with Foucaultian management of the self, the notion of the consumer as producer has a doubled valence.

Start with very elementary processes. When I walk through a supermarket, take items off the shelf, and place them in my shopping cart, I perform a productive, yet unpaid, "labor." That is perhaps obvious to me only because I can still remember my grandfather telling me about a previous time when you went to the general store, asked for a couple of pounds of flour, and the shopkeeper's assistant would measure it out behind the counter for the customer. If I now scan the products with the store's self-scanning device at the checkout counter, it is obvious to more readers that I am doing a task that the supermarket would otherwise need to pay an employee to perform. When you buy a book at Amazon.com and with

[5] See Ben Stark and David Stark, "Satisfaction Guaranteed: Megachurches as Shopping Malls," 2006.

[6] Nigel Thrift, "Re-inventing Invention: New Tendencies in Capitalist Commodification," 2006.

[7] Ash Amin and Joanne Roberts, "The Resurgence of Community in Economic Thought and Practice," 2008.

the keystrokes enter your address, credit card number, and billing information, you perform a task for which the retailer would have needed to hire an employee if you had placed the order by telephone.

My point is not to denounce my supermarket for not paying me when I walk its aisles nor to encourage you to send a bill for your unpaid keystroke time to your favorite online retailer or frequent-flier airline. It is simply to call to mind how organizations have recognized that their productive resources can be expanded if they reach beyond the formal boundaries of the organization.[8] In fact, frequently in such cases, the organizations themselves extend a subtle acknowledgment of your unpaid voluntary labor: they invite you to become a "member." Whereas one was formerly a member of a church, a synagogue, a civic association, or some other voluntary organization, now one's wallet is packed with "membership" cards of this or that frequent shopper program.

Beta testing takes this process to the next level by involving the end user as an active participant in product design. In beta testing in fields like software and website development, companies release admittedly defective products and invite the user to assist them in identifying "bugs" or glitches in the program. When the user downloads the beta release, she typically receives a message welcoming her to the testing community: "Congratulations! You've downloaded an XYZ (company name) build. This means that you've volunteered to become part of the XYZ testing community. Great! Welcome aboard. Helping out won't take much of your time, doesn't require special skills and will help improve our new product."[9] The user gets early access to new features; the company gets millions of "eyeballs" to detect flaws in the new product.

Researchers in science and technology studies have long recognized that the design process is not completed when manufacturers ship out a new product. Instead, users complete the "design process" when they resist some uses inscribed in the product, identify other potential uses, and modify the product. The telephone, the bicycle, and the tractor are famous examples.[10] All products, and especially new and unfamiliar ones, entail

---

[8] The history of firms benefiting from unpaid labor is as old as capitalism itself. But whereas in earlier times this practice was based on ascriptive status (for example, relying heavily on unpaid female labor in households) contributing to reproduction, today it is based on market participation by the customers themselves, contributing to distribution, marketing, and design.

[9] See Gina Neff and David Stark, "Permanently Beta: Responsive Organization in the Internet Era," 2003.

[10] Claude S. Fischer, *America Calling: The Social History of the Telephone until 1940*, 1992; Trevor Pinch and Wiebe Bijker, "The Social Construction of Facts and Artifacts: Or How the Sociology of Science and the Sociology of Technology Might Benefit Each Other," 1987; and Ronald

considerable "interpretive flexibility."[11] The new "user innovation communities" make this insight a part of corporate strategy. Instead of a hit-or-miss approach, they actively foster communities of users and involve their participation at ever-earlier stages of the design process.[12] This is search when you do not know what you are looking for, relying on the users to recognize it when *they* find it.

Gina Neff and I used the term *permanently beta* to refer to the organizations that emerge when the institutional barriers to user involvement in the design process are overcome. Writing in a very different context, Charles Sabel proposed the term "Moebius strip organizations"[13]—referring to the topology of the Möbius strip, which has neither an inside nor an outside. These are organizations with such fluid boundaries that it is difficult to say what is inside and what is outside.

The new social networking websites ratchet up this process to unprecedented scale and scope when they move from working with and responding to the user to building sites for which all the content is user produced. While we were doing ethnographic work at the new-media firm Net KnowHow, Monique Girard and I also did some research in one of the pioneers in the development of such sites, Bolt.com, a venture launched by Silicon Alley company Concrete Media. Bolt began as an Internet community and e-commerce site, trying to become "America's online high school newspaper." At the outset, Bolt hired a team of writers from various magazines that produced content for teens. And it paid top dollar for this talent. As an afterthought, Bolt also created a space where teens could post their own content. Because they could track the use patterns of the teenagers online, the editors were able to discover that teens were much more likely to read essays by their peers—even when they were tucked away, so to speak, on a part of the site to which it was not easy to navigate. After Bolt fired the pricey writers and adopted a user-as-producer model, traffic increased and the venture flourished. At the height of its success in 2000, Bolt's executive vice president explained, "We don't have people sitting

---

Kline and Trevor Pinch, "Users as Agents of Technological Change: The Social Construction of the Automobile in the Rural United States," 1996.

[11] Pinch and Bijker, "Social Construction of Facts and Artifacts."

[12] Eric von Hippel, "Innovation by User Communities: Learning from Open Source Software," 2001; and Raghu Garud, Sanjay Jain, and Philipp Tuertscher, "Incomplete by Design and Designing for Incompleteness," 2008. Users "consume, modify, domesticate, design, reconfigure and resist technologies," and through this process shape and are shaped by those technologies. See Nelly Oudshoorn and Trevor Pinch, "Introduction: How Users and Non-users Matter," 2003.

[13] Neff and Stark, "Permanently Beta"; and Charles F. Sabel, "Moebius-Strip Organizations and Open Labor Markets: Some Consequences of the Reintegration of Conception and Execution in a Volatile Economy," 1990.

around thinking, 'What do teens want?' It doesn't work, even if you could figure it out, it wouldn't last. You can try to write for them, but it doesn't work. Now 95 percent of our content is written by teens themselves."

Long-lived in Internet time, Bolt survived in various versions from 1996 to 2007.[14] During its tumultuous years, Bolt faced repeated organized revolts by its teen constituents, who resented the surreptitious placing of sponsors' ads into the users' activities and resisted the growing commercialization of the site. These revolts anticipated ongoing struggles at Facebook.com, which, with more powerful software, captured a huge share of first the college and then the high school social networking market. Recently, Facebook was forced to draw back from an advertising platform that tracked Facebook's member transactions on third-party partner sites and transformed them into endorsements that were then inserted on their friends' "news feeds." The company reversed its policy following a petition signed by more than fifty thousand Facebook users organized by MoveOn.org.

As hyperentrepreneurial capitalism looks for new spaces to mobilize the creative energies of "members," social networking represents an effort to capitalize not only user content but the users' personal contacts as well. Commercial social networking is an expression of the centuries-long dynamic of capitalism: the ever-greater socialization of production combined with the privatization of the profits. Social networking sites then become sites of contention over this latest effort at commodification and the intensification of the search for value.

In the context of war, poverty, and environmental catastrophe, battles such as those over Facebook doubtless seem trivial. But they are an indication, in small, of the larger social dilemmas set in motion as organizations extend their heterarchical scope beyond the formal boundaries of the firm. Of course, we prefer organizations that are responsive, and what better way to be responsive than to incorporate our participation in building the organizations themselves. Of course, we prefer organizations with at least a semblance of face-to-face community. But then should we not have a voice in the means and goals of organizations that prosper from our participation and from the structure of our communities?

I am not arguing here for a kind of denunciation in which we point our finger and say, "There, you see, at the top are the people who really

---

[14] Ironically, given its early recognition of the value of content produced by the teenagers themselves, Bolt was forced into bankruptcy by a multimillion-dollar out-of-court settlement to a lawsuit brought by Universal Media Group (UMG). UMG had sued Bolt for copyright infringement in connection with the unauthorized use of UMG's video and music content posted by users on the Bolt website. See Saul Hansell, "Universal Near Deal with Video Site on Royalties," *New York Times*, February 12, 2007.

do control these organizations. That's the problem." In fact, I believe that the problem is more challenging. The more interesting dilemma would be that the new organizational forms of hyperentrepreneurial capitalism are complex systems in which the core problems can no longer be expressed in the straightforward language of *control*. Polemically, for purposes of emphasis, perhaps it would be more accurate to think about them as systems that are out of control. Less polemically, think about them as systems in which the beneficiaries have recognized that they can increase their profits when they relinquish direct control.[15]

Old metaphors like "the reins of power" are misleading. So, too, is the notion that power is "exercised"—as if it were some kind of organizational calisthenics. These metaphors of power as something that can be held or grasped are comforting, for they suggest that if power could be seized by others who do not currently hold it, then things could be righted and brought back under control. But such notions are falsely comforting, for power in its heterarchical forms is suffused throughout the organization, distributed rather than concentrated. Moreover, even if we could locate power "at the top" and then seize it, what would we do with it? If we held on to it but kept it there, we would be re-creating a hierarchy, surely not desirable for those "at the bottom" who had sought to overturn the system. If we dispersed it, we would be creating a heterarchy, and we would then find ourselves confronting the problems of distributed authority, lateral accountability, rivalry of evaluative principles, competition of performance criteria, self-management as the management of self, and questions about who should have a voice in Möbius-strip identities when there is good cause for ambiguity about just who is and who is not a member of the organization. In other words, we would be facing exactly the processes that I have been pointing to as so difficult to bring "under control." Heterarchy thus poses problems, many of which cannot be solved at the level of the heterarchical organizations themselves.

There are ready answers to these questions: Quiet the clash of competing evaluative principles. Let there be a single metric of economic value— market value. And let there be a single metric of social values—"family values."

But there is another answer as well. Just as I have argued that the most effective response to the problems in newly emerging democracies is not less democracy but more democracy,[16] the response to the problems of

---

[15] John Seely Brown, "Introduction: Rethinking Innovation in a Changing World," 1997.

[16] David Stark and László Bruszt, "One Way or Multiple Paths? For a Comparative Sociology of East European Capitalism," 2001.

heterarchy is not less heterarchy but more—a rivalry of evaluative principles not only within organizations but more broadly in the society. As
such, the answer lies not in control but in politics, a heterarchical politics[17]
that openly challenges the market metric of value by articulating alternative principles of the valuable.

To permit one example: In addressing the question "What is the bio-
sphere worth?" Harvard biologist E. O. Wilson discusses efforts to place
a market value on its "productivity" but concludes that other metrics are
more valuable, precisely because uncertainty about the future makes such
pricing futile: "No one can guess the full future value of any kind of ani-
mal, plant, or microorganism. Its potential is spread across a spectrum of
known and as yet unimagined human needs."[18]

Challenging market dominance of the search for the valuable cannot
be a smooth process. But, precisely because that dissonance can be a productive dissonance, we can be confident in rebuking any charge that it
would curtail entrepreneurial activity. Such entrepreneurship would be
innovative and recombinant, but it would not be directed toward market
gain.[19] The friction of a truly heterarchical rivalry of evaluative principles
would generate new forms of entrepreneurship when the search for the
valuable is unleashed from the search for profits.

The problem of our unruly search is not that it has to be tamed but that
it has not been exploratory enough. We face crises not because our economic system is too diverse in its criteria of performance but because it
is not diverse enough. In our era, the socialist societies of Eastern Europe
and the Soviet Union failed not simply because they did not use market
selection mechanisms but because their social system lacked the requisite
variety for adaptability in response to changes in its environment. Communism was defeated by liberal values. But there are two very different
ways to interpret this statement, entailing divergent lessons. In the first,
communism was defeated by "the market," and the lesson is to extend
the dominance of the market logic into other domains. In the second, a
system of low diversity failed in its competition with a system of higher
diversity in which the political field, education, religion, and the arts were
organized along principles that were not subordinated to the market. In
this view, the lesson is to articulate more forcefully dissonant conceptions
of worth.

[17] For discussions of a new politics, see J. K. Gibson-Graham, *A Postcapitalist Politics*, 2006;
and Ash Amin and Nigel Thrift, *Reinventing Politics*, forthcoming.

[18] Edward O. Wilson, *The Future of Life*, 2003, p. 113.

[19] Current notions of "social entrepreneurship," which call for bringing the tools of the venture
capitalist to the nonprofit sector, are quite far from the more conflictual process I have in mind.

To face the current crises of adaptability of our own society, literally of the destruction of our natural and social environment, we need new forms of entrepreneurship, emphatically not limited to the market variant, combining new ends and means, to build policies and practices that create wealth in forms that sustain our communities and our environment. We need societal friction that generates a reflexive cognition capable of recognizing innovative solutions.

Complexity, in the field of organizations, is the interweaving of diverse evaluative principles. The assets of the firm are adaptively increased when there are multiple measures of what constitutes an asset. The same is true at the societal level. Value is amplified when there is organized dissonance about what constitutes the valuable. Times of uncertainty raise the stakes in our societal, and now global, search. To meet that challenge we must look beyond the search space of the already known. To guide that search by the quest for wealth, defined in market terms, will leave us impoverished and our planet depleted. What does it profit us to gain more wealth but lose our world?

Is it worth it? We do better when more of us with varied voices ask this question from different standpoints of what is worthy. Heterarchical search will be dissonant, but it is dissonance that leads to discovery.

Acknowledgments

I am grateful first to the toolmakers at Minotaur, the new-media workers at NetKnowHow, and the traders at International Securities who so generously welcomed me and my research collaborators, tolerated our presence and questions, and patiently explained the complexities of their working lives.

It helped enormously that I was not alone. In János Lukács I could be confident that I had the most insightful and tireless guide to explore the Hungarian shop floor. On many days, our research started at dawn, and so often, after putting his kids to bed, we would continue at his kitchen table long past midnight analyzing our field notes and trying to figure out what was happening not only at Minotaur but also more generally in those exciting times in Hungary. Of such was forged a lifetime friendship. With Monique Girard I share not only a research partnership but a life's partnership. If you know Monique, you will understand immediately her warm and glowing presence among the twentysomethings at NetKnow-How. If you do not know her, you will see her insights on every page of our joint ethnography. With my former student and now Columbia colleague and friend Daniel Beunza, I was blessed with an incomparable ethnographer. On the many days in which we did not take the subway together to the World Financial Center, Daniel would work up his field notes and we would talk about them. It is probably not an exaggeration to say that for every hour in the field we spent three hours in conversation prior to the next observations. There was much to talk about because Daniel's field notes are the best I have ever seen by any ethnographer. It has been such a pleasure seeing him become a leading figure in the social studies of finance.

For comments, criticisms, and suggestions in preparing individual chapters, I am grateful to Steve Barley, Luc Boltanski, Pierre Bourdieu, Michael Burawoy, Beverly Burris, Michel Callon, Karin Knorr Cetina, Paul Duguid, Neil Fligstein, János Kornai, David Lane, Scott Lash, Vincent Lépinay, Fabian Muniesa, Wanda Orlikowski, Alex Preda, Laurent Thévenot, Nigel Thrift, Loic Wacquant, Harrison White, Sidney Winter, and Erik Wright.

Many of the ideas in this book were developed and tested over a decade in my graduate seminar on economic sociology at Columbia. From its first meeting in the spring of 1998 to the present, the seminar has been a lively setting in which we "practice" sociology. One of my greatest joys as a teacher is to watch each year as a collection of smart and strong-minded individuals becomes a team, listening to each other and crafting concepts together. Students in the spring 2007 seminar dissected the book manuscript. Like pathologists, they discriminated the healthy tissues from the diseased and feeble. In revising, I benefited from their criticisms and suggestions as well as from the excellent advice of some of my former students. I am especially grateful to Fabien Accominotti, Pablo Boczkowski, Larissa Buchholz, Victor Corona, Amanda Damarin, Lucas Graves, Victoria Johnson, Dani Lanier-Vos, Anna Mitschele, Gina Neff, Rasmus Nielsen, Pilar Opazo, Matthias Thiemann, Zsuzsanna Vargha, and Balazs Vedres.

In revising the manuscript I benefited from insightful feedback from Patrick Aspers, Gil Eyal, Brooke Harrington, Martin Harwit, Michael Hutter, Steven Lansing, Donald MacKenzie, Mariza Peirano, and Michael Piore. At critical moments, it mattered that there were people whose judgment I respected, who really understood the project, and who were strongly supportive and encouraging. And so, I am particularly grateful to Ash Amin (director of the Institute of Advanced Study, Durham University), to Jens Beckert (codirector of the Max Planck Institute, Cologne), and to Ian Malcolm (my editor at Princeton University Press).

My research and writing would not have been possible without institutional support, especially bountiful in this case because the book spans work in different times and across different settings. For unencumbered fellowships, I am grateful to the American Council for Learned Societies (1984–85) and the John Simon Guggenheim Foundation (spring 2004). For the opportunity to work for an extended time in a community of scholars, I am grateful to the Centre de Sociologie Politique et Morale, Paris (fall 1986); the Society for the Humanities, Cornell University (1989–90); the Center for Advanced Study in the Behavioral Sciences (1995–96); the Russell Sage Foundation (2002–3); the Institute of Advanced Study, Durham, UK (fall 2007); and the Max Planck Institute for the Study of Societies, Cologne (spring 2008).

From start to finish, at every stage of research, writing, and revising, I counted on the wise counsel of four dear friends, László Bruszt, Geoff Fougere, István Gábor, and Gernot Grabher. Geoff, for example, read the drafts of chapters 1 and 5 in weekly installments, as the opportunity to discuss the work with him at the end of each week served as a strong motivation for writing. Each of them read and commented on the entire manuscript—in its multiple variants—and I frequently called on them for guidance.

If I relied on my friends for advice at each stage, I relied on Monique Girard for advice at every step. We talked about the research, about the writing of the various chapters, about the overall structure of the book, and many times, too, about the structure of particular paragraphs and sentences. Most importantly, Monique is an ever-refreshing source of new ideas. No one I know has a keener sense to spot and formulate an interesting project. Imagine enjoying a day with such an inspiring intellect ... and then imagine enjoying a lifetime.

Our children Alexa and Ben are my other major sources of inspiration. Their ideas, their laughter, and their joy of life, all has been so wonderful. Recently, they have augmented that inspirational role with the role of appreciative and helpful critics. While vacationing in Venice, Alexa and Ben asked how my book was going. I said something to the effect that it's going OK. "No, really, we want to see," they insisted. I gave each of them a chapter. Silence. And then, after a couple of minutes, Alexa asked, "do you have a pen?" Ben, meanwhile, had also started in. Slash and burn. I looked over each shoulder to see the margin comments: "unclear," "too much unnecessary information here," "don't lead with the metaphor," "needs stronger concluding sentence"—and that just on the first page. Each of them, in different ways, has a mature authorial style. So, it was a very happy father who a week later got their heavily marked-up copies. If Alexa's and Ben's editing significantly improved those chapters, their input also contributed to the book's conception. In a thoughtful conversation, for example, Ben concisely articulated the guidelines shaping the preface, and I often enjoyed talking with Alexa about the challenges of writing a book that would sharply address the issues in a particular field while also inviting a broader audience.

This book is dedicated to my parents, Talitha and Willard Stark. I am sorry that my father did not live to see the book. I think he would have enjoyed reading it, and I know that I would have enjoyed talking with him about it. He was a fine writer, with a good sense of a strong line. His beautiful singing voice carried over into the melody and rhythm of his writer's voice. I suspect that everything I learned about writing I got from him. I am happy that I have been able to discuss the book with my mother. Her curiosity about the world and her sense of social justice have, if anything, increased with age. Goldwater Republicans in 1964, by 1980 she and my father traveled to Nicaragua to protest at the American Embassy. It is one thing to chant, "One, two, three, four, we don't want your contra/Iraq/whichever war" with a crowd of thousands in New York City or Washington, DC. It takes real courage to do so at a protest with only six other demonstrators in front of the old Federal Building in Oklahoma

City. We know that our children change, grow, and develop, but we don't always recognize that our parents can do the same, sometimes at speeds that leave us behind. Forgetful of this sometimes, when my mother would ask me what I was working on, I would start out hesitatingly, wondering how she could be interested in some piece of academic sociology. But she kept me talking, and I was always impressed with an intriguing question or insightful comment from her. With this book it was the same. She has read it, and she says that it's a pretty good book.

An earlier version of chapter 3 appeared in *Environment and Planning A*, November 2002, vol. 34, no. 11, pp. 1927–1949. An earlier version of chapter 4 appeared in *Industrial and Corporate Change* 2004, vol. 13, no. 2, pp. 369–401.

Bibliography

Abbott, Andrew. 1992. What do cases do? Some notes on activity in sociological analysis. Pp. 53–82 in *What is a case? Exploring the foundations of social inquiry*, ed. Charles C. Ragin and Howard S. Becker. London and New York: Cambridge University Press.

Abolafia, Mitchell. 1996. *Making markets: Opportunism and restraint on Wall Street*. Cambridge, MA: Harvard University Press.

Abolafia, Mitchell Y., and Martin Kilduff. 1988. Enacting market crisis: The social construction of a speculative bubble. *Administrative Science Quarterly* 33:117–193.

Agre, Philip E. 1965. Conceptions of the user in computer systems design. Pp. 67–106 in *The social and interactional dimensions of human-computer interfaces*, ed. Peter J. Thomas. New York: Cambridge University Press.

Akerlof, George A. 1970. The market for "lemons": Quality uncertainty and the market mechanism. *Quarterly Journal of Economics* 84 (3): 488–500.

Alberts, David S., John J. Garstka, and Frederick P. Stein. 2000. *Network centric warfare: Developing and leveraging information superiority*, 2nd ed. revised. Washington, DC: U.S. Department of Defense, Command and Control Research Program.

Alberts, David S., and Richard E. Hayes. 2003. *Power to the edge*. Washington, DC: U.S. Department of Defense, Command and Control Research Program.

Allen, Peter M., and J. M. McGlade. 1987. Modeling complex human systems: A fisheries example. *European Journal of Operational Research* 24:147–167.

Amin, Ash, and Patrick Cohendet. 2004. *Architectures of knowledge: Firms capabilities, and communities*. Oxford: Oxford University Press.

Amin, Ash, and Joanne Roberts. 2008. The resurgence of community in economic thought and practice. Pp. 11–34 in *Communities of Practice: Community, economic creativity, and organization*, ed. Ash Amin and Joanne Roberts. Oxford: Oxford University Press.

Amin, Ash, and Nigel Thrift. 1992. Neo-Marshallian nodes in global networks. *International Journal of Urban and Regional Research* 16:571–587.

———. Forthcoming. *Reinventing politics*.

Arbib, Michael A. 2000. Warren McCulloch's search for the logic of the nervous system. *Perspectives in Biology and Medicine* 43 (2): 193–216.

Arnoldi, Jakob. 2004. Derivatives: Virtual values and real risks. *Theory, Culture and Society* 21 (6): 23–42.

Arthur, W. Brian. 1989. Competing technologies, increasing returns, and lock-in by historical events. *Economic Journal* 99 (394): 116–131.

———. 1994. *Increasing returns and path dependence in the economy.* Ann Arbor: University of Michigan Press.

———. 2007. The structure of invention. *Research Policy* 36 (2): 274–287.

Ashcraft, Karen Lee. 2001. Organized dissonance: Feminist bureaucracy as hybrid form. *Academy of Management Journal* 44 (6): 1301–1322.

Bach, Jonathan, and David Stark. 2002. Innovative ambiguities: NGOs' use of interactive technologies in Eastern Europe. *Studies in Comparative International Development* 37:3–23.

———. 2004. Link, search, interact: The co-evolution of NGOs and interactive technologies. *Theory, Culture and Society* 21 (3): 101–117.

Bacon, Francis. [1620] 1960. *Novum organum (The new organ).* Indianapolis: Bobbs-Merrill.

Baker, Wayne. E. 1984. The social structure of a national securities market. *American Journal of Sociology* 89:775–811.

Barry, David, and Clauss Rerup. 2006. Going mobile: Aesthetic design considerations form Calder and the Constructivists. *Organization Science* 17 (1): 262–276.

Barsade, Siegal. 2002. The ripple effect: Emotional contagion in groups. *Administrative Science Quarterly* 47:644–675.

Baum, Dan. 2005. Battle lessons: What the generals don't know. *New Yorker*, January 17, pp. 42–48.

Bechky, Beth. 2003. Sharing meaning across occupational communities: The transformation of understanding on a production floor. *Organization Science* 14 (3): 312–320.

Beckert, Jens. 1996. What is sociological about economic sociology? Uncertainty and the embeddedness of economic action. *Theory and Society* 25:803–40.

———. 1999. Agency, entrepreneurs, and institutional change: The role of strategic choice and institutionalized practices in organizations. *Organization Studies* 20 (5): 777–99.

Benkler, Yochai. 2006. *The wealth of networks: How social production transforms markets and freedom.* New Haven, CT: Yale University Press.

Beunza, Daniel, and Raghu Garud. 2007. Calculator, lemmings, or frame-makers? The intermediary role of securities analysts. Pp. 13–39 in *Market Devices*, ed. Fabian Muniesa, Yuval Millo, and Michel Callon. Blackwell Synergy (special issue of *Sociological Review* 55 [2]).

Beunza, Daniel, and David Stark. 2003. The organization of responsiveness: Innovation and recovery in the trading rooms of Wall Street. *Socio-economic Review* 1:135–16.

———. 2005. Resolving identities: Successive crises in a trading room after 9/11. Pp. 293–320 in *Wounded city: The social impact of 9/11*, ed. Nancy Foner. New York: Russell Sage Foundation Press.

Bijker, Wiebe E. 1995. *Of bicycles, Bakelites, and bulbs: Toward a theory of sociotechnical change.* Cambridge, MA, and London: MIT Press.

Bijker, Wiebe E., Thomas P. Hughes, and Trevor J. Pinch. 1990. *The social construction of technological systems: New directions in the sociology and history of technology*. Cambridge, MA, and London: MIT Press.

Boczkowski, Pablo. 2001. Affording flexibility: Transforming information practices in online newspapers. PhD dissertation, Department of Science and Technology Studies, Cornell University.

———. 2004. *Digitizing the news: Innovation in online newspapers*. Cambridge, MA: MIT Press.

Boltanski, Luc, and Ève Chiapello. 2005. *The new spirit of capitalism*. London: Verso.

Boltanski, Luc, and Laurent Thévenot. 1991. *De la justification: Les economies de la grandeur*. Paris: Gallimard.

———. 1999. The sociology of critical capacity. *European Journal of Social Theory* 2:359–377.

———. 2006. *On justification: The economies of worth*. Princeton, NJ: Princeton University Press.

Bourdieu, Pierre. 1977. *Outline of a theory of practice*. Cambridge: Cambridge University Press.

———. 1986. Habitus, code, et codification. *Actes de la recherche en sciences sociales* 64:40–44.

Bowker, Geoffrey, and Susan Leigh Star. 1994. Knowledge and infrastructure in international information management: Problems of classification and coding. Pp. 187–213 in *Information acumen: The understanding and use of knowledge in modern business*, ed. Lisa Bud-Frierman. London: Routledge.

———. 2000. *Sorting things out: Classification and its consequences*. Cambridge, MA: MIT Press.

Brandenburger, Adam. 2007. The power of paradox: Some recent developments in interactive epistemology. *International Journal of Game Theory* 35:465–492.

Brown, John Seely. 1997. Introduction: Rethinking innovation in a changing world. Pp. ix–xxviii in *Seeing differently: Insights on innovation*, ed. John Seely Brown. Boston: Harvard Business School Press.

Brown, John Seely, and Paul Duguid. 1998. Organizing knowledge. *California Management Review* 40:90–111.

———. 2000. *The social life of information*. Boston: Harvard Business School Press.

———. 2001a. Creativity versus structure: A useful tension. *MIT Sloan Management Review* 42:93–95.

———. 2001b. Knowledge and organization: A social-practice perspective. *Organization Science* 12:198–213.

Bruszt, László. 2002. Market making as state making: Constitutions and economic development in postcommunist Eastern Europe. *Constitutional Political Economy* 15:53–72.

Bruszt, László, and David Stark. 2003. Who counts? Supranational norms and societal needs. *East European Politics and Societies* 17 (1): 74–82.

Bryan, Dick, and Michael Rafferty. 2006. *Capitalism with derivatives: A political economy of financial derivatives, capital and class.* New York: Palgrave Macmillan.

———. 2007. Financial derivatives and the theory of money. *Economy and Society* 36 (1): 134–158.

Burawoy, Michael. 1979. *Manufacturing consent: Changes in the labor process under monopoly capitalism.* Chicago: University of Chicago Press.

Burns, Tom, and G. M. Stalker. 1961. *The management of innovation.* London: Tavistock.

Burt, Ronald. 1995. *Structural holes: The social structure of competition.* Cambridge, MA: Harvard University Press.

———. 2005. *Brokerage and closure.* Oxford: Oxford University Press.

Buxbaum, Richard M. 1993. Is "network" a legal concept? *Journal of Institutional and Theoretical Economics* 149 (4): 698–705.

Callon, Michel. 1998a. An essay on reframing and overflowing: Economic externalities revisited by sociology. Pp. 244–269 in *The Laws of the Markets*, ed. Michel Callon. Oxford: Blackwell Publishers.

———. 1998b. Introduction: Embeddedness of economic markets in economics. Pp. 1–57 in *The Laws of the Markets*, ed. Michel Callon. Oxford: Blackwell Publishers.

———. 2003. The increasing involvement of concerned groups in R&D policies: What lessons for public powers? Pp. 30–68 in *Science and innovation: Rethinking the rationales for funding and governance*, ed. A. Geuna, A. J. Salter, and W. E. Steinmueller. Cheltenham, UK: Edward Elgar.

———. 2007. What does it mean to say that economics is performative? Pp. 311–357 in *Do economists make markets? On the performativity of economics*, ed. Donald MacKenzie, Fabian Muniesa, and Lucia Siu. Princeton, NJ: Princeton University Press.

Callon, Michel, Cecile Meadel, and Vololona Rabeharisoa. 2002. The economy of qualities. *Economy and Society* 31 (2): 194–217.

Callon, Michel, Yuval Millo, and Fabian Muiesa, eds. 2007. *Market devices.* Malden, MA: Blackwell.

Callon, Michel, and Fabian Muniesa. 2005. Economic markets as calculative collective devices. *Organization Studies* 26 (8): 1229–1250.

Callon, Michel, and Vololona Rabeharisoa. 2003. Research in the wild and the shaping of new social identities. *Technology in Society* 25:193–204.

Camic, Charles. 1987. The making of a method: A historical reinterpretation of the early Parsons. *American Sociological Review* 52:421–39.

Castells, Manuel. 1996. *The rise of the network society.* Cambridge, MA: Blackwell Publishers.

Clark, Andy. 1993. *Associative engines: Connectionism, concepts, and representational change.* Cambridge, MA: MIT Press.

———. 1997. *Being there: Putting brain, body, and world together again.* Cambridge, MA: MIT Press.

———. 1999. Leadership and influence: The manager as coach, nanny, and artificial DNA. Pp. 47–66 in *The biology of business: Decoding the natural laws of enterprise*, ed. John H. Clippinger. San Francisco: Jossey-Bass.

———. 2003. *Natural-born cyborgs: Minds, technologies, and the future of human intelligence*. Oxford: Oxford University Press.

Clark, Gordon L., Maryann P. Feldman, and Meric S. Gertler. 2000. *The Oxford handbook of economic geography*. Oxford: Oxford University Press.

Clippinger, John H. 1999. Tags: The power of labels in shaping markets and organizations. Pp. 67–88 in *The biology of business: Decoding the natural laws of enterprise*, ed. John H. Clippinger. San Francisco: Jossey-Bass.

Clouse, Abby. 2008. Narratives of value and the antiques roadshow: A game of recognitions. *Journal of Popular Culture* 41 (1): 3–20.

Cohen, Michael D. 1981. The power of parallel thinking. *Journal of Economic Behavior and Organization* 2:285–306.

———. 1983. Conflict and complexity: Goal diversity and organizational search effectiveness. *American Political Science Review* 78:435–451.

Conrad, Michael. 1983. *Adaptability*. New York: Plenum Press.

Contractor, Noshir S., and Peter R. Monge. 2002. Managing knowledge networks. *Management Communication Quarterly* 16:249–258.

Corbridge, Stuart, and Nigel Thrift, eds. 1994. *Money, power and space*. London: Blackwell Publishers.

Damarin, Amanda. 2004. Fit, flexibility, and connection: Organizing employment in emerging web labor markets, New York City 1993–2003. PhD dissertation, Department of Sociology, Columbia University.

DeLanda, Manuel. 1991. *War in the age of intelligent machines*. New York: Swerve Editions.

———. 2006. *A new philosophy of society: Assemblage theory and social complexity*. London: Continuum International Publishing Group.

Derman, Emanuel. 2007. Modeling and its discontents. Paper presented at the Conference on Uncertainty, Center on Organizational Innovation, Columbia University, September 2007.

Desrosières, Alain. 1994. Official statistics and business: History, classification, uses. Pp. 168–186 in *Information acumen: The understanding and use of knowledge in modern business*, ed. Lisa Bud-Frierman. London: Routledge.

———. 1998. *The politics of large numbers: A history of statistical reasoning*. Cambridge, MA: Harvard University Press.

Dewey, John. [1938] 1998. Analysis of reflective thinking. Pp. 137–144 in *The essential Dewey, volume 2: Ethics, logic, psychology*, ed. Larry A. Hickman and Thomas M. Alexander. Bloomington: Indiana University Press.

———. [1938] 1998. The pattern of inquiry. Pp. 169–179 in *The essential Dewey, volume 2: Ethics, logic, psychology*, ed. Larry A. Hickman and Thomas M. Alexander. Bloomington: Indiana University Press.

———. 1939. *Theory of valuation*. Chicago: University of Chicago Press.

DiMaggio, Paul, ed. 2001. *The twenty-first-century firm: Changing economic organization in international perspective.* Princeton, NJ: Princeton University Press.

DiMaggio, Paul J., and Walter W. Powell. 1983. The iron cage revisited: Institutional isomorphism and collective rationality in organizational fields. *American Sociological Review* 48 (2): 147–160.

———. 1991. Introduction. Pp. 1–38 in *The new institutionalism in organizational analysis*, ed. Walter W. Powell and Paul J. DiMaggio. Chicago: University of Chicago Press.

Dodds, Peter Sheridan, Duncan J. Watts, and Charles F. Sabel. 2003. Information exchange and the robustness of organizational networks. *Proceedings of the National Academy of Sciences* 100 (21): 12516–12521.

Dorf, Michael C., and Charles F. Sabel. 1998. A constitution of democratic experimentalism. *Columbia Law Review* 98:267–529.

Dosi, Givoanni, and Bruce Kogut. 1993. National specificities and the context of change: The coevolution of organization and technology. Pp. 249–262 in *Country Competitiveness: Technology and the organization of work*, ed. Bruce Kogut. New York: Oxford University Press.

Dourish, Paul. 2004. *Where the action is: The foundations of embodied interaction.* Cambridge, MA: MIT Press.

Dourish, Paul, and Graham Button. 1998. On technomethodology: Foundational relationships between ethnomethodology and system design. *Human-Computer Interaction* 13 (4): 395–432.

Dow, Sheila, and John Hillard, eds. 1995. *Keynes, knowledge and uncertainty.* Aldershot, UK: Edward Elgar.

Dreyfus, Laurence. 1996. *Bach and the patterns of invention.* Cambridge, MA: Harvard University Press.

Dunbar, Nicholas. 2000. *Inventing money: The story of long-term capital management and the legends behind it.* New York: John Wiley & Sons.

Dupuy, Jean-Pierre. 1989. Common knowledge, common sense. *Theory and Decision* 27:37–62.

———. 1994. The self-deconstruction of convention. *Substance: A Review of Theory and Literary Criticism* 23 (2): 86<n->98.

———. 2000. *The mechanization of the mind: On the origins of cognitive science.* Princeton, NJ: Princeton University Press.

Epstein, Steven. 1995. The construction of lay expertise: AIDS activism and the forging of credibility in the reform of clinical trials. *Science, Technology, & Human Values* 20:408–437.

———. 1997. Activism, drug regulation, and the politics of therapeutic evaluation in the AIDS era. *Social Studies of Science* 27:691–726.

Espeland, Wendy Nelson, and Michael Sauder. 2007. Rankings and reactivity: How public measures recreate social worlds. *American Journal of Sociology* 113 (1): 1–40.

Espeland, Wendy Nelson, and Mitchell L. Stevens. 1998. Commensuration as a social process. *Annual Review of Sociology* 24:313–43.

Eymard-Duvernay, François. 1994. Coordination des échanges par l'entreprise et qualité des biens. Pp. 331–358 in *Analyse économique des conventions*, ed. André Orlean. Paris: PUF.

Favereau, Olivier, Olivier Biencourt, and Francois Eymard-Duvernay. 2002. Where do markets come from? From (quality) conventions. Pp. 213–252 in *Conventions and structures in economic organization: Markets, networks and hierarchies*, ed. Olivier Favereau and Emmanuel Lazega. Cheltenham, UK: Edward Elgar.

Favereau, Olivier, and Emmanuel Lazega, eds. 2002. *Conventions and structures in economic organization: Markets, networks and hierarchies*. Cheltenham, UK: Edward Elgar.

Fischer, Claude S. 1992. *America calling: The social history of the telephone until 1940*. Berkeley: University of California Press.

Fleming, Lee. 2001. Recombinant uncertainty in technological search. *Management Science* 47:117–132.

Fligstein, Neil. 1990. *The transformation of corporate control*. Cambridge, MA: Harvard University Press.

———. 1996. Markets as politics: A political-cultural approach to market institutions. *American Sociological Review* 61 (4): 656–673.

———. 1997. Social skill and institutional theory. *American Behavioral Scientist* 40 (4): 397–405.

———. 2001. *The architecture of markets: An economic sociology of capitalist societies*. Princeton, NJ: Princeton University Press.

Fontana, Walter, and Leo Buss. 1994. "The arrival of the fittest": Toward a theory of biological organization. *Bulletin of Mathematical Biology* 56 (1): 1–64.

———. 1996. The barrier of objects: From dynamical systems to bounded organizations. Pp. 56–116 in *Barriers and boundaries*, ed. J. Casti and A. Karlqvist. Reading, MA: Addison-Wesley.

Franz, K. 2005. *Tinkering: Customers reinvent the early automobile*. Philadelphia: University of Pennsylvania Press.

Friedland, Roger, and Robert R. Alford. 1991. Bringing society back in: Symbols, practices, and institutional contradictions. Pp. 232–266 in *The new institutionalism in organizational analysis*, ed. Walter W. Powell and Paul J. DiMaggio. Chicago: University of Chicago Press.

Fullbrook, Edward, ed. 2001. *Intersubjectivity in economics: Agents and structures*. London and New York: Routledge.

Gábor, István R. 1979. The second (secondary) economy. *Acta Oeconomica* 22 (3–4): 291–311.

Galison, Peter L. 1997. *Image and logic: A material culture of microphysics*. Chicago: University of Chicago Press.

Galison, Peter L., and Emily Thompson, eds. 1999. *The architecture of science*. Cambridge, MA: MIT Press.

Galloway, Alex. 2006. *Protocol: How control exists after decentralization*. Cambridge, MA: MIT Press.

Garud, Raghu, Sanjay Jain, and Philipp Tuertscher. 2008. Incomplete by design and designing for incompleteness. *Organization Studies* 29 (3): 351–371.

Garud, Raghu, and Peter Karnøe. 2001. Path creation as a process of mindful deviation. Pp. 1–40 in *Path dependence and creation*, ed. Raghu Garud and Peter Karnøe. Mahwah, NJ: Lawrence Erlbaum Associates.

———. 2003. Bricolage versus breakthrough: Distributed and embedded agency in technological entrepreneurship. *Research Policy* 32 (2): 277–300.

Gibson-Graham, J. K. 2006. *A postcapitalist politics*. Minneapolis: University of Minnesota Press.

Girard, Monique, and David Stark. 2007. Socio-technologies of assembly: Sense-making and demonstration in rebuilding Lower Manhattan. Pp. 145–176 in *Governance and information: The rewiring of governing and deliberation in the 21st Century*, ed. David Lazer and Viktor Mayer-Schoenberger. New York and Oxford: Oxford University Press.

Gladwell, Malcom. 1999. The science of the sleeper. *New Yorker*, October 4, pp. 48–55.

———. 2000. Designs for working. *New Yorker*, December 11, pp. 60–70.

Godechot, Olivier. 2000. Le bazar de la rationalite. *Politix* 13:17–56.

Gould, Glenn. 1994. Forgery and imitation in the creative process. *Grand Street* 13 (2): 53–62.

Grabher, Gernot. 1994. *Lob der Verschwendung* [In praise of waste: Redundancy in regional development]. Berlin: Edition Sigma.

———. 1997. Adaptation at the cost of adaptability? Restructuring the Eastern German regional economy. Pp. 107–134 in *Restructuring networks: Legacies, linkages, and localities in postsocialism*, ed. Gernot Grabher and David Stark. London and New York: Oxford University Press.

———. 2001. Ecologies of creativity: The village, the group, and the heterarchic organisation of the British advertising industry. *Environment & Planning A* 33:351–374.

———. 2002a. Cool projects, boring institutions, and temporary collaboration in social context. *Regional Studies* 36:205–214.

———. 2002b. The project ecology of advertising: Tasks, talents and teams. *Regional Studies* 36:245–262.

Grabher, Gernot, and David Stark. 1997. Organizing diversity: Evolutionary theory, network analysis, and the postsocialist transformations. Pp. 1–32 in *Restructuring networks: Legacies, linkages, and localities in postsocialism*, ed. Gernot Grabher and David Stark. London and New York: Oxford University Press.

Graham, Benjamin, and David L. Dodd. 1934. *Security analysis: Principles and techniques*. New York: McGraw-Hill.

Grandclément, Catherine. 2008. Wheeling one's groceries around the store: The invention of the shopping cart, 1936–1953. Pp. 233–251 in *Food chains: From farmyard to shopping cart*, ed. Warren Belasco and Roger Horowitz. Philadelphia: University of Pennsylvania Press.

Grandori, Anna, and Santi Furnari. 2008. A chemistry of organization: Combinatory analysis and design. *Organization Studies* 29 (3): 459–485.

Granovetter, Mark S. 1985. Economic action and social structure: The problem of embeddedness. *American Journal of Sociology* 19:481–510.

Hagel, John III, and John Seely Brown. 2005. Productive friction: How difficult business partnerships can accelerate innovation. *Harvard Business Review* 83 (2): 82–91, 148.

Hagstrom, Peter, and Gunnar Hedlund. 1998. A three-dimensional model of changing internal structure in the firm. Pp. 166–191 in *Dynamic firm: The role of technology, strategy, organization and region*, ed. Alfred Chandler, Peter Hagstrom, and Orjan Solvell. London and New York: Oxford University Press.

Hamilton, Gary G., and Robert C. Feenstra. 1995. Varieties of hierarchies and markets: An introduction. *Industrial and Corporate Change* 4 (1): 51–91.

Hannan, Michael T. 1986. Uncertainty, diversity, and organizational change. Pp. 73–94 in *Behavioral and social sciences, fifty years of discovery: In commemoration of the fiftieth anniversary of the "Ogburn report,"* ed. Neil J. Smelser and Dean R. Gerstein. Washington, DC: National Academy Press.

Hannan, Michael T., L. Polos, and Glen Carroll. 2007. *Logics of organization theory: Audiences, codes, and ecologies*. Princeton, NJ: Princeton University Press.

Hansen, Thomas F. 2003. Is modularity necessary for evolvability? Remarks on the relationship between pleiotropy and evolvability. *BioSystems* 69:83–94.

Hargadon, Andrew. 2003. *How breakthroughs happen*. Boston: Harvard Business School Press.

Heath, Christian, Marina Jirotka, Paul Luff, and Jon Hindmarsh. 1995. Unpacking collaboration: The interactional organization of trading in a city dealing room. *Computer Supported Cooperative Work* 3:147–165.

Hedlund, Gunnar. 1986. The hypermodern MNC: A heterarchy. *Human Resource Management* 25:9–35.

———. 1993. Assumptions of hierarchy and heterarchy, with applications to the management of the multinational corporation. Pp. 211–236 in *Organization Theory and the Multinational Enterprise*, ed. Sumantra Ghoshal and D. Eleanor Westney. London: Macmillan.

Hedlund, Gunnar, and Dag Rolander. 1990. Action in heterarchies—new approaches to managing the MNC. Pp. 15–46 in *Managing the global firm*, ed. Christopher A. Bartlett, Yves Doz, and Gunnar Hedlund. London and New York: Routledge.

Hennion, Antoine. 1997. Baroque and rock: Music, mediators and musical taste. *Poetics* 24:415–435.

———. 2004. The pragmatics of taste. Pp. 131–144 in *The Blackwell companion to the sociology of culture*, ed. Mark Jacobs and Nancy Hanrahan. Oxford and Malden, MA: Blackwell.

Herlocker, Jonathan L. 1999. Algorithmic framework for performing collaborative filtering. Pp. 230–237 in *Proceedings of the 22nd International Conference on Research and Development in Information Retrieval.* New York: ACM.

Hofstadter, Douglas R. 1979. *Gödel, Escher, Bach.* New York: Basic Books.

Holland, John. 1992. Complex adaptive systems. *Daedalus* 121 (1): 17–30.

Hull, John C. 1996. *Options, futures, and other derivative securities.* Englewood Cliffs, NJ: Prentice Hall.

Hutchins, Edwin. 1995. *Cognition in the wild.* Cambridge, MA: MIT Press.

Hutchins, Edwin, and Tove Klausen. 1991. Distributed cognition in an airline cockpit. Pp. 15–34 in *Distributed cognition and communication at work,* ed. Y. Engestrom and D. Middleton. Cambridge: Cambridge University Press.

Hutter, Michael, and Günther Teubner. 1993. The parasitic role of hybrids. *Journal of Institutional and Theoretical Economics* 149:706–715.

Introna, Lucas D., and Frenando M. Ilharco. 2006. On the meaning of screens: Towards a phenomenological account of screeneness. *Human Studies* 29 (1): 57–76.

Jacob, Francois. 1977. Evolution and tinkering. *Science* 196:1161–1166.

Kahl, Steve. 2008. The dynamics of categorization. Manuscript, University of Chicago.

Kait, Casey, and Stephen Weiss. 2001. *Digital hustlers: Living large and falling hard in Silicon Alley.* New York: HarperCollins.

Kauffman, Stuart A. 1989. Adaptation on rugged fitness landscapes. Pp. 527–618 in *Lectures in the science of complexity,* vol. 1, ed. D. Stein. Reading, MA: Addison-Wesley, Longman.

———. 1993. *The origin of order: Self-organization and selection in evolution.* London: Oxford University Press.

Kellogg, Katherine C., Wanda J. Orlikowski, and JoAnne Yates. 2006. Life in the trading zone: Structuring coordination across boundaries in postbureaucratic organizations. *Organization Science* 17 (1): 22–44.

Kelly, John, and David Stark. 2002. Crisis, recovery, innovation: Learning from 9/11. Environment and Planning A 34:1523–1533.

Kennedy, David. 2006. *Of war and law.* Princeton, NJ, and Oxford: Princeton University Press.

Kidder, Tracy. 1981. *The soul of a new machine.* Boston: Little, Brown, and Company.

Kirzner, Israel M. 1982. Uncertainty, discovery, and human action: A study of the entrepreneurial profile in the Misesian system. Pp. 139–159 in *Method, process, and Austrian economics: Essays in honor of Ludvig von Mises,* ed. I. M. Kirzner. Lexington, MA: D. C. Heath.

Kline, Ronald, and Trevor Pinch. 1996. Users as agents of technological change: The social construction of the automobile in the rural United States. *Technology and Culture* 37:763–795.

Knight, Frank H. 1921. *Risk, uncertainty and profit.* Boston: Houghton Mifflin Company.

Knorr-Cetina, Karin. 1981. Introduction: The micro-sociological challenge of macro-sociology: Towards a reconstruction of social theory and methodology. Pp. 1–47 in *Advances in social theory and methodology: Toward an integration of micro- and macro-sociologies*, ed. Karin Knorr-Cetina and Aaron V. Cicourel. London: Routledge & Kegan Paul.

———. 2002. The market as an epistemic institution. Paper presented at the New York Conference on Social Studies of Finance, Columbia University.

Knorr Cetina, Karin, and Urs Bruegger. 2002. Global microstructures: The virtual societies of financial markets. *American Journal of Sociology* 107:905–50.

Knorr Cetina, Karin, and Alex Preda. 2001. The epistemization of economic transactions. *Current Sociology* 49:27–44.

Kogut, Bruce, and Anca Metiu. 2001. Open source software development and distributed innovation. Oxford Review of Economic *Policy* 17:248–264.

Kogut, Bruce, Weijan Shan, and Gordon Walker. 1992. The make-or-cooperate decision in the context of an industry network. Pp. 348–365 in *Networks and organizations*, ed. Nitin Nohira and Robert G. Eccles. Cambridge, MA: Harvard Business School Press.

Kogut, Bruce, and Udo Zander. 1992. Knowledge of the firm, combinative capabilities, and the replication of technology. *Organization Science* 3:383–97.

Konrad, George, and Ivan Szelenyi. 1979. *The intellectuals on the road to class power*. New York: Harcourt, Brace and Jovanovich.

Kornai, János. 1980. *Economics of shortage*. Amsterdam: North-Holland.

Kunda, Gideon. 1993. *Engineering culture: Control and commitment in a high tech corporation*. Philadelphia: Temple University Press.

Kunda, Gideon, and John Van Mannen. 1999. Changing scripts at work: Managers and professionals. *Annals of the American Academy of Political and Social Science* 561:64–80.

Ladeur, Karl-Heinz. 1997. Towards a legal theory of supranationality: The viability of the network concept. *European Law Journal* 3 (1): 33–54.

Lamont, Michèle, and Laurent Thévenot, eds. 2000. *Rethinking comparative cultural sociology: Repertoires of evaluation in France and the United States*. Cambridge and New York: Cambridge University Press.

Landau, Martin. 1969. Redundancy, rationality, and the problem of duplication and overlap. *Public Administration Review* 29 (4): 346–58.

Lane, David. 1995. Models and aphorisms. *Complexity* 1 (2): 9–13.

Lane, David, and Robert Maxfield. 1996. Strategy under complexity: Fostering generative relationships. *Long Range Planning* 29:215–231.

Latour, Bruno. 1986. Powers of association. Pp. 261–277 in *Power, action, and belief: A new sociology of knowledge*, ed. John Law. London and Boston: Routledge & Kegan Paul.

———. 1987. *Science in action: How to follow scientists and engineers through society*. Cambridge, MA: Harvard University Press.

———. 1988. *The Pasteurization of France*. Cambridge, MA: Harvard University Press.

————. 1991. Technology is society made durable. Pp. 103–131 in *A sociology of monsters: Essays on power, technology, and domination*, ed. John Law. London and Boston: Routledge & Kegan Paul.

————. 2005. *Reassembling the social*. Oxford: Oxford University Press.

Latour, Bruno, and Steve Woolgar. 1979. *Laboratory life: The social construction of scientific facts*. Los Angeles: Sage.

Lemieux, Thomas, W. Bentley MacLeod, and Daniel Parent. 2007. Performance pay and wage inequality. Working Paper Series, May, National Bureau of Economic Research, Cambridge, MA.

Lenoir, Timothy. 2000. All but war is simulation: The military-entertainment complex. *Configurations* 8 (3): 289–335.

————. 2002a. Authorship and surgery: The shifting ontology of the virtual surgeon. Pp. 283–308 in *From energy to information: Representation in science, art, and literature*, ed. Linda Henderson and Bruce Clarke. Stanford, CA: Stanford University Press.

————. 2002b. The virtual surgeon. Pp. 28–51 in *Semiotic flesh: Information and the human body*, ed. Phillip Thurtle. Seattle: University of Washington Press.

————. 2003. Programming theaters of war: Gamemakers as soldiers. Pp. 175–198 in *Bombs and bandwidth: The emerging relationship between IT and security*, ed. Robert Latham. New York: New Press.

Leonard-Barton, Dorothy. 1995. *Wellsprings of knowledge: Building and sustaining the sources of innovation*. Boston: Harvard Business School Press.

Lépinay, Vincent. 2002. Finance as circulating formulas. Paper presented at the New York Conference on Social Studies of Finance, Columbia University.

Lester, Richard K., and Michael J. Piore. 2004. *Innovation: The missing dimension*. Cambridge, MA and London: Harvard University Press.

Lettvin, J. Y., H. R. Maturana, W. S. McCulloch, and W. H. Pitts. 1959. What the frog's eye tells the frog's brain. *Proceedings of the Institute of Radio Engineering* 47:1940–1951.

Levinthal, Daniel A., and James G. March. 1993. The myopia of learning. *Strategic Management Journal* 14:95–112.

Levy, Thierry. 2001. The theory of conventions and a new theory of the firm. Pp. 254–272 in *Intersubjectivity in economics: Agents and structures*, ed. Edward Fullbrook. London and New York: Routledge.

Lewis, David K. 1969. *Conventions: A philosophical study*. Cambridge, MA: Harvard University Press.

Lewis, Michael. 1999. How the eggheads cracked. *New York Times*, January 24.

Leyshon, Andrew, and Nigel Thrift. 1997. *Money/space: Geographies of monetary transformation*. London and New York: Routledge.

Long, Norton E. 1958. The local community as an ecology of games. *American Journal of Sociology* 64 (3): 251–261.

MacKenzie, Donald. 2000. Long-term capital management and the sociology of finance. *London Review of Books*, April 13.

———. 2002. Risk, financial crises, and globalization: Long-term capital management and the sociology of arbitrage. Manuscript, University of Edinburgh.

———. 2006. *An engine not a camera: How financial models shape markets.* Cambridge, MA: MIT Press.

———. 2007. Is economics performative? Option theory and the construction of derivatives markets. Pp. 54–86 in *Do economists make markets? On the performativity of economics,* ed. Donald MacKenzie, Fabian Muniesa, and Lucia Siu. Princeton, NJ: Princeton University Press.

MacKenzie, Donald, and Yuval Millo. 2003. Negotiating a market, performing theory: The historical sociology of a financial derivatives exchange. *American Journal of Sociology* 109:107–145.

MacKenzie, Donald, Fabian Muniesa, and Lucia Siu. 2007. Introduction. Pp. 1–23 in *Do economists make markets? On the performativity of economics,* ed. Donald MacKenzie, Fabian Muniesa, and Lucia Siu. Princeton, NJ: Princeton University Press.

Manovich, Lev. 2001. *The language of new media.* Cambridge, MA: MIT Press.

Manville, Brook. 1999. Complex adaptive knowledge management: A case from McKinsey & Company. Pp. 89–112 in *The biology of business: Decoding the natural laws of enterprise,* ed. John H. Clippinger. San Francisco: Jossey-Bass.

March, James G. 1991. Exploration and exploitation in organizational learning. *Organization Science* 2:71–87.

Marcus, George E. 1998. *Ethnography through thick and thin.* Princeton, NJ: Princeton University Press.

Martin, Ron. 1999. The new economic geography of money. Pp. 2–27 in *Money and the space economy,* ed. Ron Martin. Chichester, UK: John Wiley & Sons.

McCulloch, Warren S. [1945] 1965. A heterarchy of values determined by the topology of nervous nets. Pp. 40–44 in *Embodiments of mind,* ed. W. S. McCulloch. Cambridge, MA: MIT Press. Originally published in 1945 in *Bulletin of Mathematical Biophysics* 7 (2) :89–93.

———. 1960. The reliability of biological systems. Pp. 264–481 in *Self-organizing systems,* ed. M. G. Yovitz and S. Camerons. New York: Pergamon Press.

McCulloch, Warren. S., and Pitts, Walter H. 1943. A logical calculus of the ideas immanent in nervous activity. *Bulletin of Mathematical Biophysics* 5:115–33.

McKenzie, Jon. 2001. *Perform or else: From discipline to performance.* New York: Routledge.

Meyer, John W., and Brian Rowan. 1977. Institutionalized organization: Formal structure as myth and ceremony. *American Journal of Sociology* 83 (2): 340–363.

Meyerson, Debra, Karl E. Weick, and Roderick M. Kramer. 1996. Swift trust and temporary groups. Pp. 166–195 in *Trust in Organizations,* ed. R. M. Karmer and T. R. Tyler. Thousand Oaks, CA: Sage.

Miller, Daniel. 2005. Materiality: An introduction. Pp. 1–50 in *Materiality,* ed. Daniel Miller. Durham, NC, and London: Duke University Press.

Miller, Peter, and Ted O'Leary. 2007. Mediating instruments and making markets: Capital budgeting, science, and the economy. *Accounting, Organizations, and Society* 32 (7–8): 701–734.

Millo, Yuval. 2001. Safety in numbers: How exchanges and regulators shaped index-based derivatives. Paper presented at the New York Conference on Social Studies of Finance, Columbia University.

Millo, Yuval, and Donald MacKenzie. In press. The usefulness of inaccurate models: The emergence of financial risk management. *Accounting, Organizations and Society.*

Miltner, Robert. 2001. Where the visual meets the verbal: Collaboration as conversation. *Enculturation* 3.

Mirowski, Philip. 2001. *Machine dreams: Economics becomes a cyborg science.* London and New York: Cambridge University Press.

Mische, Ann. 2008. *Partisan publics: Communication and contention across Brazilian youth activist networks.* Princeton, NJ: Princeton University Press.

Mische, Ann, and Harrison White. 1998. Between conversation and situation: Public switching dynamics across networks. *Social Research* 65 (3): 695–724.

Möllering, Guido. 2006. *Trust: Reason, routine, reflexivity.* Amsterdam: Elsevier.

Monge, Peter R., and Noshir N. Contractor. 2003. *Theories of communication networks.* New York: Oxford University Press.

Moreau, C. P., A. B. Markaman, and D. R. Lehmann. 2001. "What is it?" Categorization flexibility and consumers' responses to really new products. *Journal of Consumer Research* 27:489–498.

Morin, Edgar. 1974. Complexity. *International Social Science Journal* 26:555–82.

Muniesa, Fabian. 2000. Un robot walrasien: Cotation électronique et justesse de la découverte des prix. *Politix* 13:121–154.

———. 2002. Reserved anonymity: On the use of telephones in the trading room. Paper presented at the New York Conference on Social Studies of Finance, Columbia University.

———. 2007. Market technologies and the pragmatics of prices. *Economy and Society* 36 (3): 377–395.

Muniesa, Fabian, Yuval Millo, and Michel Callon, eds. 2007. *Market devices.* Blackwell Synergy (special issue of The Sociological Review 55 [2]).

Neff, Gina. 2004. Organizing uncertainty: Individual, organizational and institutional risk in New York's Internet industry, 1995–2003. PhD dissertation, Department of Sociology, Columbia University.

———. 2005. The changing place of cultural production: The location of social networks in a digital media industry. *Annals of the American Academy of Political and Social Science* 597 (1): 134–152.

Neff, Gina, and David Stark. 2003. Permanently beta: Responsive organization in the Internet era. Pp. 173–188 in *Society online: The Internet in context*, ed. Philip E. N. Howard and Steve Jones. Thousand Oaks, CA: Sage.

Neff, Gina, Elizabeth Wissinger, and Sharon Zukin. 2005. Entrepreneurial labor among cultural producers: "Cool" jobs in "hot" industries. *Social Semiotics* 15 (3): 307–334.

New York New Media Association. 2000. *3rd New York New Media Industry Survey.*

Obstfeld, David. 2005. Social networks, the tertius iungens orientation, and involvement in innovation. *Administrative Science Quarterly* 50 (1): 100–130.

O'Mahony, Siobhan. 2002. The emergence of a new commercial actor: Community managed software projects. PhD dissertation, Stanford University.

O'Neill, Michael. 2007. "My vision quickening": Dante and romantic poetry. Pp. 45–66 in *Dante rediscovered: From Blake to Rodin*, ed. David Bindman, Stephen Hebron, and Michael O'Neill. Grasmere, UK: Wordsworth Trust.

Orlikowski, Wanda J. 2002. Knowing in practice: Enacting a collective capability in distributed organizing. *Organization Science* 13 (3): 249–73.

———. 2007. Sociomaterial practices: Exploring technology at work. *Organization Studies* 28 (9): 1435–1451.

Orlikowski, Wanda, and C. S. Iacono. 1999. The truth is not out there: An enacted view of the "digital economy." Pp. 352–380 in *Understanding the digital economy: Data, tools, and research*, ed. E. Brynjolfsson and B. Kahin. Cambridge, MA: MIT Press.

Oudshoorn, Nelly, and Trevor Pinch. 2003. Introduction: How users and nonusers matter. Pp. 1–28 in *How users matter: The co-construction of users and technologies*, ed. Nelly Oudshoorn and Trevor Pinch. Cambridge, MA: MIT Press.

Padgett, John F. 2001. Organizational genesis, identity, and control: The transformation of banking in Renaissance Florence. Pp. 211–257 in *Networks and markets*, ed. James Rauch and Alessandra Casella. New York: Russell Sage Foundation.

Padgett, John F., and Christopher K. Ansell. 1993. Robust action and the rise of the Medici, 1400–1434. *American Journal of Sociology* 98:1259–1319.

Page, Scott E. 2007. *The difference: How the power of diversity creates better groups, firms, schools, and societies.* Princeton, NJ: Princeton University Press.

———. 2008. Uncertainty, difficulty, and complexity. *Journal of Theoretical Politics* 20 (2): 115–149.

Perrow, Charles. 2002. Disaster prevention and mitigation. Manuscript, Yale University.

Pinch, Trevor. 1986. *Confronting nature: The sociology of solar-neutrino detection.* Dordrecht: Kluwer Publishers.

Pinch, Trevor, and Wiebe Bijker. 1987. The social construction of facts and artifacts: Or how the sociology of science and the sociology of technology might benefit each other. Pp. 17–50 in *The social construction of technology*, ed. Wiebe Bijker, Thomas Hughes, and Trevor Pinch. Cambridge, MA: MIT Press.

Pinch, Trevor, and Frank Trocco. 2004. *Analog days: The invention and impact of the Moog synthesizer*. Cambridge, MA: Harvard University Press.

Piore, Michael J., and Charles F. Sabel. 1984. *The second industrial divide*. New York: Basic Books.

Pitts, Walter H., and Warren S. McCulloch. 1947. How we know universals: The perception of auditory and visual forms. *Bulletin of Mathematical Biophysics* 9:127–47.

Podolny, Joel M., and Marya Hill-Popper. 2004. Hedonic and transcendent conceptions of value. *Industrial and Corporate Change* 13:61–89.

Podolny, Joel M., and Karen L. Page. 1998. Network forms of organization. *Annual Review of Sociology* 24:57–76.

Podolny, Joel M., and Toby E. Stuart. 1995. A role-based ecology of technological change. *American Journal of Sociology* 100:1224–1260.

Poincaré, Henri. [1908] 1982. *Foundations of science*. Washington, DC: University Press of America.

Poon, Martha. In press. From New Deal institutions to capital markets: Commercial consumer risk scores and the making of subprime mortgage finance. In *Accounting, organizations, and society*.

Porteus, David. 1999. The development of financial centers: Location, information externalities and path dependence. Pp. 95–114 in *Money and the space economy*, ed. Ron Martin. Chichester, UK: John Wiley & Sons.

Powell, Walter W. 1990. Neither market nor hierarchy: Network forms of organization. *Research in Organizational Behavior* 12:295–336.

———. 1996. Inter-organizational collaboration in the biotechnology industry. *Journal of Institutional and Theoretical Economics* 152:197–215.

Powell, Walter W., and Jason Owen-Smith. 1998. Universities and the market for intellectual property in the life sciences. *Journal of Policy Analysis and Management* 17:253–277.

Powell, Walter W., Douglas R. White, Kenneth W. Koput, and Jason Owen-Smith. 2005. Network dynamics and field evolution: The growth of interorganizational collaboration in the life sciences. *American Journal of Sociology* 110 (4): 1132–1205.

Power, Michael. 2007. *Organized uncertainty: Designing a world of risk management*. Oxford: Oxford University Press.

Pratt, Andy C. 2000. New media, the new economy, and new spaces. *Geoforum* 31:25–36.

Preda, Alex. 2006. Socio-technical agency in financial markets: The case of the stock ticker. *Social Studies of Science* 36 (5): 753–782.

Pryke, Michael. 2008. Money's eyes: The visual preparation of financial markets. Manuscript, The Open University.

Rediker, Marcus. 2004. *Villains of all nations: Atlantic pirates in the Golden Age*. Boston: Beacon Press.

Reuf, Martin. 1999. The emergence of organizational forms: A community ecology approach. *American Journal of Sociology* 106:658–714.

Reverre, Stephane. 2001. *The complete arbitrage deskbook*. New York: McGraw-Hill.

Ricoeur, Paul. 2005. *The course of recognition*. Cambridge, MA: Harvard University Press.

Rocha, Luis M. 1999. Evidence sets and contextual genetic algorithms: Exploring uncertainty, context and embodiment in cognitive and biological systems. PhD dissertation, State University of New York at Binghamton. UMI Microform 9734528.

———. 2001. Adaptive webs for heterarchies with diverse communities of users. Paper presented at the conference From Intelligent Networks to the Global Brain: Evolutionary Social Organization through Knowledge Technology, Brussels, July 3–5. LAUR 005173.

Ross, Andrew. 2003. *No collar: The humane workplace and its hidden costs*. New York: Basic Books.

Sabel, Charles, F. 1990. Moebius-strip organizations and open labor markets: Some consequences of the reintegration of conception and execution in a volatile economy. Pp. 23–54 in *Social theory for a changing society*, ed. Pierre Bourdieu and James Coleman. Boulder, CO, and New York: Westview Press and the Russell Sage Foundation.

———. 1997. Design, deliberation, and democracy: On the new pragmatism of firms and public institutions. Pp. 101–149 in *Liberal institutions, economic constitutional rights, and the role of organizations*, ed. K.-H. Ladeur. Baden-Baden: Nomos Verlagsgesellschaft.

Sabel, Charles F., and Jane Prokop. 1996. Stabilization through reorganization? Some preliminary implications of Russia's entry into world markets in the age of discursive quality standards. Pp. 151–191 in *Corporate governance in central Europe and Russia*, vol. 2, ed. Roman Frydman, Andrzej Rapaczynski, and Cheryl Gray. World Bank/Central European University Privatization Project Publication. Budapest: CEU Press.

Sabel, Charles F., and Jonathan Zeitlin. 1997. Stories, strategies, structures: Rethinking historical alternatives to mass production. Pp. 1–33 in *World of Possibilities: Flexibility and mass production in Western industrialization*, ed. Charles F. Sabel and Jonathan Zeitlin. Cambridge: Cambridge University Press.

Sack, Warren. 2005. Discourse architecture and very large-scale conversations. Pp. 242–282 in *Digital Formations*, ed. Robert Latham and Saskia Sassen. Princeton, NJ: Princeton University Press.

Sassen, Saskia. 1997. The spatial organization of information industries. Pp. 33–52 in *Globalization: Critical reflections*, ed. J. H. Mittelman. London: Lynne Rienner.

———. 2004. The locational and institutional embeddedness of electronic markets. Pp. 224–246 in *Markets in historical contexts: Ideas and politics in the modern world*, ed. Mark Bevir and Frank Trentmann. London: Cambridge University Press.

Schelling, Thomas C. 1960. *The strategy of conflict*. London: Oxford University Press.

Schivelbusch, Wolfgang. 1995. *Disenchanted night: The industrialization of light in the nineteenth century*. Berkeley: University of California Press.

Schumpter, Joseph A. 1934. *The theory of economic development*. Cambridge, MA: Harvard University Press.

Sen, Amartya. 1990. *On ethics and economics*. Oxford: Oxford University Press.

———. 1993. Capability and well-being. Pp. 30–53 in *The quality of life*, ed. Martha Nussbaum and Amartya Sen. Oxford: Oxford University Press.

Shardanand, Upendra, and Pattie Maes. 1995. Social information filtering: Algorithms for automating word of mouth. Paper presented at the Conference on Human Factors in Computing Systems, Chicago.

Sheller, Mimi. 2004. Mobile publics: Beyond the network perspective. *Environment and Planning D: Society and Space* 22 (1): 39–52.

Simon, Herbert. 1969. *The sciences of the artificial*. Cambridge, MA: MIT Press.

Smith, Charles. 1990. *Auctions: The social construction of value*. Berkeley: University of California Press.

———. 2001. *Success and survival on Wall Street: Understanding the mind of the market*. New York: Rowman and Littlefield.

Sperber, Dan, and Deirdre Wilson. 1996. *Relevance: Communication and cognition*. Malden, MA, and Oxford: Wilely-Blackwell.

Staber, Udo, and Jörg Sydow. 2002. Organizational adaptive capacity: A structuration perspective. *Journal of Management Inquiry* 11 (4): 408–424.

Star, Susan Leigh, and James Griesemer. 1989. Institutional ecology, translations, and boundary objects: Amateurs and professionals in Berkeley's Museum of Vertebrate Zoology, 1907–1939. *Social Studies of Science* 19:387–420.

Stark, Ben, and David Stark. 2006. Satisfaction guaranteed: Megachurches as shopping malls. Center on Organizational Innovation Working Papers, Columbia University.

Stark, David. 1985. The micropolitics of the firm and the macropolitics of reforms: New forms of workplace bargaining in Hungarian enterprises. Pp. 247–273 in *States vs. markets in the world-system*, ed. Peter Evans, Dietrich Rueschemeyer, and Evelyne Huber Stephens. Beverly Hills: Sage Publications.

———. 1986. Rethinking internal labor markets: New insights from a comparative perspective. *American Sociological Review* 51:492–504.

———. 1989. Coexisting organizational forms in Hungary's emerging mixed economy. Pp. 137–168 in *Remaking the economic institutions of socialism*, ed. Victor Nee and David Stark. Stanford, CA: Stanford University Press.

———. 1990. Privatization in Hungary: From plan to market or from plan to clan? *East European Politics and Societies* 4 (3): 351–392.

———. 1992. Path dependence and privatization strategies in East Central Europe. *East European Politics and Societies* 6 (1): 17–53.

———. 1996. Recombinant property in East European capitalism. *American Journal of Sociology* 101:993–110.

———. 2001. Ambiguous assets for uncertain environments: Heterarchy in postsocialist firms. Pp. 69–104 in *The twenty-first century firm: Changing economic organization in international perspective*, ed. Paul DiMaggio. Princeton, NJ: Princeton University Press.

Stark, David, and László Bruszt. 1998. *Postsocialist pathways: Transforming politics and property in East Central Europe*. Cambridge and New York: Cambridge University Press.

Stark, David, and László Bruszt. 2001. One way or multiple paths? For a comparative sociology of East European capitalism. *American Journal of Sociology* 106 (4): 1129–1137.

Stark, David, and Victor Nee. 1989. Toward an institutional analysis of state socialism. Pp. 1–31 in *Remaking the economic institutions of socialism: China and Eastern Europe*, ed. Victor Nee and David Stark. Stanford, CA: Stanford University Press.

Stark, David, and Balazs Vedres. 2006. Social times of network spaces: Network sequences and foreign investment in Hungary. *American Journal of Sociology* 111 (5): 1367–1411.

Stark, David, Balazs Vedres, and László Bruszt. 2006. Rooted transnational publics: Integrating foreign ties and civic activism. *Theory and Society* 35 (3): 323–349.

Suchman, Lucy. 2000. Located accountabilities in technology production. Paper presented at the Workshop on Heterarchy, Santa Fe Institute.

———. 2007. *Human-machine reconfigurations: Plans and situated actions*, 2nd ed. Cambridge and New York: Cambridge University Press.

Swedberg, Richard. 2007. *Principles of economic sociology*. Princeton, NJ: Princeton University Press.

Sydow, Jörg, Lars Lindkvist, and Robert DeFillippi. 2004. Project-based organizations, embeddedness and repositories of knowledge. *Organization Studies* 25 (9): 1475–1488.

Terranova, Tiziana. 2000. Free labor: Producing culture for the digital economy. *Social Text* 18:33–58.

Teubner, Günther. 1991. Beyond contract and organization? The external liability of franchising systems in German law. Pp. 105–132 in *Franchising and the law: Theoretical and comparative approaches in Europe and the United States*, ed. Christian Joerges. Baden-Baden: Nomos Verlagsgesellschaft.

Thévenot, Laurent. 1984. Rules and implements: Investment in forms. *Social Science Information* 23:1–45.

———. 2001. Organized complexity: Conventions of coordination and the composition of economic arrangements. *European Journal of Social Theory* 4:405–425.

———. 2007. The plurality of cognitive formats and engagements: Moving between the familiar and the public. *European Journal of Social Theory* 10 (3): 409–423.

Thompson, E. P. 1971. The moral economy of the English crowd in the eighteenth century. *Past and Present* 50:76–136.

———. 1982. Time, work-discipline, and industrial capitalism. Pp. 299–309 in *Classes, power, and conflict*, ed. Anthony Giddens and David Held. Berkeley: University of California Press.

Thrift, Nigel. 1994. On the social and cultural determinants of international financial centres: The case of the City of London. Pp. 327–355 in *Money, power and space*, ed. S. Corbridge, N. J. Thrift, and R. L. Martin. Oxford: Blackwell.

———. 1999. The place of complexity. *Theory, Culture, and Society* 16 (3): 31–69.

———. 2000. Pandora's box? Cultural geographies of economies. Pp. 689–704 in *The Oxford Handbook of Economic Geography*, ed. G. L. Clark, M. P. Feldman, and Meric S. Gertler. Oxford: Oxford University Press.

———. 2001a. "It's the romance not the finance that makes the business worth pursuing": Disclosing a new market culture. *Economy and Society* 30:412–432.

———. 2001b. Software writing cities. Address to the Taub Urban Research Center, New York University, February 26.

———. 2004a. Movement-space: The changing domain of thinking resulting from the development of new kinds of spatial awareness. *Economy and Society* 33 (4): 582–605.

———. 2004b. Remembering the technological unconscious by foregrounding knowledges of position. *Environment and Planning D: Society and Space* 22 (1): 175–190.

———. 2005. *Knowing capitalism*. London: SAGE Publications.

———. 2006. Re-inventing invention: New tendencies in capitalist commodification. *Economy and Society* 35 (2): 279–306.

Tilly, Charles. 2006. *Why?* Princeton, NJ: Princeton University Press.

Turkle, Sherry. 1998. *Life on the screen*. New York: Simon & Schuster.

Urry, John. 2004. The "system" of automobility. *Theory, Culture and Society* 21 (4–5): 25–39.

Uzzi, Brian. 1997. Social structure and competition in interfirm networks: The paradox of embeddedness. *Administrative Science Quarterly* 42:35–67.

———. 1999. Embeddedness in the making of financial capital: How social relations and networks benefit firms seeking financing. *American Sociological Review* 64:481–505.

Vallas, Steven P. 2006. Empowerment redux: Structure, agency, and the remaking of managerial authority. *American Journal of Sociology* 111 (6): 1677–1717.

Van den Bulte, Christophe, and Rudy K. Moenaert. 1998. The effect of R&D team co-location on communication patterns among R&D, marketing and manufacturing. Manuscript, Marketing Department, Wharton School, University of Pennsylvania.

Vedres, Balazs, Laszlo Bruszt, and David Stark. 2004. Organizing technologies: Genre forms of online civic association in Eastern Europe. Pp. 171–188 in *Cultural production in a digital age*. (Special issue of the *Annals of the American Academy of Political and Social Science*.)

Vedres, Balazs, and David Stark. 2008. Opening closure: Intercohesion and entre-preneurial dynamics in business groups. Center on Organizational Innovation Working Papers, Columbia University.

Velthuis, Olav. 1999. The changing relationship between economic sociology and institutional economics: From Talcott Parsons to Mark Granovetter. *American Journal of Economics and Sociology* 58 (4): 629–649.

———. 2005. *Talking prices: Symbolic meanings of prices on the markets for contemporary Art*. Princeton, NJ: Princeton University Press.

von Goldammer, Eberhard, Joachim Paul, and Joe Newbury. 2003. Heterarchy—hierarchy: Two complementary categories of description. *Vordenker Webforum for Innovative Approaches in Science, Economy and Culture*. August. http://www.vordenker.de/heterarchy/a_heterarchy-e.pdf.

von Hippel, Eric. 2001. Innovation by user communities: Learning from open source software. *Sloan Management Review* 42:82–86.

von Neumann, John. 1956. Probabilistic logics and the synthesis of reliable organizations from unreliable components. Pp. 43–98 in *Automata studies*, ed. C. E. Shannon and J. McCarthy. Princeton, NJ: Princeton University Press.

Wagner, Gunter P., and Lee Altenberg. 1996. Complex adaptations and the evolution of evolvability. *Evolution* 50 (3): 967–976.

Wark, McKenzie. 2004. *A hacker manifesto*. Cambridge, MA: Harvard University Press.

Weick, Karl E. 1977. Organization design: Organizations as self-designing systems. *Organizational Dynamics* 6:31–45.

———. 1979. *The social psychology of organizing*, 2nd ed. Reading, MA: Addison-Wesley.

———. 1993. The collapse of sensemaking in organizations: The Mann Gulch disaster. *Administrative Science Quarterly* 38:628–652.

———. 1995. *Sensemaking in organizations*. Thousand Oaks, CA: Sage.

Weick, Karl, and Karlene H. Roberts. 1993. Collective mind in organizations: Heedful interrelating on flight decks. *Administrative Science Quarterly* 38 (3): 357–382.

Weitzman, Martin L. 1998. Recombinant growth. *Quarterly Journal of Economics* 113 (2): 331–360.

Wenger, Etienne. 1998. *Communities of practice: Learning, meaning, and identity*. Cambridge: Cambridge University Press.

White, Harrison C. 1981. Where do markets come from? *American Journal of Sociology* 87:983–38.

———. 1992a. Agency as control in formal networks. Pp. 92–117 in *Networks and organizations*, ed. Nitin Nohira and Robert G. Eccles. Cambridge, MA: Harvard Business School Press.

———. 1992b. Cases are for identity, for explanation, or for control. Pp. 83–104 in *What is a case? Exploring the foundations of social inquiry*, ed. Charles C. Ragin and Howard S. Becker. London and New York: Cambridge University Press.

———. 1992c. *Identity and control.* Princeton, NJ: Princeton University Press.

———. 1993. Values come in styles, which mate to change. Pp 63–91 in *The origins of values,* ed. Michael Hechter, Lynn Nadel, and Richard E. Michod. New York: Aldine de Gruyter.

———. 2002. *Markets from networks: Socioeconomic models of production.* Princeton, NJ: Princeton University Press.

Williamson, Oliver. 1981. The economics of organization: The transaction cost approach. *American Journal of Sociology* 87 (3): 548–577.

Wilkinson, John. 1997. A new paradigm for economic analysis? *Economy and Society* 26 (3): 305–339.

Wilson, Edward O. 2003. *The future of life.* New York: Vintage Books.

Wittgenstein, Ludwig. 1999. *Tractatus logico-philosophicus,* trans. C. K. Ogden. Mineola, NY: Dover Publications.

Wolfe, Tom. 1987. *The bonfire of the vanities.* New York: Farrar, Straus and Giroux.

Yates, JoAnne. 1989. *Control through communication: The rise of system in American management.* Baltimore: Johns Hopkins University Press.

———. 2005. *Structuring the information age: Life insurance and technology in the 20th Century.* Baltimore: John Hopkins University Press.

Zaheer, Srilata A. 1997. Acceptable risk: A study of global currency trading rooms in the US. Working Paper 97-22, Wharton Financial Institutions Center, Philadelphia.

Zaheer, Srilata, and Elaine Mosakowski. 1997. The dynamics of the liability of foreigners: A global study of survival in financial services. *Strategic Management Journal* 18:439–464.

Zaloom, Caitlin. 2003. Ambiguous numbers: Trading and technologies in global financial markets. *American Ethnologist* 30:258–272.

———. 2004. The discipline of the speculator. Pp. 253–269 in *Global assemblages: Technology, politics and ethics as anthropological problems,* ed. Aihwa Ong and Stephen Collier. New York: Blackwell.

———. 2006. *Out of the pits: Traders and technology from Chicago to London.* Chicago: University of Chicago Press.

Zelizer, Viviana A. 1985. *Pricing the priceless child: The changing social value of children.* New York: Basic Books.

———. 1996. Payments and social ties. *Sociological Forum* 11 (3): 481–495.

———. 1998. The proliferation of social currencies. Pp. 58–68 in *The laws of the markets,* ed. Michel Callon. Oxford: Blackwell Publishers.

———. 2004. Circuits of commerce. Pp. 122–135 in *Self, social structure, and beliefs: Explorations in sociology,* ed. Jeffrey C. Alexander, Gary T. Marx, and Christine L. Williams. Berkeley and Los Angeles: University of California Press.

———. 2007. *The purchase of intimacy.* Princeton, NJ: Princeton University Press.

Index

friction: bountiful/generative, 16, 18–19,
109–11; in economics, 182; recombinant
processes as, 182 (*see also* recombinant
innovation)
Friedland, Roger, 12n

Galison, Peter L., 109n.26, 192–94
General Dynamics, 60n
generative redundancy, 159–60
genetic code, 30–31
Girard, Monique, 81, 156n.46, 208
Gladwell, Malcolm, 170n
Grabher, Gernot, 94n.10
Griesemer, James, 109–10, 194

Hagel, John, III, 182
Hann, Mike, 146n
Hannan, Michael, 178–80
Hedlund, Gunnar, 19n.43
heterarchy: allocative efficiency in the
short run sacrificed for dynamic efficiency in the long run, 178, 183; as an
organizational form, conception of,
5–6, 19; complex coordination through
discursive pragmatics in, 108–11; distributing intelligence and lateral accountability, 20–23; as a metaphor for
organization, 27–31; military organizations and, 199–202; more heterarchy as
the answer to problems created by,
210–12; as organizing dissonance, 23–27;
problems created by, 204–10; self-
management in, 113–14
hierarchy: as an organizational model,
23–24, 27–28; heterarchy as flattening,
25 (*see also* heterarchy); origin of the
term, 28
Hobbes, Thomas, 12
Holiday, Billie, 180
Holland, John, 180
Hungary: civic associations in, study of,
198n.88; independent labor movement,
organizational innovation to thwart, 45–
47; mixed economy of, 45; mixed organizational forms in, 47; modes of economic coordination operating in, 70–71;
postsocialist, 76–77; the second economy,

47, 73–75, 179n.42; semiautonomous
subcontracting work partnership in (*see*
enterprise work partnership)
Hutchins, Edwin, 177n.38, 187n.63
hyperentrepreneurial capitalism, 206–10

identities, new attributions of, 188–90
indeterminate situations: analysis of in case
studies, 32–34; economic sociology and,
9–10, 14–15
innovation: among new-media firms (*see*
NetKnowHow; Silicon Alley); analytic
and interpretive modes, distinction between, 2–3; design, as the source of, 101;
organizational, 81–83; re-cognition, 125,
139–42, 187–90; recombinant (*see* recombinant innovation); reflexive cognition
and the paradoxical process of, 4–5; rivalry
as a source of, 106; technological, 90–91;
in the trading room, basis of, 124–25
institutional analysis: classification in, 166–
69; economic sociology, as a theoretical
approach within, 163–64; founding statement of, 166–67; new institutionalism,
11n.22, 16, 165n, 167–68, 183–84; practical
action, grounding in a theory of, 183–84;
the Soviet system in terms of, 179n.43
International Securities, 34, 119; 9/11,
response to, 153–55; trading room of,
120–21, 130–31 (*see also* trading room)
Internet consulting firms. See NetKnow-
How; Silicon Alley
Investors Group (IG), 139–41

Jacob, Francois, 180

Kádár, János, 49
Kauffman, Stuart, 20
Kelly, John, 156, 200n.92
Knight, Frank, 14–15, 17
Knorr Cetina, Karin, 122–25, 133, 142–43
knowledge management, 174
Kogut, Bruce, 15n.32
Kunda, Gideon, 204

Lamont, Michèle, 10n.19
Lane, David, 14, 20, 175, 188–90